MY STORY

JULIE COUILLARD
MY STORY

McCLELLAND & STEWART

Original title: Mon histoire
Copyright © 2008 Les Éditions de l'homme

All rights reserved
Published under arrangement with Les Éditions de l'homme,
Montreal, Quebec, Canada

English-language translation copyright © 2008 by McClelland & Stewart Ltd.

Written with Serge Rivest

Translated from the French by Michael Gilson

Library and Archives Canada Cataloguing in Publication

Couillard, Julie
  My story / Julie Couillard.

ISBN 978-0-7710-2292-0

1. Couillard, Julie. 2. Motorcycle gangs – Québec (Province).
3. Montréal Region (Québec) – Biography. I. Title.

FC641.C69A3 2008   971.4'2704092   C2008-904194-1

We acknowledge the financial support of the Government of Canada
through the Book Publishing Industry Development Program and that of the
Government of Ontario through the Ontario Media Development
Corporation's Ontario Book Initiative. We further acknowledge the support
of the Canada Council for the Arts and the Ontario Arts Council for our
publishing program.

Typeset in Sabon by M&S, Toronto

Printed and bound in Canada

McClelland & Stewart Ltd.
75 Sherbourne Street
Toronto, Ontario
M5A 2P9
www.mcclelland.com

1 2 3 4 5   12 11 10 09 08

This book is dedicated to all women who, like me, have had their reputations and lives destroyed by the wagging tongues of men in power, and who, to defend themselves, have had to give up their right to privacy.

To all those who have suffered during this scandal that was fabricated from beginning to end, and particularly to those close to me: I thank them for their tolerance and their understanding in light of the fact that they will see, through no fault of their own, aspects of their private lives exposed in this book.

Contents

Introduction

Since May 7, 2008, so much has been written about me in the newspapers that I sometimes feel I've contributed to the depletion of Canada's forests. I've been called the "Mata Hari of the 450," a "twenty-first-century Gerda Munsinger," a gold digger, a praying mantis who consumes her mates after lovemaking, and more. This insidious rumour mill would have it that I exhibited all manner of vulgar behaviour while in the company of Canada's minister of foreign affairs, Maxime Bernier, that I sought to control his communications strategy and write his speeches, that I engaged in influence peddling, and that I posed a serious threat to Canada's national security.

From the outset of the so-called Bernier-Couillard affair, a scandal-obsessed media delighted in perpetrating the worst drivel and falsehoods imaginable, without ever taking the trouble to verify their sources. As the old journalists' joke goes, "Why let the facts stand in the way of a good story?"

Not content to limit their accusations to my own person – as the most elementary precepts of decency would demand – many of these gossipmongers took it upon themselves to attack members of my family as well, violating their privacy and casting doubt upon their integrity.

That media hounding created a living hell for me and my loved ones. I was portrayed as a "biker's chick," a prostitute, a thief, the lowest of the low. I had to go into hiding, like a common criminal. My house was literally under siege, and I was forced to take refuge in an apartment in downtown Montreal for several weeks. On the rare occasions that I went out, I had to hide my face behind huge dark sunglasses.

I was forced into silence during that time, because anything I might have said would have been used against me, so strong was the presumption of my guilt. People were ready to take every last rumour manufactured about me as gospel – for in the court of public opinion, insinuations, half-truths, and even outright lies can be introduced as evidence.

The time for delusional innuendo is over. I have allowed these assertions and actions to go on for months. Now, my turn has come. To speak out. To tell my story, the way I lived it – in other words, my true story.

Readers of this book will be hard-pressed to recognize the monster that the press depicted time and again during that infernal summer of 2008. Not that I would ever claim to be perfect – far from it. Like everyone has, I have made mistakes. I have dealt with failure. I have had regrets. And I have been afraid. Throughout my short life, however, I have never tried to be anyone other than myself. I have never been party to any nefarious plot, secret plan, or evil machinations for or against anyone whatsoever.

In these pages, I tell the true story of my journey, from my birth in a modest Montreal neighbourhood to my brief romance with a Canadian federal cabinet minister to the aftermath of that relationship, which deprived me of my freedom of movement and threw my life into disarray for quite some time. This book is not the fruit of wild imaginings, but my honest view of the account of my life.

Mixed Roots

"My mother became pregnant . . . so they got married."

My earliest, most powerful memory of childhood was the day our dog Butch died, not far from our home on Mazarin Street in Ville-Émard. I must have been three or four. Like many smaller dogs, Butch was mesmerized by the sight of a moving vehicle. That morning, it was a bus that he'd decided to run after. I remember the impact: sudden, quick, clean. There was no pool of blood, no slow, agonizing death. He was struck in the head and killed instantly. It was the first time I'd ever mourned.

I've always felt love, mingled with a kind of wonderment, for animals. When I was little, I was fascinated by the slightest little creature, and stirred by a desire to protect it and care for it. I remember one day finding a blue jay that had fallen from its nest. I picked it up, tended its wounds, and fed it until it learned to fly again – which was a good thing, because before long our cat Frigolo would have made a meal out of it.

My affection for animals wasn't always requited, however. Once, I managed to capture a little flying squirrel. My sister and I pitched a tent in the backyard and zipped him up inside.

It was supposed to be his house. We left him some grass and a bit of food. The next morning, I was all excited at the prospect of visiting my new tenant (or rather my prisoner), but I soon saw that the tent zipper had been slightly opened and realized that he'd run out on me during the night.

My childhood years, from my birth on June 21, 1969, until I was four, were spent in Ville-Émard, a working-class neighbourhood in the southwest part of the Island of Montreal nestled between the Lachine Canal and the De l'Aqueduc Canal, and bounded by the present-day boroughs of Verdun, LaSalle, and Notre-Dame-de-Grâce.

My parents, Marcel Couillard and Diane Bellemare, were barely sixteen years old when they met. Two years later, my mother became pregnant with my sister, so they got married. This was 1966, just before the flower-power revolution and the more liberal mores that were to ensue. But in Quebec, the puritanical attitudes of the years of Great Darkness under Premier Maurice Duplessis still held sway, and my parents were disgraced.

The circumstances of their marriage – and what happened later between her and my father probably had just as much to do with it – caused my mother to repeat an admonition throughout my teenage years: "Whatever you do, don't make the mistake of marrying the first man you meet!" And in my mind, out of that warning grew a panicky fear of getting pregnant and having to go down the same road as she.

I have fairly mixed roots. Although I have a typically French family name, my father's ancestors were mainly Irish and Scottish. I remember my great-grandmother, whom I got to know later and who lived in Halifax. She was a tall Irishwoman, five feet ten, while her daughter (my paternal grandmother) was a green-eyed redhead barely five feet tall, but heavy-set. My great-grandfather, whom I never knew, had Scottish roots.

On my mother's side, my grandparents, Jean-Paul Bellemare and Simone Henri, were both old-stock francophone Quebecers, although my grandfather, through his mother, had First Nations blood.

My family and I never spent much time with my father's parents, even though they lived practically around the corner, in neighbouring LaSalle. My grandmother Gloria wasn't a mean sort, but she had somewhat of an icy demeanour, and on top of that had never really accepted that her son had married a francophone. As for my grandfather Bernard, who was a sailor for much of his life and died of cirrhosis of the liver, he was an alcoholic, and this surely contributed to his driving people away. He used to come home drunk and beat his wife and children. My father was the eldest, and as he got older he would step in more often, but the situation regularly turned against him. He left home at sixteen, burned his bridges, and would not see his family again for many years.

With my mother's parents, it was like night and day. These were the grandparents kids were supposed to have: loving and ready to spoil us at every opportunity. When we went over for family visits, grandpa Jean-Paul would take my sister, Johanne, and me out a lot. We would go to the movies and see films like *Godzilla*. He would buy us all sorts of treats – candied apples and other goodies – which invariably drew an affectionate rebuke from my grandmother: "You'll spoil their supper!" she'd say. All through my childhood, my grandma Simone and I were very close. She was a petite woman, generous, warm, and open-minded. When my family, after living for a few years in Lorraine, moved back to Ville-Émard, onto the same street as her, we saw each other very often – practically every day.

My grandfather was a bus driver, and I remember him only in his retirement years.

For as long as I can remember, my grandparents lived at the same address: 7130 D'Aragon Street in Ville-Émard. They rented a two-bedroom apartment on the second floor of an eight-plex. They were tenants all their lives, which I never really understood, because I'm sure they had the means to buy a small house. They weren't rich, but they had a stable income and their home was always clean, elegant, and well kept.

My first brush with fame occurred when I was barely a year old. It was in much more pleasant circumstances than those of the second, which was to come many years later, in 2008. Montreal's Télé-Métropole, now the flagship station of the TVA network, used to run a contest to find the cutest baby of the month. My mother entered my name, sending along a picture of me hungrily devouring a piece of chicken. I was declared the winner, and my mother's grand prize was a gift certificate for a baby clothing store.

When they first got married, both my parents held down regular jobs. My father was a lithographer at the *Gazette,* and my mother worked for Chargex, the credit-card company that eventually became Visa. I can still remember how, when my sister and I were little, my mother would bring home these bits of cardboard with the Chargex logo on them. We'd spend hours making up all kinds of games with that precious treasure.

That was how it was in my earliest childhood: a tranquil atmosphere in the humblest of surroundings. Until one day in 1973, when our parents made a big announcement: my sister and I would get to live in a new house. The family was moving to Lorraine, then a burgeoning suburban town in what is today known as Montreal's northern ring. I was four years old.

2

Life in Lorraine

"Whenever my parents started fighting, I would fall asleep right away."

I don't remember exactly why my parents decided to leave the city and settle in the suburbs. I imagine they were simply attracted by the improved quality of life and the chance to raise their children in a healthier environment, closer to nature.

The first place we lived in Lorraine was a spacious, brand new Georgian-inspired house on De Reims Boulevard, a nice, quiet stretch of road in a pleasant, comfortable neighbourhood. Even though I was still very young, I could clearly see that Lorraine was a big change from Ville-Émard, where the houses stood cheek by jowl on either side of narrow streets. Suddenly, we not only had a big, modern house but also a huge yard with trees and flowers and space to play, away from the street, without fear of passing cars.

My two most cherished childhood memories date back to those years. Once, when I was still very young, we went on a family picnic at the lakeshore. It was a beautiful summer day, bathed in sunshine – one of those rare times when it seems like everything is in its ideal place. Another time, during our last winter in Lorraine – I was ten – we went on a long walk one evening after a huge snowfall. My father was pulling a sled, and we kept running up behind him to try and jump on, but at the last minute he would tug hard on the cord and we would tumble into the freshly fallen snow, laughing our heads off.

Not long after we moved to Lorraine, my mother became pregnant again. The birth of my brother, Patrick, was a significant moment for me; I had always loved my dolls, and now I would have a real live one to play with! I have fond memories of rocking him, giving him his bottle, and "helping" my mother change his diapers. My kid brother and I were always close and remain so to this day.

It was while she was pregnant with Patrick that I saw my mother cry for the first time. I gleaned from a conversation she'd just had with my father that she had found a lipstick-stained cigarette butt in the car. Since neither my father nor my mother smoked, it wasn't hard to put two and two together. I think that was the point when I started to realize my father's true nature. The cigarette butt incident was the first sign, and others would confirm and clarify my suspicions as the years went by. I remember going to my father and telling him to stop making my mother cry.

My father's infidelity was not the only source of embarrassment for his family. He was a profoundly dysfunctional man in many ways. My father could easily spend hours on trivial daily tasks that would take most people just a few minutes – getting up in the morning, showering and shaving, dressing.

For example, it wasn't unusual for him to say, on a Saturday or Sunday morning, "Girls, how about we go horseback riding today?" I loved horses, and I would start to fidget impatiently, waiting for the moment to arrive. But the day would drag on and nothing would happen, until finally we would pile into the car and set off in a rush. Once we were on the road, my mother would say, "It's not worth it. We'll be too late. It'll be dark by the time we get there, and they won't want to bring the horses out." Sometimes, if we were lucky, the ranch owner would saddle the horses and bring them out for a half-hour, rather than the minimum one hour, so that we children wouldn't be disappointed. But often they would tell us it was too late, and we'd have to turn around and go home. On the way back, the litany of complaints would begin again.

"You had your daughters looking forward to this all day and you couldn't even keep your promise!" my mother would say.

"Next time we'll go earlier."

"We can't count on you to do anything!"

And on it would go, for a long time. Meanwhile, I would sleep in the car. Whenever my parents started fighting, I would fall asleep right away. It was an escape – my way of pretending that it wasn't happening.

Monday mornings at school, our teacher would usually ask one of the kids what he or she had done on the weekend. In this fairly upscale neighbourhood, all the children had active, fulfilling lives. Once, when I was unlucky enough to be asked the dreaded question, I said – even though it was a patent lie – "My dad took us all to the ranch. The horses were magnificent and the ride was amazing."

I was seven years old at the time, the age of reason, when we first learn how to tell right from wrong. I remember coming home from school that afternoon, lying down on the embankment in front of our house, and looking up at the clouds. I was fully cognizant of the fact that I had told a lie in class. At that moment, I told myself that I couldn't continue to mingle fantasy with reality, to believe in what I'd wished for rather than in what had really happened. I decided that the next time I was asked to tell the class about my weekend, I was going to tell the truth. If we hadn't done a damn thing, then we hadn't done a damn thing, period. From that moment on, I stopped covering for family members and making them out to be better than they were.

I didn't grow up in a household where the parents said to themselves, "Not in front of the children – we'll settle this some other time." Whenever the tension went up a notch between my mother and father, things always had to come out in the open, right then and there. There was no way they were going to talk it over later. Not that they were ever violent; they never beat us, thank God, and we never suffered any real physical or even verbal abuse of any kind. But there was no affection. No "I love you"s, no kisses, no loving gestures, no affectionate nicknames like in so many other families. When I look back on my childhood today, I realize that I missed out on those things. But at the time, since I had never known anything else, it was hard for me to put a name to the vague unease that I felt – a sort of nostalgic longing for something that had never existed in my world, that is, a close-knit family that would gather at mealtimes, playfully tease one another, talk about the little things that worried them or their plans for the future.

Around the same time, a week before my first communion, something happened that drove home the reality of how fragile life is. One spring morning, when my sister and I had the day off from school and were home alone, the phone rang. It was the hospital. While driving to work in downtown Montreal, our mother had been in a serious accident in the Ville-Marie Tunnel, a pile-up involving more than twenty-five vehicles. The force of the impact had smashed her teeth, and her upper lip was split open. The hospital staff said the fur coat she was wearing probably saved her from even more serious injury. She had a huge bruise on her upper body where the seatbelt had left its imprint.

Our mother had had emergency surgery, they said, but she was now out of danger. After we'd hung up the phone, Johanne and I suddenly realized that we hadn't thought to ask about our younger brother, who had left the house with my mother as usual – she always dropped him off at daycare on her way to work. What if, for some reason or other, she hadn't left Patrick at the daycare centre? What if the worst had happened? We were beside ourselves with worry. After a while – which seemed like an eternity – we finally found out that our brother was safe and sound at the daycare. But during that brief, horrible spell of not knowing, my sister and I went through hell.

It was the first time I had been forced to face, if not the reality, at least the possibility, of death. That day, I realized quite clearly that my mother could have died, and my brother as well. I was overcome by anxiety. I had never thought about these kinds of things before. And yet, twenty or so years later, death was to come knocking at my door again, and far more brutally.

3

Money Problems

"Little girls need to love their fathers."

wo years after we moved to Lorraine, my father decided
to leave his job as a lithographer and go into business
for himself as a building contractor. I still wonder today
how someone who lacked the necessary organizational sense
and discipline could have seriously considered a career as a
businessman. It was a disastrous decision that was to result in
a long period of instability and financial problems for him and
for our family.

One of his first decisions as a contractor was to build a big
house for the entire family on Ronchamp Road, quite close to
where we lived. To that end, he sold the house on De Reims
Boulevard, but when the time came for the new owners to
move in, construction of our new house wasn't yet complete.
Far from it.

We therefore went to stay for a few weeks with my father's
brother, Wayne, who lived in the next town over, Bois-des-
Filion. I remember hating that time. My aunt had several cats,
and I remember one of them scratched Patrick's face, which is

probably one reason why we didn't stay very long in those less-than-hospitable surroundings.

We left and went back to live in Lorraine for about ten months, in a semi-detached house that my father had rented. Then, a full year after giving up our house on De Reims, we finally moved into our new home on Ronchamp Road. It was in a beautiful location: a huge, well-shaded property in a crescent, in the heart of a very pleasant neighbourhood. I quickly made new friends. It was the summer of my seventh birthday.

In this brand new neighbourhood, resplendent with tall old-growth trees, dense woods, lush green parks, and gurgling streams, I spent some of the best times of my childhood. It was an amazing, fairy-tale world with all kinds of wondrous things to discover. In the summertime, my friends and I were always playing in the woods, building clubhouses out of pine branches, studying insects, and looking for puffballs that we would crush into clouds of dust. We'd tear off pieces of birch bark to make parchments and on them write imaginary proclamations inspired by medieval tales. There was a lot of clay in the soil, and we'd use it to make sculptures and little pots that we would paint once the clay had set.

Wintertime was also busy. We'd go skating behind our school for hours on end, until we were exhausted. And since there was still plenty of undeveloped land in the surrounding area back then, the whole family would go cross-country skiing too. This we enjoyed immensely, especially since the trails were laid out on fairly uneven terrain, which made for lots of hills and curves.

I attended only one school in Lorraine: École le Carrefour, which was about two kilometres from our house – if we walked along the road. But in summer as well as winter, we used to take a shortcut along a little trail that ran straight through a pretty patch of woods, where both broad-leaved trees and firs grew. The spot was perfectly emblematic of the city of Lorraine, where nature was never far away. That trail was my scenic route to school, the one I loved best and would remember forever.

Not long after we moved into the new house, my father's company started construction on a twenty-four-unit apartment building in the neighbourhood, which he thought would be very profitable. But before long, everything fell apart. The electrical contractor he'd hired asked him to pay him up front for his full expenses – several tens of thousands of dollars. Naively, my father agreed. The same day, the contractor cashed the cheque and declared bankruptcy. Not only had my father lost what was a huge sum of money for the time, but he was out of working capital as well. He was stuck with an unfinished building that had no roof and, obviously, not a single electrical wire. And because he could no longer secure credit, it was impossible for him to continue with the construction project.

Had he decided to go bankrupt himself and wind up his company, my father probably would have been able to cut his losses. But he stubbornly insisted on continuing. He hurriedly sold off what was left of the apartment building work site and sold the house on Ronchamp Road for far below its market value. He put all the furniture into storage and moved the whole family to a house that he'd managed to rent for three months at the foot of Mont Habitant, in Saint-Sauveur.

My father never truly recovered from this financial disaster. While he unsuccessfully tried to get back on an even keel, my mother started working nights as a waitress at the restaurant

La Flamberie, in addition to her regular day job. I don't think we ever went hungry, but I still remember clearly that when my mother's parents came to visit, they often had an armful of groceries with them. And sometimes, my grandpa would buy me clothes or shoes.

For the first time in my life, I gained a vague understanding of the value of money – or at least the hardships that can result from a lack of it. And by that I don't mean only the absence of material comforts. My father's financial troubles exacerbated the tensions between my parents and forced us to move several times in the space of only a few months. As a result, during these years I often felt the weight of instability, worry, and insecurity pressing down on me.

By this time I was ten years old, and naturally it was easy for me to identify the guilty party. But little girls need to love their fathers. I was upset by what he was putting us through, and I couldn't understand why he was the way he was. But I felt incapable of holding a grudge. Pity is probably the emotion that best describes what I felt for him at the time. I saw my father as a victim of circumstance – just a poor guy who'd had a run of bad luck. He was barely into his thirties, and I had the confused impression that life had cut him a raw deal.

4

Waltz of the Bailiffs

"Ambition didn't come to me, as it does for many people, from parents who pushed me to succeed, but from a deep-seated yearning to escape from the life I was stuck living."

At the end of that summer, after six years in the suburbs and a fairly comfortable lifestyle, my family and I went back to Ville-Émard to live in a small rented three-bedroom apartment on D'Aragon Street, where I shared a room with Patrick. A few months later, we moved to a ground-floor apartment right across the street; it was a little roomier, and we had the use of part of the basement. Still, moving back to Ville-Émard was nothing less than going back to square one, and a terrible admission of failure.

Lorraine had always been fun for me. I'd made good friends there, and there was no shortage of entertaining things to do. It was a stimulating environment. The idea of leaving upset me, but I didn't have much choice.

Although I don't think that at ten years old I had any real sense of class differences, as soon as we arrived in Ville-Émard I quickly realized that there was quite a gulf between my former and my present surroundings – one that was evident even in the way people talked. In the suburbs, everyone spoke fairly good French. But on my first day at École Saint-Jean-de-Matha, as I started Grade 5, I was struck by my classmates' accents, and the way they said "*moé*" and "*toé*" instead of "*moi*" and "*toi*." I wasn't used to this, and I remember going home that evening and telling my mother I hated the way it sounded.

There was some consolation in this exile. Moving back to Ville-Émard brought me closer to my best friend, Lucie.* She lived just a couple of minutes away from my grandparents', and I would see her whenever we made the trip from Lorraine to visit them. We got along great. She had a wonderful family. Her parents were friendly and funny, and I had a lot of fun whenever I spent time with them. Now, not only was she going to be my new neighbour, but we were in the same Grade 5 class at Saint-Jean-de-Matha.

For years after that, Lucie and I were joined at the hip. We had a great rapport, and I remember that even after we were old enough to be interested in boys, we kept on – more or less in secret – playing with our Barbies and their ubiquitous companion, Ken. It was with Lucie that I discovered my new neighbourhood, starting with Curé Albert-Arnold Park, on Hamilton Street, where we'd play after school and on weekends or holidays. We both lived near Des Trinitaires Boulevard, which runs beside Angrignon Park – one of Montreal's most expansive green spaces – so we spent a lot of time there too. It was a great place to walk our pet dogs, Fanny and Max, a female and a male from the same litter that our families had adopted at the same time. A few years after that, we'd spend summer days playing baseball and football in Angrignon Park

---

* Not her real name.

with friends from the neighbourhood. Still later, in our teen years, we'd often go out with my brother and Lucie's cousin, a boy who was the same age as Patrick and was in the same class. We'd take them to the Alexis-Nihon shopping centre and buy them treats with the pocket money we earned doing odd jobs around the neighbourhood, such as babysitting.

To get to Lucie's and my grandmother's, I often took the alleyway that ran behind our building, between D'Aragon and Hamilton Streets. For years, we played ball hockey there with friends from an Italian family who lived not far away. It wasn't one of those dark, dingy alleys characteristic of some other Montreal neighbourhoods. Just the opposite: it was bright and sunny and bordered to the east by huge back-yards where many Hamilton Street residents, most of them Italian, tended magnificent gardens that filled the air with wonderful fragrances. I remember one of them, a widower named Mr. Joseph, would plant a huge vegetable garden every summer and guard it jealously.

After we moved back to Ville-Émard, my mother very quickly found a job with the Montreal Catholic School Commission. She was a secretary in the principal's office at École Pierre-Dupuy, at the corner of De Lorimier and Ontario Streets in eastern Montreal. It was a rough neighbourhood, and she became quite committed to helping troubled youth.

Meanwhile, my father's situation was becoming increasingly precarious. He described himself as a businessman, but exactly what business he was in was far from clear. I know that he ran a restaurant for a while, but as with all of my father's ventures, it didn't last long. It was difficult to know exactly what he was up to because he was hardly ever at home. Despite his absence, we still suffered the consequences of his troubles; the collapse of his construction business was beginning to catch up with him in a big way.

As mentioned, my father had not only refused to declare bankruptcy after being cheated by an electrical contractor, but he'd also pledged to repay his creditors every last cent they were owed. Since he was taking his time making good on that promise, they eventually decided to resort to extreme measures.

More than once, we had our phone cut off. The phone bill had gotten out of hand because of the many long-distance calls my father made for business. I still have a painful memory of the humiliation I felt one day at school when a friend told me she'd tried to call me the night before but got a recorded message saying the number she had called was no longer in service.

Not long after we moved back to Ville-Émard, the bailiffs started showing up at our door, one after another. My father had neglected to follow the legal steps that might have prevented this from happening. I remember my mother once having to rush over to her parents' to borrow two thousand dollars so our furniture wouldn't be confiscated. Another time, the bailiffs even showed up with a moving truck, ready to load it with the furniture they'd come to seize.

But since my father was never home and my mother worked, more than once I had to answer the door myself. The first time it happened, the bailiff strode through the entire house, taking inventory of every last piece of furniture. When he went into my bedroom, still taking notes, I asked, "Why are you doing that?"

"Because we're coming to take your bed away," he replied.

When my mother came back, she reassured me and said, "That's not how these things work." There were rules to be followed before things could get to that point. Then she explained that the notice of seizure had to be a certain colour, otherwise the bailiff couldn't come inside the house, and if it wasn't the right colour, I was to refuse to allow him to enter. I could even threaten to call the police. Although her words were meant to soothe me – and in a way prepare me to face the music the next time a bailiff came calling – these were the kinds of situations that create insecurity in a child's head.

I would see my mother crying, worried sick. There was no way out for her. I was twelve years old and I was ashamed of my father. Soon after that, my sister and I started telling our mother that we would all be better off without him, that we could manage on our own, that she should leave him. It would be several years yet before she would find the courage to do so.

I remember later, when I was fifteen, going out to look for my father one night and finding him in a bar. I made sure he couldn't see me and watched him sitting at a table, chatting up a girl barely in her twenties.

He was what I would call a periodic alcoholic. I don't remember ever seeing him get drunk at home, but when he went out for a drink, he was like a bottomless pit. Worse, he would drive his car back home. He always managed to buy a new car every couple of years and very often managed to wreck it in no time. Once, I went with my boyfriend at the time to fetch him from a bar. When we found my father, he was already pretty far gone, but he flat out refused to leave his car outside the bar and let us drive him home. We followed him in my boyfriend's truck, fingers crossed. On the Ville Marie Expressway, we watched as he weaved from one lane to another, and when he got to the La Vérendrye exit, he barely made it – his car nearly rode up onto the concrete barrier. I still wonder how he arrived home in one piece that night. I guess his number wasn't up, simple as that.

What with all the family instability and financial hardship, my early teen years were a very trying time. There was also the fact that by then, my relationship with my mother was starting to fray at the edges as well. Of course, she was going through hell. I can only imagine all the stress she must have been under, being for all practical purposes a single mother, raising her family herself, running the household, and going to work every morning – whatever the circumstances. She was under enormous pressure. I suppose from time to time she had to blow off steam one way or another, and for some reason, I always seemed to be the one on the receiving end. As a result, we were often at each other's throats. Once, she blew her stack for some reason and actually threw me out of the house. She had a better rapport with my sister than me, and I felt more or less rejected by her. So I began spending most of my free time away from the house, over at Lucie's or with other friends in the neighbourhood.

The events of that period in my life kindled in me a sort of ambition born of insecurity. I began repeating a kind of mantra: "Don't ever rely on anybody but yourself in life – otherwise you'll probably find yourself in deep shit." Ambition didn't come to me, as it does for many people, from parents who pushed me to succeed, but from a deep-seated yearning to escape from the life I was stuck living.

5

Petit Mal

"I floated up and out of my body and saw myself as if in a movie."

When I was seven, my Grade 2 teacher at École le Carrefour in Lorraine began complaining to my mother that I was often absent-minded in class. My mother scolded me, but I continued to drift off, and the teacher had a hard time bringing me back. One day, she asked me a question in class and when I didn't answer, she came over to my desk and snapped her fingers in front of my face. There was no reaction: I didn't even blink.

In fact, I had (and still have) epilepsy. These early episodes were the mild form known as petit mal or absence seizures, as opposed to the more serious grand mal, or tonic-clonic form, characterized by violent convulsions. It was not until several years later, however, that I was properly diagnosed.

About a week after the finger-snapping incident at school, I had an absence seizure at home. I was about to pour myself a glass of water. My hand stayed on the faucet, the water kept running, and I remained motionless. It was as if someone had pressed a pause button.

Over time, the seizures grew in intensity. All of a sudden, I would become disoriented, oblivious to where I was or what was happening to me. Everything seemed disconnected and made no sense. I would feel rotten and would start to cry. It was like I was losing my memory, and I would eventually pass out. The only times the seizures were somewhat controllable were when my mother or another close relative or friend was nearby, and I would feel relatively safe. When I started puberty, around the age of twelve, the seizures worsened again. Every month when I had my period, I would lose a lot of blood and feel very weak, and have a seizure.

For years, I underwent every test imaginable at the Montreal Children's Hospital: electrocardiograms, electroencephalo-grams, red blood cell counts, white blood cell counts. The results were always normal, but I kept on having seizures. From my perspective as a child, all doctors were geniuses. "If the doctors can't figure out what's wrong with me," I thought, "maybe it means I have some rare disease and I'm going to die from it soon."

Eventually, after poring over all the data that had accumu-lated in my file over the years, some doctors considered the possibility that my illness was mental in origin, perhaps related to some trauma I had suffered in my infancy. Eventually – and reluctantly – I started seeing a therapist. I was deeply ashamed of having to resort to this, because I was convinced, as many people still are, that only crazy people needed to see a shrink. I remember shouting at my mother when I found out she'd told my grandmother the news. She tried to reason with me, but to no avail. "She's going to think I'm crazy," I kept saying. The only person to whom I'd confessed my secret was my best friend, Lucie. And since the idea of having to see a therapist made me extremely nervous, she offered to come with me.

We took the number 112 bus to the nearby neighbourhood of Verdun, where the psychologist's office was. I don't really remember all the details of our conversation, but one thing was certain: I was scared to death of the doctor, because I was convinced he was there to judge me. According to what I'd been told, or at least what I'd understood, he was going to assess whether I was emotionally and intellectually "normal" and based on that assessment make a diagnosis. So I tried to appear strong and give him the impression that I was coping just fine with the hard times we were going through at home, including the fact that my father was rarely there. My greatest fear was that I was going to be institutionalized. I thought, "That's what they do with crazy people, right?" I'd been to the children's hospital so many times for tests; this time I was sure I was going to wind up in a psychiatric hospital.

On the way back from that first visit, riding the bus to the Jolicoeur metro station, where we were due to catch the number 36 bus home, I felt another episode coming on. I sensed it was going to be more intense than any I had ever experienced. There was also an acute feeling of panic, brought on by the fact that I was in unfamiliar, public surroundings, and that the only person with me was someone my own age, which didn't provide the same sense of security I would have felt had my mother been there, for example.

Anyone with any experience with epilepsy knows that the worst thing a sufferer can do when they feel a seizure aura is to panic, stiffen, and try to fight the seizure; this only makes things much worse. But I still had no idea at that point that I had epilepsy. All I knew was that I was feeling an alarming sense of insecurity and anxiety, and there was nothing I could do about it.

As soon as we got off the bus and walked into the metro station, I felt my legs weaken dangerously and go out from under me. I collapsed. I was having a full-blown panic attack. I couldn't breathe.

And then something strange happened. At the very moment I fell to the floor, I floated up and out of my body and saw myself as if in a movie, from above – as if I were stuck to the ceiling of the metro station. I could see Lucie leaning over my body, crying and screaming, "Somebody call an ambulance! Call an ambulance!" Then a lady came over, bent down, and started slapping my face, saying I was having an overdose. Then Lucie started hitting *her*, yelling, "No, no! She's sick and the doctors don't know what's wrong with her!" Then I saw my mother enter the scene from one side of the station and the ambulance drive up on the other. I saw the attendants pick up my body, wrap it in a red blanket, lay it on a stretcher, and strap it down. Then they lifted the stretcher into the ambulance and closed the doors.

I clearly remember, at that moment, the horrible sensation that I was dying. I thought of all the people I loved: my closest family members, my grandparents. But I also had the distinct feeling that there was an attentive presence near me. With all the naïveté of a twelve-year-old girl, I prayed to – or rather shouted at – God (or whatever entity was present) about something that was supposed to happen the next weekend: my first ever school dance. I'd been excitedly looking forward to it for days, and there was no way I was going to miss it. At that point, it was the most important thing in my young life. So I said to God, "You can't do this to me! I don't know anything about life. I've never even danced with a boy. I beg of You, let me live!" But at the same time, it felt so good, floating weightless in that softness, not feeling my body yet fully aware of everything. I felt ready to die.

I woke up in the children's hospital. They told me I'd stopped breathing for a while because of the panic attack and that the oxygen supply to my brain had been briefly cut off. My face was blue and swollen. But I was about to find out the true nature of my illness.

Dr. Kenneth Silver, a distinguished Montreal neurologist, examined me soon after I was admitted. He looked at my file and was the first to theorize that I might be suffering from epilepsy. He ran some tests, and the diagnosis was confirmed.

Although being able to put a name to my illness was comforting in a way, at first the news came as a shock to me, and soon it became a source of considerable anxiety. After all, I'd just learned that there was something wrong with my brain, and that wasn't the slightest bit comforting. I began to fear that I could never be normal, that I was condemned to a certain brand of madness. I wondered whether I would be able to do well at school, and if I would be viewed as less intelligent than the other kids. These doubts became a real obsession.

As soon as I was discharged from the hospital, I rushed to the local library and began reading everything I could about epilepsy. One thing I learned was that notable historical figures such as Nostradamus, Napoleon, and Einstein – who weren't exactly imbeciles – had suffered from epilepsy. This was very reassuring. It meant that my intellect would remain intact, and I wasn't an idiot because I was suffering from epilepsy.

As soon as his diagnosis was confirmed, Dr. Silver prescribed Tegretol, and from that point on I began to be able to control my seizures. But it took a few years before the condition could be completely controlled. During adolescence, because our body mass and hormone concentrations are constantly changing, the daily dosage of medication must be altered frequently. Nevertheless, my seizures eventually grew less violent, and less frequent. And because I was better informed about my condition, I quickly learned to conquer my fear whenever I felt a seizure coming on. All I had to do was take a step back, enter into a meditative state, listen to reason, and take deep breaths. Gradually, I learned to get through the seizures without losing consciousness, except on days when I didn't eat well, did too much exercise, or was too tired, in which case they were harder to control. On the advice of my doctor, I began to follow a more stable, balanced lifestyle.

But I was not yet completely immune to a relapse. A few years after that worst episode, when I was fifteen, I had another serious seizure, at school this time. It was a very humiliating experience; I remember the unease I felt as I saw the strange looks I was getting from my classmates and when, back at school the next day, the episode was the sole subject of conversation. An epileptic seizure isn't a particularly nice thing to see: loss of motor control, convulsions, foaming at the mouth, and all the rest. Very quickly, I not only had to learn to deal with my condition but also to fashion a sort of shell to protect myself from the judgment of others.

I still have to take my medication today, but I've learned to live with my illness, and it is well under control. I haven't had any seizure auras since I was eighteen. I think the experience has taught me a great deal, however. First, the episode in the metro station and my strange out-of-body experience convinced me – a girl from a family that didn't practise religion aside from attending mass on Christmas Eve – that there is something beyond death and our humble existence as human beings. During that episode, I could see and hear everything, I was capable of thought and analysis, but I could no longer feel my body, and I experienced a feeling of wellness that is difficult to describe. I drew and kept from that experience a sense of spirituality that I had not even come close to before.

Second, my epilepsy taught me never to feel sorry for myself, and never to play the victim. Yes, I have been through difficult situations because of it, and it has restricted my career options. But, I realized quickly back then, countless people were in much more painful situations than mine: diabetics forced to inject themselves with insulin daily; burn victims who have known hellish suffering and who will never again see their real faces in the mirror; accident victims who have lost the use of one or more limbs. The price I would have to pay to live a normal life – taking a few pills a day, following a stable regimen, eating right, and limiting my alcohol intake – was not too high, all things considered.

6

First Kisses

"I wasn't in any hurry to lose my innocence."

When I was twelve, I started my first year of high school at Polyvalente Notre-Dame-du-Bon-Conseil, on Beaulieu Street in Ville-Émard. At the time it was a brand new, clean building, with a huge asphalt schoolyard. It was for Secondary I and II students, while École Honoré-Mercier, on Desmarchais Boulevard, was for students in the last three years of high school.

The year was 1981, and the Quebec education ministry had just decreed that the passing grade in every high school subject would henceforth be 60 per cent, rather than 50 per cent. The news led to widespread student protests, especially in Montreal. In our part of the city, the students at Polyvalente Saint-Henri, which was in a rougher part of town, spearheaded the movement. One morning, they decided to go on strike, and they went around to all the neighbouring high schools to get other students to join them.

When the striking students arrived at Notre-Dame-du-Bon-Conseil, we were in math class. I don't recall the teacher's name, but I clearly remember that she was pregnant. All of a sudden, a tough-looking young guy of sixteen or seventeen burst into the classroom. He looked pretty agitated and was swinging a stick, making a racket and yelling, "Everybody outside!" He strode up to the teacher and shoved her violently against the blackboard. Several of us shouted at him that she was pregnant and he should be careful. He then started hitting everything in sight with his stick again – walls, desks, and chairs. Some of his henchmen soon joined him, and they forced us to leave the school, threatening us in the process. It was the first time in my life that I'd seen the brute force of an uncontrolled mob in action. We were still young children, being pushed around by young adults, and scared out of our wits.

That day, the incensed strikers ransacked everything in their path, leaving graffiti on walls here and there and causing significant damage. It was a horrible sight; you'd have sworn that Attila's armies had swept through on a raiding party. We were all deeply upset and saddened by the vandalism.

The strike actions went on for nearly two weeks. But after that first day, as soon as the school authorities were advised that striking students were on their way, the bell would ring and we would all be herded out into the schoolyard. Then they would lock all the doors to make sure the strikers couldn't return to vandalize the premises. The school administration also had a huge iron fence built around the building, and even had barbed wire installed to block access to the second-floor windows. These security devices are still there, a constant reminder of a turbulent episode in the history of my old school. To this day it looks more like a prison than a place of learning.

Although by this time I had reached puberty, I still felt very much like a little girl, and that was fine by me. A lot of girls my age, including Lucie and others in the neighbourhood, much preferred playing with their Barbie dolls to looking at boys. In my case, I can't help but wonder whether this had something to do with my parents' strained relationship and my feeling that adults' lives were just too complicated. At any rate, I was comfortable just being a kid. The prospect of growing up didn't seem particularly exciting.

My first more-or-less sensual contact with the opposite sex happened on my twelfth birthday. We had a little party at our house, and among the guests was a boy who had come with one of my friends. He was a little bit older, maybe fourteen. He came up to me and kissed me, and stuck his tongue in my mouth. My reaction was sheer disgust: "Yecch! What are you doing?" I cried. I was really shocked.

The first guy I went out with steadily, about a year after that, was one of Lucie's neighbours, Sylvain Béchard.* He was cute, with blond hair and blue eyes, shy, and not very talkative. I'd known him for years. I shared my first French kiss with him. We would walk hand in hand through the neighbourhood, giving each other *gros becs*, which is what we used to call these "tongue kisses" that brought on strange new pleasurable sensations. But during the few months that we went out together, things never went any further than that.

I was fourteen when I met my first real boyfriend, Michel Dubé.† We were together for almost five years. He was almost two years older than me, and I knew he wasn't a virgin. He put

---

* Not his real name.
† Not his real name.

quite a bit of pressure on me to sleep with him. One day, a bit exasperated, I said to him, "If you don't find me adventurous enough, big guy, just go off and have your fun with somebody else. There are plenty of other girls. I won't mind." I wasn't in any hurry to lose my innocence. Of course, there was the ever-present fear of an unwanted pregnancy, but I was also well aware that one's first sexual experience is an important step in life, and I wasn't ready to take that step. After that he was more patient.

Throughout most of my teenage years, Michel and I were part of a gang of ten or so kids who had a lot in common and did all kinds of things together. In the summer, we'd often hang out in Saint-Jean-de-Matha Park, right behind the church of the same name, watching baseball games or attending events like the Saint-Jean-Baptiste Day celebrations. Lucie and her boyfriend, Frédéric* (Michel's best friend), whom she eventually married and had three children with, were part of the same group. Most of them lived in Old Ville-Émard, so we would often get together with them in the evening or when we had the day off school.

A few years later, when the boys in the gang started driving, we widened our party territory. Michel had a truck that his father had bought him, and Carl,† another of our friends, drove an old Chevrolet Impala with a huge engine that made a hellish noise. We would drive out along Saint-Patrick Street, next to the Côte-Saint-Paul neighbourhood, where there was a level crossing, and the guys would race their cars. It wasn't so much the speed that they got a kick out of; what they really liked was to get air as they accelerated over a bump and flew over the train tracks. Sometimes, we'd go to a parking lot next to one

---

* Not his real name.
† Not his real name.

of the many abandoned factories in the neighbourhood. The guys would noisily rev their engines with the brakes on to see who could make the best smoke show. Over the course of one summer, Michel wore out three whole sets of tires doing that. If any of their parents had got wind of what they were up to, some of the guys would surely have spent the rest of the summer on foot.

Our summer fun wasn't always that spectacular. Often, we'd spend the day at the local waterslides or even drive all the way to Lake George in New York State. On the way down, we'd stop at an abandoned quarry where there was a lake. It was a beautiful shade of blue, like you'd see in the tropics. There was a fairly high cliff that we loved jumping off, which was foolhardy, to say the least, since there were rocks just underneath the surface, and we had to be sure to hit the water in a precise spot between them.

Later, after we'd finished high school, several of us would often set out on a Friday night with our boyfriends on what we called a "nowhere trip." We'd pack our bags and start driving with no particular destination in mind, taking back roads. We might end up in the Eastern Townships, the Laurentians or who knows where. We'd rent connecting rooms in some little motel – our base camp for the weekend. During the day, we'd enjoy whatever the natural surroundings had to offer, and at night we'd hit the local pub. So that they wouldn't go broke buying beers in the bar, the guys would start drinking well before we left the motel while we girls got ready, so often we'd be the designated drivers for the trip back to the motel. I have very fond memories of that time, when we didn't know the meaning of the word *responsibility*.

When I was fourteen, I started Secondary III at Honoré-Mercier. This too was a very happy time for me. Like

Notre-Dame-du-Bon-Conseil, where I'd spent the previous two years, Honoré-Mercier was in an attractive, newer building. It also had an excellent music program, with top-notch equipment and services. There was a fine auditorium with excellent acoustics, where the students regularly gave band concerts. During my three years there, I tried my best to learn a number of instruments: flute, xylophone, and especially trombone, but I didn't really have a gift for music – woodwinds and brass were particularly hard to learn – and in the end I had to give it up.

I was never what one would call a model student. I had good grades but not outstanding ones, especially in subjects that demanded memory skills. I simply didn't view my studies as that important compared to my other pursuits. I had a steady boyfriend, a group of female friends that I spent a lot of time with, and I worked on weekends – none of which left much time for schoolwork.

Like any student, I enjoyed some subjects more than others, and the teacher usually had a lot to do with how much I liked the course. On our first day of Secondary IV studies, we learned that the French teacher, who had a reputation for being very strict, was on sick leave that semester. The substitute was Jean,* a young man in his early thirties with longish hair. All the girls had crushes on him from day one. He was pretty easygoing, completely different from anything we'd seen in a teacher up to then, and didn't hesitate to stray from the standard curriculum. The first day, he pulled out a copy of the French translation of Richard Bach's New Age classic, *Jonathan Livingston Seagull*. Every day he would read an excerpt aloud, then ask questions

---

* Not his real name.

to get our impressions, and see what analogies we could draw between Jonathan's ambitions and ordeals and our own lives. Jean understood that we were all going through profound changes, being at an age when we were learning about life and struggling with all kinds of questions about ourselves. He helped us put our uncertainties into words. Looking back, I suppose his teaching methods could have been described as "interactive" – long before the term became trendy. They were a breath of fresh air in an educational system that was mostly geared toward the lecture format, where teachers almost always dispensed the course content in mechanical fashion, and we were expected to absorb it without asking too many questions.

Meanwhile, at home, things weren't any rosier between my parents. My father was still staying out until late at night, while my mother kept on working, struggling to make ends meet and raise her family as best she could. By this time I was completely fed up with life in this tense environment, where an argument was likely to erupt at any moment. I had only one thing in mind: get out as soon as I could. I started working part-time, evenings and weekends, having firmly decided to save enough money to strike out on my own. My first job was as a sales clerk and cashier at Tip Top Tailors in the Alexis-Nihon Plaza. Later, I worked at Bata Shoes, in that same shopping mall, and at the Le Château clothing store at 2020 University.

Although they didn't pay particularly well, these jobs were an enjoyable experience for me throughout my teenage years. They brought me into contact with people, something I still enjoy. My co-workers were friendly and fun. And, of course, I was at an age when I was keenly interested in style and trends, so being entitled to an employee discount from all these shops was nothing to be sneezed at either.

From around my sixteenth birthday until I finished high school about a year later, I worked at the Leather Ranch, in what is now the Promenades Cathédrale, a shopping mall built underneath Christ Church Cathedral, on Sainte-Catherine Street. The job paid much better than other retail positions would have because I earned a commission – and since it was a leather-goods store, each sale was worth quite a bit.

One Saturday morning, the owner of the chain, an American from Atlantic City whose name I don't recall, dropped by the store. I remember the store manager being very nervous, while we, the sales staff, had a good laugh watching him bend over backwards to please the "big boss." The chain owner had decided to add furs to the collections, and as head buyer he had come to Montreal to visit the Salon de la fourrure, a fur products trade show being held at Place Bonaventure.

He strode around, looking a bit arrogant, inspecting the premises. Then he came up to me. "Do you work here?" he asked.

"Yes," I said.

"How would you like to spend the weekend trying on some beautiful coats?"

That was how I got my first experience working as a model, something I would do regularly a few years later. I got into a taxi with my manager and the chain owner, and we went to Place Bonaventure. At the trade show, we stopped at every stand. My job was to try on each fur coat that he picked out. I was extremely nervous, because I was well aware that these first steps in the fashion industry could open doors for me, and fulfill my hope of becoming a successful model. I had never even been part of a fashion show, and at first I found the work difficult. I had to move around inside the heavy fur coats to show how large the skirt was, because volume is a key criterion for a coat's value. After trying on a few coats, though, I became quite sure of myself, and in the end I did a pretty good job.

The "big boss," who had struck me at first as being somewhat smug, turned out to be a nice guy. He was an eccentric who had the financial means to act the way he did. Around his neck, he wore a heavy gold chain, from which he'd hung a huge pendant depicting a three-dimensional pharaoh's head; it looked very heavy. He noticed me staring at it and told me with a hearty laugh how he'd acquired it. One night, he'd won more than one hundred thousand dollars at a casino. He had gone straight to the jewellery store next door and spent all his winnings on the pendant.

On Sunday afternoon, the show was winding down. Before heading back to Atlantic City, the chain owner stopped at a stand that was selling sable coats. One of them, in pale brown, was simply stunning. He had me try it on. It was ankle-length, with magnificent, plush fur, a broad collar, an ample hood, and flutter sleeves. The coat was so roomy that even when I reached out both my arms as far as I could, the fur was far from being stretched taut. How much for this fabulous item? Eighty thousand U.S. dollars. This was 1985, and for that price one could buy a decent house! Wearing that coat gave me the feeling that I'd instantly leapt several rungs higher up the social ladder.

In the end, the boss told me that I'd shown off the sable coat so well that he'd decided to buy it for his wife. That day was quite an eye-opener for me: I had never in my wildest dreams imagined that a coat could cost so much, let alone that there were people who could afford to buy them.

The next day, it was back to reality – until one of my girlfriends called and told me to have a look at the front page of the fashion section of that morning's *La Presse*. There I was, twirling proudly in the sable coat!

Having worked at a number of part-time jobs throughout most of my teenage years, by the time I graduated high school, just a few weeks before I turned seventeen, I had saved up a tidy sum of money. It allowed me to think seriously about escaping the stifling atmosphere of my family nest.

7

Floodwaters Rising

"People were paddling in canoes in the street."

September 1986: I had enrolled in humanities at Cégep André-Laurendeau, in LaSalle, hoping to become a lawyer. My mother approved of my plan, but had made it clear to me that she didn't have the means to pay for the long years of university that it required. And even though I had a fair bit of money saved up, I knew full well that I wouldn't manage without a student loan. I was fearful of later beginning my professional life with a large debt on my shoulders – and what was more, I wasn't completely sure that my career choice was the right one. So rather than commit myself fully to that option, I decided to interrupt my studies temporarily and go to work in a law office to see if I would enjoy the legal profession. Looking back, I see very clearly that, on top of the financial insecurity, my decision was hastened by the prospect of my having to keep on living with my parents if I were to continue my studies.

I was seventeen that fall. By then I had been going out with Michel for more than three years. We'd started talking about maybe moving in together, or even buying a home. Michel's father was a plumber, and he supplemented his income by buying buildings, renovating them, and reselling them. He had explained the key criteria to consider when planning to buy an apartment building, and the calculations to be made, especially in terms of the relationship between the asking price and the expected rental income.

We had been looking at two adjoining duplexes on Sainte-Marie Street, between Côte-Saint-Paul Road and Saint-Rémi Street, in the Saint-Henri neighbourhood. They belonged to an older gentleman who had a large real estate portfolio that he had decided to liquidate. I'm sure he found us very likeable because we were so young. When we met with him, he explained that he too had started buying property when he was fairly young, and that he felt like giving us a leg up by offering us a good price on the two buildings. We paid $49,000 for each duplex, a total of $98,000. It was a real bargain.

Michel's father, who had secured all his mortgage loans from the Caisse populaire de Ville LaSalle, estimated the market value of each of our properties at $69,000, which represented net assets of $40,000. That meant it wouldn't be difficult to get our mortgage approved. The only problem was that I wasn't yet of legal age, so I couldn't be an official party to the transaction. Michel was therefore the only one to sign the mortgage loan, even though I had contributed $2,000, my share of the down payment, a ridiculously low sum.

My mother was dead set against my leaving home before I turned eighteen. In hindsight, I think she was worried that I was about to make the same mistake that she had, some twenty years earlier. Given what eventually transpired, I have to admit that she may not have been entirely wrong. At any rate, this proved to be one of the rare times in my life when my father intervened on my behalf; he advised my mother to let me make my own way in the world. In truth, she didn't have much choice in the matter.

So, shortly before Christmas, Michel and I moved into a two-bedroom apartment on the ground floor of one of the two duplexes, which we set about gradually renovating and furnishing, splitting the costs as we had agreed.

Then, one day in early June 1987 – a few weeks before my eighteenth birthday – disaster struck. I had invited my grandmother to come over for dinner that evening and see my new home. We were doing the dishes together afterward, and it had started to rain – so heavily that we couldn't see more than half a metre in front of us through the window. Water started pouring into the apartment from everywhere, and at one point I had to pick up my little poodle, Lady, and set her on top of the kitchen table. Realizing that the situation might become dangerous, I called my sister to ask her if her boyfriend could come and get us – he had a pickup truck with an engine that was sealed, and therefore waterproof. He arrived very soon, and got my grandmother and me out of there. As we drove through the streets, I could see that the water was up to the fenders on either side of the pickup, as if we were in a boat. Around us, people were paddling in canoes in the street. The car that Michel and I owned, a little Ford Escort hatchback, had been swept away by the current.

Our neighbours across the street, an elderly couple, were far less fortunate. The water pressure was so strong that they weren't able to open their front door. After strenuous effort and with the help of some neighbours, Michel managed to break a window that was already completely submerged. The water had nearly reached the ceiling by the time they were finally able to rescue the couple from their house. Once they were in the ambulance, however, the poor man had a heart attack and died.

The flooding had been caused by the heavy rain, of course, but was made worse by a defect in the city sewer system. The sewage pumps hadn't worked – there had been a power outage and the generators had failed to take over – so the storm drains had backed up. The damage to our two properties was considerable: the water level had risen to almost two metres inside our apartment, and all the furniture we'd recently bought was ruined. Moreover, the ground in front of the house had collapsed, taking with it the foundation walls around the one-metre-high dirt-floor basement.

The insurance company decided that because the damage had resulted from a natural disaster, we weren't entitled to the slightest compensation. When my father learned of this, he put me in touch with a well-respected claims adjuster who had worked for many years for the City of Montreal and knew all about the municipal sewer system and other underground infrastructure. The adjuster painstakingly analyzed the circumstances of the disaster and unequivocally concluded that the city was at fault. Armed with the findings of that study, Michel and I filed a new claim and began the necessary renovations after securing a loan from the caisse populaire.

At the time, I had been working for several months in a law office on Saint-Jacques Street in Old Montreal, and things were going well for me. I had started out as the receptionist but had soon been given some responsibility for corporate cases, and I was a quick learner. But someone had to stay at home on a full-time basis to handle the claim with the city administration, to look after the renovations, and to find new tenants (we had let our tenants out of their leases because their apartments were no longer inhabitable). Since Michel was earning a lot more than me as a plumber's apprentice, we agreed that it would be best if I quit my job and took on all these new responsibilities.

I therefore assumed full management of the crisis, including supervising the renovations, all while trying to do as much of the job as possible with Michel in the evenings to keep the contractors' bills down. When I say that I was a 100 per cent full partner, these aren't just words; I committed myself fully to all the manual labour involved in the renovations. I demolished bathrooms with a sledgehammer, put up wallboard, did plastering, cut tiles, spread grout, and painted walls and ceilings.

I also took care of all the accounting for the two buildings, which until then had been mostly done by Michel and his father. Looking at the books, I realized that the income from the three rents we were collecting was more than enough to cover the mortgage payments. All the same, Michel was asking me to pay him $225 per month in rent, even though his income was much higher than mine. This got me thinking that perhaps I tended to be too trusting of people who didn't deserve it. But we were so busy during that time that I didn't dwell on those thoughts.

The renovations went fairly well, and by the morning of July 14, new carpeting was rolled out on the floors of our apartment, ready to be tacked down. Then the rain started falling again. Anyone who was living in Montreal at the time remembers what happened next: a deluge the likes of which the city had never seen. The damage to our buildings was even worse than after the previous month's flooding. We lost everything once again, but this time our credit had run out, and there was no way we could consider renovating again. Our only option was to liquidate our properties and try as best we could to cut our losses.

In those days, there were real estate investors who would buy out the mortgages on damaged properties. A real estate agent approached us, offering to put our buildings on the market, and we accepted. She quickly found us a buyer: a company was willing to purchase our buildings, but their price meant that we would lose five thousand dollars on our investment. We wanted to submit a counter-offer, but the agent talked us out of it, convincing us that the buyer would reject it. When we went to the notary's office to sign the documents, we realized that the real estate agent for the investment firm that was buying our property was also a partner in that firm. Not only that: our agent was fully aware of this, but had not told us anything. Though I was hardly a specialist in this type of transaction, it wasn't hard to see that there was a conflict of interest. How could our agent have negotiated in good faith on our behalf when she was clearly in league with the buyer's agent? I asked the notary, "How can it be that the buyer's agent is the one buying our buildings?"

The notary asked the buyer to leave the office so that he could confer with Michel and me in private. Once they were gone, I asked, "Is this legal?"

"Has the buyer's agent signed any sort of declaration stating that she is one of the prospective buyers?" the notary asked.

"Not at all. I knew nothing about it until now. We never would have dealt with her had we known," I replied.

"Then you're in the right," the notary said. "There are some remedies available to you. You're entitled to file a complaint with the Quebec Real Estate Brokers and Agents Association. Or I could simply annul the transaction right here and now."

But I had another idea. I went to see our real estate agent and told her point blank, "You have a choice. Either you don't take a penny in commission, or you add five thousand dollars to the purchase price. Otherwise I'm going to ask the notary to put everything in trust, and we'll see each other in court."

I saw her flinch when I raised the possibility of entrusting the matter to the judicial system. In the end, the buyer paid the commission. But the most important thing was that we were no longer selling at a loss. At the end of the day, Michel and I weren't out any money. Not long after, we were among a handful of injured parties who saw their insurance claims through to the end, and we won our case against the city. We were awarded forty thousand dollars in compensation for our losses.

Throughout this period, from our initial purchase of the buildings in Saint-Henri through the management of the mortgage and our claim before the City of Montreal, I had placed my trust in Michel. Blindly. It was a mistake.

8

Breakup

"The only boyfriend I'd ever had had just cheated me out of twenty thousand dollars."

Not long after the great flood of July 14, 1987, and the disposal of our property, my father found us an apartment in a building that he partly owned in the Notre-Dame-de-Grâce neighbourhood, popularly referred to as NDG. Soon after we moved in, Michel received the cheque for forty thousand dollars from the City of Montreal.

Even before he collected the compensation from the city, though, I had begun to observe a marked change in Michel's behaviour. He started going out more often than usual, which was strange, because he was basically a homebody and had never been that fond of alcohol. He began going to bars with friends on a regular basis and staying out until very late at night. It was as if he'd decided to live the bachelor life that he'd never known.

At first, I didn't make a big deal about it. After all, we'd just gone through a difficult period that had subjected us both to quite a bit of stress: the purchase of the buildings, the renovations, administering the tenant leases, and worst of all, the two spells of bad luck that had arrived one after the other and had forced us to dispose of our buildings in a rush. It was a lot to deal with for a young man barely into his twenties, and I understood Michel's need to let off some steam. I'd known him for a long time, and I trusted him.

But as time wore on, Michel kept going out, three or four nights a week. He would stay out until the bars closed, more often than not coming home at four in the morning, even though he had to be up at six to go to work. Little by little, we stopped doing things together, even on weekends, because he would spend most of his days off in bed, recovering from the excesses of the previous days.

Before long, I began to be seriously worried and started confiding in my female friends. One day, one of them said to me: "Julie, Michel's a partier, it's obvious."

"No way," I replied. "That's not his thing."

At first, I refused to believe the explanations I heard sometimes. Neither Michel nor I had ever been big partiers. Nevertheless, several signs led me to believe that he must have been taking something – speed, or who knows what – to be able to stay awake all day at work.

My girlfriends then told me that some of the people Michel was hanging out with were well known for partying hard. So I decided to confront him. "What are you talking about?" he scoffed. "I don't do drugs. What do you take me for?"

"In that case, explain to me how you manage to put in an entire day at work – doing such a physically demanding job, too – on barely two hours' sleep," I retorted.

At the time, Michel was an apprentice plumber for a janitorial company that specialized in apartment buildings. It was a tough job, and the hours were long.

"I take speed, caffeine pills, stuff like that. But don't worry about it. I'm young, I can handle it. You don't have to worry."

On the contrary, I *was* worried – very. With each passing day, I saw my Michel turning into the polar opposite of the man I knew and loved. And it was disconcerting to see how fast the change was happening. To tell the truth, he was on a downward spiral, and I was becoming afraid of him. This was all the more surprising because just a few weeks earlier he had given me an engagement ring and asked me to marry him. Since his behaviour clearly proved to me that he wasn't comfortable in the relationship, I had said no: I wasn't ready, we were too young, I didn't want to get married, and that was that. He told me to keep the ring anyway, as a pledge, a testimonial to his commitment. In the ensuing weeks, he continued living the wild life, spending his evenings away from home and coming back at ungodly hours, in a mess.

Finally, one night I said to him, "Look, if you plan to keep on living like this, we'd be better off going our separate ways, at least for a while. If you want to live a bachelor's life, go ahead. You do what you have to do, but it'll be without me. And when you're done, we'll get back together if we're really meant to be together." He didn't take the news well at all.

A few days later, the forty-thousand-dollar cheque from the city arrived – made out to Michel only, of course, because he'd been the sole signer on the mortgage loan and therefore the only official owner. He moved out of the apartment, telling me that he would do the right thing and give me half the amount in short order. But in the meantime, his father told him, "The cheque's in your name, son. Anyway, you and that girl are history. The law's on your side. Nobody will be able to come after you. You keep the money, and that's it." And like a good son, that's exactly what he did.

The only boyfriend I'd ever had had just cheated me out of twenty thousand dollars. What made the pill that much harder to swallow was the fact that it had been my father who had helped us find the claims expert who had pleaded our cause before the City of Montreal. Had it not been for him, we wouldn't have received a penny in compensation. It was also my father who had found us a place to live, rent-free, after the July 14 flood.

I learned later that Michel had gone on a serious binge and that nearly all of the forty thousand dollars was blown in just a few weeks. One night, in the grip of remorse, he called me. I don't know if he was drunk or high; I never tried to find out. His voice was thick and pasty, as if he'd swallowed a bite of hot potato. He was crying his eyes out on the other end of the phone line. He said he had five thousand dollars left and he was ready to come and give it to me. I exploded. "If you think you can buy back your conscience for five thousand bucks when you owe me twenty thousand, you can take that five thousand and shove it where the sun don't shine," I told him. "You know what? You're going to carry the weight of what you did for the rest of your life. That's how you're going to pay. And at least I'll have the satisfaction of knowing that if we ever run into each other on the street, you won't have any other choice but to look down at your boots, you thieving bastard." Then I hung up on him.

A few months later, I got a letter from him, and in the envelope was all the jewellery I'd given to him as presents during our nearly five years together. In the letter, he wrote that he'd recently heard that a star player with the Montreal Canadiens, a very popular hockey player at the time, was a regular at the same LaSalle bar that I went to, and that he "had the hots for me." He added that there was no way he could compete with somebody of that calibre and that I'd never go back to him, so he was giving up on us ever getting back together. That was the end of our story.

That first relationship had given me a taste of all the disillusionment that I'd seen my mother experience with my father. There was precious little I could take from my time with Michel that could change my low opinion of men.

9

One Bourbon, One Scotch, One Beer

"As I walked past, holding a tray with twelve beers on it, the idiot grabbed me by the waist and sat me down on his lap."

After the breakup with Michel, I quickly moved out of the apartment in NDG and rented a small loft on Allard Street in Ville-Émard. I was single, without a job, and desperately needed to make some money, fast. I became a real estate agent, after a crash course at a school run by Jean-Guy Leboeuf, who had been a candidate for the leadership of the Union Nationale and was later elected to the National Assembly in 1976 as a member of that party.

This was the late 1980s, however, and the real estate market had begun a downturn that was to last several years. After a very short stint trying to sell residential buildings, which I didn't much like, I decided to try my luck with the commercial market, which at the time wasn't in such bad shape. I did a good deal of prospecting in downtown Montreal, found a client who had some magnificent spaces for rent near Saint-Mathieu Street, not far from the old Forum, and made an agreement with him. He started out asking $26 per square foot for these rental properties, and when I brought him a tenant who was prepared to pay $20, he told me to forget it. But his stubborn attitude didn't last: the commercial rental market soon went into a difficult phase as well, and before long my client told me that if I could find someone willing to pay $12 per square foot, he'd be interested in making a deal.

I quickly came to the conclusion that as a beginner in the industry my chances of earning an acceptable income were slim; under those market conditions, even the most experienced agents were having difficulty closing major deals. I was going to have to change jobs quickly if I was to have any hope of supporting myself. Before long, I was selling new cars at a Subaru dealership in LaSalle.

I can't claim that automobile mechanics was one of my strong suits – I didn't even know how to do an oil change. But I was pretty good at selling, so good that by my second month at the dealership, I was voted salesperson of the month. This came at some cost, however; the hours were very long, and the economy was in the doldrums, which meant that many of the sales I made were never finalized, because the customers failed to get credit approval. The banks were extremely averse to risk, and their criteria were strict. In the automobile sales business, the bulk of salespeople's income comes from commissions, so I concluded that I didn't have much of a future in that line of work either.

I turned next to the restaurant industry – at least the tips made for attractive income potential. So I found myself working for several months as a waitress at the Picasso restaurant, on Saint-Jacques Street in NDG. It was always full, at all hours of the day and night, so there were plenty of tips to be had.

It was hard-earned pay, though. It was wintertime, the front doors were poorly insulated, and customers were coming and going all the time, so there were constant cold drafts. Our feet were forever frozen as we walked across the ice-cold terrazzo floor. The pace was insane and the hours were very long. My shift started at five in the evening and ended at five in the morning. But the pay was good.

While working at Picasso, I started studying to become a dental assistant, at École Pierre-Dupuy in the city's east end. This meant that after leaving the restaurant in the wee hours, I would go home and sleep for an hour or two, then leave the house to spend most of the day in class, and return home to try to grab a bit more sleep before the next shift at the restaurant. Eventually, I abandoned my studies on the advice of my doctor; he said I was starting to show all the symptoms of mononucleosis. I couldn't keep up that kind of regimen or my health would surely suffer. I have to admit that there was another factor that strongly influenced my decision to give up on a career in dentistry. This was the late 1980s, at the height of public fears about AIDS, and antiretroviral drugs had yet to be developed. I had worked briefly in a dentist's office in LaSalle, and one day I had cut my finger while cleaning an instrument. I was so worried about getting infected that I put an end to my plans.

The Picasso restaurant was on the ground floor of the building on Saint-Jacques, and the basement was occupied by a strip club called Les Amazones. After closing time, the staff – the waitresses, the bouncers, and a few of the dancers – would come upstairs for a bite to eat. I found them friendlier and less demanding than the average customer, no doubt because they worked in the service industry as well. I made friends with one of the waitresses, Katie. One night she said to me, "Julie, I hope you don't mind my asking . . . how much do you clear in a week?"

"I don't know, five or six hundred bucks," I replied.

"If you're interested, I can get you a job waitressing down-stairs. It's three nights a week, plus the occasional Sunday, and you'll make between $275 and $300 a night just in tips."

Basically, she was telling me that I could double my salary while cutting my hours in half. The offer was tempting, but I wasn't too thrilled at the idea of working in a strip club. I had always profoundly mistrusted the world of exotic dancers and their clients. For one reason or another, I'd always had the impression that if the United States had never had a woman president, it was in large part because there were so many strip clubs projecting such a negative image of women. But Katie was reassuring. "The waitresses' uniform isn't provocative at all," she said. "Black slacks, white shirt – it's super conserva-tive. The dancers have their own dressing room and they stick to their own area inside the club."

In the end, the lure of a decent paycheque won out, and I gave it a try. But my greatest fears were soon realized, and my already limited patience was brutally put to the test. As anyone would expect, the place was full of loud, drunken customers who talked incessantly, flirting with and harassing the female staff – and not just the dancers.

One Friday night, a customer sitting at the bar, who clearly had long since exceeded the legal blood-alcohol limit, got it into his head that he was going to get me to dance for him – at any price. He pulled out a hundred-dollar bill, then a second, and a third. "Sir," I said, doing my best to keep my cool and remain polite, "there are plenty of dancers here. That's their job. I only serve drinks. I don't dance." But the drunk wouldn't hear of it. He insisted – and then raised the stakes, pulling out more hundred dollar bills, convinced that I would finally give in. I decided to ignore him and went to fill my order at the end of the bar.

In this type of establishment, the beer and drink trays are huge; they can carry the equivalent of a case of beer. Each waitress has to pay up front for all the drinks her customers have ordered, out of her pocket. If she spills the contents of her tray for any reason, she has to cover the loss.

While the barmaid was filling my drink tray, the stubborn customer, despite his state of advanced intoxication, just wouldn't give up. He kept on upping his offer, and was now prepared to spend more than one thousand dollars to see me dance. He was even ready to compromise: "You can keep your bra and panties on," he said.

I left the bar with my order. As I walked past, holding a tray with twelve beers on it, the idiot grabbed me by the waist and sat me down on his lap. Bottles and glasses flew in all directions and shattered all over the place. Before I even had time to react, the bouncers swept in, grabbed the customer, and without further ado, dragged him up the stairs and out of the club.

The next day, I wasn't in any mood to go to work, so I called in sick. I went in the day after that, on the Sunday – typically a slow night. Not long before closing time, however, I had a seizure. I decided life was sending me a message: earning a good wage is all very well, but not if you're going to have to pay with your health. My career as a strip club waitress was over.

My brief stint – barely a month – in that business had validated all my preconceived notions. In those days, dancers could easily earn between two thousand and three thousand dollars a week, but in the end, for the majority of them, it just wasn't worth the effort. True, some women who dance in clubs manage to stay grounded, especially those who do it with a specific goal in mind – to pay for their education or some project or other. They amass the required funds and get out as soon as they can. But they're the exceptions. The reality is that to get up the nerve to go out on stage and gyrate nude in front of complete strangers, most dancers rely on alcohol or drugs. But eventually, they develop a dependency, and the pattern is reversed; they keep dancing to be able to buy the drugs they need. And in many cases, unfortunately, this vicious circle ruins one life after another.

At Les Amazones I had got to know Norman,* one of the bouncers. We hit it off right away, and soon after I quit working there, we started going out. He had a little apartment in NDG but didn't sleep there very often. Before long, he'd moved in with me.

Norman wasn't exactly rolling in money, to say the least. He drove an old car – I forget which make and model – that was so beat up there were holes in the floor that let snow in during the winter. It was a real menace to society. Norman had quit his job at Les Amazones at the same time as me and was working in a computer store for a pittance. Since his financial situation was precarious, I lent him some money so that he could make a down payment on a small used car.

---

* Not his real name.

10

Steroids

*"He grabbed me by the throat and lifted me off the floor,
my head against the wall. He was literally choking me. I
had the presence of mind to knee him in the crotch."*

In my short spell at Les Amazones, I'd been able to amass a
tidy sum, but I didn't exactly have enough to take a year off
and sail around the world. I had to find more work, and
fast. I soon got myself a job as a receptionist for a company
that made jeans and ready-to-wear apparel for women.

After a few weeks, the designer (who went on to win a prize
at the Rose d'Or fashion awards a few years later) noticed me
and before long was regularly asking me to be a fit model for
her designs. She didn't have to ask twice; I loved doing it. I
would slip on the clothes and she would do the final adjust-
ments before okaying them for production. Then one day she
asked if I'd like to be part of a photo shoot for the in-house
magazine, which was sent out to retailers so they could choose
which collections they wanted to carry. I was so enthusiastic at
the prospect that I rushed to sign the necessary documents in
case she changed her mind.

Shortly thereafter, the company manager called me into his office and told me that he'd bought the distribution rights to a famous European denim brand. He was a good-looking man, very seductive, in his early thirties. Very well off too – and he wasn't shy about demonstrating it, to impress young women like me. There were several pairs of jeans lying around the office, and he asked me to try a few on. Then he explained that he was planning a major advertising blitz to launch the brand in North America, that the commercial would be shot in Europe, and that he thought I was the ideal candidate to be the face of the campaign. I told him I was interested and then asked him to have a contract drawn up. I planned to have a lawyer look it over, because I knew next to nothing about that side of the business. I assured him that once that was taken care of, we could go ahead.

The next day or maybe the day after, he asked me to go back and see him in his office, after five o'clock, to talk about the deal. "Contract's right there," he said, nodding toward some pages. He didn't ask me to read it, and he didn't offer me a copy. "There's just one small condition you have to be aware of that's not spelled out in the contract."

Then he started telling me about a room at the Sheraton. Strawberries and champagne. Let's just say it didn't take me long to see where this was going. The guy may have been attractive, but he'd just fallen way down on the charm scale. I let him finish up his spiel and then I said, "So, just to get this straight: I sleep with you, and I get the contract?" I spun on my heel, headed for the door, and just before I got to it, turned back around, looked him up and down, shot him a taunting little smile, and said, "I might have gone to bed with you just for the fun of it. But, see, if I did it for the money, I'd feel awfully dirty in the morning." And I left. When I went back in to work the next day, there was a letter waiting for me on my desk, thanking me for my "excellent and loyal services" and adding that, unfortunately, they would no longer be required.

Some time later, it came to my attention that several of the photos I'd posed for, which were to be published in the in-house magazine, had appeared in mainstream publications like *Chatelaine* and *Allure* without my consent. I went to see a lawyer to see what recourse I had, but he explained that given the wording of the contract, my options were limited. So I let it go. But at least the episode taught me something: if people were willing to use pictures of me to publish them in magazines, I might actually have a future in fashion and advertising – as long as I surrounded myself with people I could trust. I started looking for an agent who could find me modelling contracts. I ended up choosing Agence Scoop, a small operation that at the time was run by a former model out of her Old Montreal loft.

Meanwhile, I was still living with Norman in the loft on Allard Street. His financial situation had improved quite a bit since we'd started going out. He'd found himself a new day job that paid better, and he was also a bouncer at Thursday's, a bar on Crescent Street in downtown Montreal. He had decent income from the two jobs and had even managed to buy himself a Porsche – used, mind you, but still . . .

I can't say that things were going all that well for me, though. I was still trying to find my way. I knew I wanted to go back to school, but I didn't have the means to pay for three or four years of university. So I decided to study hotel management at LaSalle College, on Sainte-Catherine Street in the western part of downtown. I was attracted to the program because the courses were so diverse (accounting, statistics, marketing, wine appreciation, and more) and it offered a chance to gain all manner of practical knowledge that would end up being quite useful in life, even if it turned out that I didn't want a job in the hotel industry.

Norman thought it was a great idea, and since I had supported him financially early in our relationship, he offered to return the favour. He suggested that I study full-time and take the intensive program, which was shorter. He would pay the rent and incidental expenses, so I could concentrate on my studies. And since I didn't own a car, we would move downtown so I could be close to the college.

As planned, we moved out of the little loft on Allard Street and into an apartment on the corner of Atwater and Sainte-Catherine streets, just a short walk from LaSalle College. Everything went as we had hoped. I loved my coursework, I had no money issues, and Norman and I had a fulfilling relationship.

Norman wasn't what you would call a bad guy, but he had an obsession with bodybuilding. He was particularly fixated on his chest measurements. He was nearly six foot two and had a very attractive body, but he was convinced that he was sunken-chested and that made him less virile. He wanted a physique like Arnold Schwarzenegger's. To add bulk, he occasionally used anabolic steroids, like many friends with whom he worked out at the gym. He'd taken them for several months at the beginning of our relationship. He put on plenty of muscle, of course, but it was hardly worth the effect it had on his personality. As with so many bodybuilders who rely on "the juice," the drugs gave Norman a feeling of power, but they also made him irritable and sometimes even paranoid. He knew perfectly well that I was against that sort of thing, so when he started taking steroids again, he did so in secret. But the effect on his personality was so obvious that I could tell he was using them again.

One morning, I was having breakfast at the kitchen table, sitting in the chair Norman normally sat in at suppertime. He was collapsed in an armchair, watching TV. Suddenly he turned to me and said, in an extremely aggressive voice, "What are you doing sitting in my chair? You know that's where I usually sit." It was ridiculous. It was obvious he was looking for an argument.

"Yeah . . . except at the moment you're not eating," I answered.

"It's still my spot. Get out of my chair!"

Now, if you prod me in the morning before I've had a chance to drink my coffee, the odds are excellent that you'll hit a nerve. So I just lost it and let fly: "Okay, that's it, mister. You were living under my roof, you were in deep shit, and I moved heaven and earth to help you out of it. I let you share my home. And now you've got the gall to treat me like dirt?! Well, I'm not going to take it anymore!"

He got up and came toward me. He grabbed me by the throat and lifted me off the floor, my head against the wall. He was literally choking me. I had the presence of mind to knee him in the crotch. He let go and collapsed to the floor. All of a sudden, as if struck by the realization of what he was doing, he started crying.

Playing the battered woman really isn't my style. I took a few moments to catch my breath, then went and found some big garbage bags and without a word marched into the bedroom. I methodically emptied the contents of my drawers into the bags, went to the bathroom and picked up my things, and quickly got dressed. Through it all, I didn't utter a word. I completely ignored him. Seeing me in that state – cold, emotionless – he must have said to himself, "If you think this is the way it's going to be, forget it. *I'm* going to be the one kicking *you* out." He picked up my bags, flung the door open, and threw them outside. Quite the performance.

I was out in the street, no home, no job, and no financial support from Norman. With the money I had left, I had two options: pay the balance owing on my tuition fees at LaSalle College, or rent a new place and buy new furniture. Obviously, option two prevailed. In the end, I wasn't authorized to sit the final exams, even though I'd done all my coursework.

I went back to live in Ville-Émard, in the same building I'd left when I decided to move in with Norman. During that time, I'd let Agence Scoop know I was still available to work as a model, but things weren't working out particularly well on that score. So I started registering with casting agencies and auditioning to be an extra in films and TV programs. The work paid quite well, and most of the time it was interesting, despite the long hours spent waiting for the crew to set up.

It was at this time that I played a role on the popular hidden-camera show *Surprise sur prise*. The "victim" was comic actor Serge Thériault, and the gimmick had his tennis partner luring him to a house where a family of nudists lived. I played the part of the daughter (I was then in my early twenties) who leaves the room, telling Thériault, "I'm just going to slip into something a little more comfortable and be right back." Rather than returning before the cameras in the nude, as he was expecting, I showed up a few seconds later wearing a huge sweater, wool stockings, and big boots. The whole experience was a lot of fun. The people were very friendly and everyone had a great time on set.

Despite these occasionally interesting episodes, I was starting to feel like I was just spinning my wheels, wasting time. I began to seriously consider a change of scene, some way to widen my horizons and maybe steer my life in a new direction.

I had an uncle (my father's brother) who at the time was living in California, not far from San Diego. I'd last seen him when I was eight or nine. But I remember my parents once telling me when I was little that if ever "something awful happened," my uncle and aunt would be the ones to take care of me. I got in touch with my uncle, and he was very encouraging; he said there were plenty of modelling agencies in California and urged me to come out to the West Coast and try my luck. This was sometime in June 1992, a few days before my twenty-third birthday. I decided to take the rest of the summer to think about it.

Tony

"I never felt there was the slightest reason why I should be afraid of him. He had solved a huge problem for me, even though he owed me no favours."

That summer, I spent many a night soaking up the downtown Montreal bar scene. I had made friends with two girls about my age, and we hung out a lot at a trendy spot on De la Montagne Street. One Thursday evening, we'd shown up there fairly early for ladies' night, and some guy we'd never seen before came up to us. He was a real jerk, a loudmouth who kept trying to impress us but was succeeding only in ruining our evening. He was the perfect stereotype of a kind of Italian man one occasionally runs into in downtown Montreal bars – full of himself and trying to pass himself off as a mobster.

While this performance went on, for the better part of fifteen minutes, a man at the end of the bar – early forties, the picture of elegance – sat silently sipping his drink, casting the occasional glance at this asshole who was getting on our nerves (and in fact was now seriously harassing one of my friends). I couldn't take it any more, so I finally said, "Listen,

I don't know you, but I have something to tell you. I'm a lot more afraid of that guy over there, sitting at the end of the bar not saying a word, than I am of you, just yapping away like a dog, all bark and no bite."

The guy at the end of the bar simply looked up and said, in English, "Beautiful *and* smart, I like that." Then he turned around and said to the braggart, "I think you should leave the ladies alone." Our "friend" left the bar immediately, and we never saw him again.

The man who had just come to our rescue was Tony Volpato, who many people claimed was a key figure in the Montreal mafia. At the time, that didn't impress me one way or the other. I was barely into my twenties and didn't know very much about underworld intrigue. At any rate, I never got the feeling that speaking to this man was dangerous in any way. He immediately bought us all a drink and remained seated at the bar, without moving or saying another word. It wasn't until a week later, in the same bar, that he came over and introduced himself.

Contrary to what some newspapers have claimed, I was never romantically involved with Tony Volpato, and he never made any advances. But I grew to appreciate him; he was a gentleman, discreet and distinguished, and he always treated me – indeed, every woman he met – with the utmost respect. We went out to dinner two or three times, but it was never just the two of us. We were always in a group, and I was his guest. I remember showing up to meet him on one of these occasions, and he was sitting with mafia kingpin Frank Cotroni. Word was that he and Tony were very close. Tony introduced me, and we spent a few minutes chatting with him; then he slipped out before the other guests arrived. I imagine people assumed Tony and I were a couple because we were seen together on social occasions. Never mind the fact that there is a world of difference between having dinner with a man and going to bed with him. One thing is certain: during the short time that we were in touch, Tony did me a huge favour, for which I remain grateful to this day.

That summer, Norman was doing everything he could to try to get back together with me, although I had made it very clear to him that I could not forgive him for his violent behaviour and there was no way I would ever go back to him. His insistence eventually became worrisome: he started to show up at my apartment door late at night, usually drunk out of his mind. He would ring the bell and call me on the phone in tears, begging me to open the door. He'd also been threatening men who had made the mistake of coming up to talk to me in bars or elsewhere. It was becoming unliveable. I opened up to Tony about it: "It's completely insane. I've left him, I've started my life over, and I don't want to have anything to do with him. But he's still harassing me – and not just me. It's got to the point that guys don't dare talk to me anymore because he's threatened them and they're afraid. My life is a nightmare."

"Let me take care of it," Tony said quietly.

He asked me for Norman's phone number, and called him to invite him to have a drink with the two of us at a bar called Di Salvio, on Saint-Lawrence Boulevard. Everyone arrived at the appointed hour. Tony began explaining to Norman that it wasn't particularly courteous of him to be harassing me and even trying to intimidate men who seemed interested in me. "You can't force anyone to love you," he told him. "Just be a man and leave her alone. There are so many fish in the ocean. Just go fishing somewhere else."

Norman got the picture. I'm sure he knew exactly who he was dealing with – more than I did, at any rate. He was afraid; that much was clear. He never bothered me again, and I felt like a considerable weight had been lifted off my shoulders. I ran into him a few years later, and I could see that he had changed his ways. He was married, with children, and he showed me pictures of his family. We still hear from each other occasionally and remain on good terms.

As for Tony, I've seen him on a few occasions over the years, almost always by accident. In the late 1990s, when I was managing my construction company and his family ran a tile store in Montreal, we did some business together. At the time, and subsequently as well, a few people asked me why I wasn't afraid something bad might happen to me because I was dealing with "someone like him." I finally realized he had a reputation, and got some idea of the nature of that notoriety. But the fact is, Tony Volpato has always been more than decent with me and I never felt there was the slightest reason why I should be afraid of him. He had solved a huge problem for me, even though he owed me no favours. I still run into him now and again, in restaurants or other settings, and it's always a pleasure to see him. He is a man I respect highly. I don't have any reason to feel otherwise.

With summer drawing to a close, my intentions were growing clearer. In Montreal, the professional avenues I'd chosen didn't seem to be leading anywhere. What I needed was a change, a chance to explore new possibilities. I was determined to try my luck elsewhere. In early September, I headed for California.

Hotel California

"But I had another reason for wanting to abandon my California dream: a few weeks before leaving Montreal, I had met a man named Gilles Giguère."

During the summer, I had met a guy in a bar downtown; his name was Steve,* and he was a football player for the Montreal Machine.† In the off-season, he lived near Santa Barbara, which is about halfway between Los Angeles and San Francisco. We had hit it off pretty well and exchanged addresses and phone numbers. "If you ever plan to come out to California," he had said, "let me know." Shortly before I left, I got in touch with him, and he invited me to come and stay with him for a week at his parents' house.

As soon as I got there, I was very impressed by the area, a beautiful stretch of land between the mountains and the Pacific, with Spanish colonial architecture and vast fields of wild-flowers in yellow, pink, and purple hues. But I was far less

---

* Not his real name.

† The Machine, Montreal's short-lived franchise in the World League of American Football, played for two seasons, 1991 and 1992.

impressed by my host, who turned out to be nothing like the gentleman I had met just a few weeks earlier in Montreal. He immediately assumed that I was going to hop in the sack with him, based on the mere fact that we were going to spend a week under the same roof. I realized there was a world of difference between the mindsets of Americans and Canadians, especially in men's attitudes toward women.

I called that house "the lair of the father-king." If Steve's father felt like drinking a beer, he didn't bother getting up to get one from the fridge; he asked his wife to fetch him one, as if he was ordering it in a bar. It didn't matter if she was already busy doing something. And I was particularly shocked by the fact that Steve's mother, who enjoyed having a cigarette right after supper – her only one of the day – had to go outside to smoke it, despite the fact that her husband puffed cigars in the house all day long. The poor man couldn't stand the smell of cigarettes.

Needless to say, I cut short my Santa Barbara sojourn and caught the first train to San Diego. My uncle and aunt welcomed me warmly, and I was overjoyed to meet their daughter, my little cousin, who was just six or seven years old at the time. They immediately gave me a tour of the city and its main attractions, including the famous San Diego Zoo and SeaWorld.

My uncle, who was a ventilation and air conditioning systems engineer for a large company, was often away on business. Since my aunt also worked all day long (she was a grade school teacher), she more or less assigned the son of one of her mother's friends – who was also named Steve – to accompany me and show me the sights. Steve was about my age, very kind, reserved, and hard-working. He took me to some beautiful spots in San Diego and the surrounding area and introduced me to his friends.

San Diego isn't a large metropolis like Los Angeles or San Francisco, but it has a spectacular skyline. A nighttime walk on the beach offered a breathtaking panorama, with the moon's reflection shimmering in the waves on one side and the bright lights of the downtown skyscrapers on the other. It was impressive. I found it hard to believe that these two worlds could coexist so close to each other.

After a few days, I called a few casting agencies, and the prospects looked good. Among other things, I auditioned for a part on *Beverly Hills, 90210,* the new season of which hadn't yet started production. I then got a callback, and the second audition was a bit more demanding: I had to give a few line readings and improvise a bit. As soon as I was called in for an interview, I had to fill out a fairly detailed form, which asked for a great deal of personal information. Since I wasn't a U.S. citizen and obviously didn't have a green card, I tried to get around the law by putting down my aunt's social security number. But when I went to a third audition, the agency representative looked at me and said, "We ran a check, and the number you gave us doesn't match your name." Caught red-handed, I had no choice but to tell the truth. No, I wasn't American. No, I didn't have a green card either. I had come to California to try my luck and see whether I was cut out for a career in the U.S. entertainment industry. "What you have to understand," the rep told me gently, "is that this is an American production. If I want the producers to hire you, I have to prove that no American actress would be able to do a better job than you. That's not going to be easy. And even if it works, your papers would have to be in order."

So I went back to my aunt and uncle's, only slightly disappointed; I was pretty sure that had it not been for that slight complication, which was basically a technicality, I would have had a good shot at landing the part and that, all in all, there might be a future for me in the States. Only half joking, my aunt said I should just marry Steve, which would automatically make me a U.S. citizen. But I wasn't interested in playing that game. Instead, I decided I would go back to Montreal and try to get a green card through other channels, as soon as I could. I was very optimistic about my chances. I even managed to find an American lawyer who was prepared to work on my behalf and fast-track the process of securing the infamous work permit.

At the same time, though, I realized that the longer I remained in the United States, the less comfortable I felt. Before returning to Montreal, I decided to visit Los Angeles and walk up and down some of its legendary streets, like Sunset Boulevard and Rodeo Drive. My immediate reaction was "much ado about nothing"; I was far from impressed by all the faux wealth, which probably hid a world of loneliness and broken ambitions. The legendary aura of the silver screen didn't stand the test of reality. And next to all that Tinseltown glamour, in the small towns around Los Angeles, I found an unhealthy mentality driven by fear: fear of strangers, of the police, of government, and generally of anything that wasn't white, Anglo-Saxon, and Protestant.

On top of that, I had my own fears. I was afraid of taking the plunge into the unknown. If I came back, I would have to find a place to live in Los Angeles, where I didn't know a soul. I knew that the world I hoped to work in was tough, competitive, ruthless. I had heard all the horror stories about young women who aspired to a career in the movies but became ensnared in abusive situations and came to a bad end. Beyond talent and a motivation to work, I wondered, did I have the necessary tenacity and strength of character to survive in that cutthroat world?

I started feeling homesick. I missed so many things about my hometown: dinners with friends and family, even trivial things like having a hot dog at a Lafleur restaurant. But I had another reason for wanting to abandon my California dream: a few weeks before leaving Montreal, I had met a man named Gilles Giguère.

13

Gilles

"Our eyes met and something went boom! Like a bolt of lightning."

I have already said so, outside the pages of this book, and I unhesitatingly say it again: Gilles Giguère was the love of my life, the man with whom I spent my happiest days, and whose loss remains the most painful wound I have ever suffered, one that will never completely heal. No man since has held the place that Gilles did in my heart. The bar had been set far too high.

I first met Gilles in the least romantic setting imaginable: a Lafleur restaurant on Notre-Dame Street in east-end Montreal, where I'd gone one evening to have a hot dog with a girlfriend. He was sitting alone at a table, wearing clothes that couldn't have been more ordinary: paint-spattered jeans and T-shirt, and work boots, the typical apparel of a construction worker on his way home from his job. But Gilles could have been wearing a tuxedo that night, for the effect he had on me.

It was his eyes that attracted me, right away: big pale-brown almond eyes that somehow seemed familiar – I was positive I'd seen them before, maybe in another life. The rest didn't matter in the slightest. Our eyes met and something went boom! Like a bolt of lightning. I didn't even notice his face. All I could focus on was those eyes, brimming with gentleness and goodness and wielding a strange power over me.

Was it love at first sight? I have no doubt that it was – that's how, in hindsight, I would describe what happened to me that night. But at the time I didn't sense it as such, probably because it was a sensation I had never experienced before. Strangest of all, our relationship was strictly platonic for around a year.

Very soon, I came to consider Gilles my best friend, the kind of friend I could go out to a restaurant with and enjoy a long dinner, talk about any subject under the sun, turn the world upside down and change it, and then change it all over again. The kind of friend I would go to the movies with. If I felt like going out, having a drink or having a wild time, it was always with Gilles. I spent almost all my free time with him for a year, and during that time, he never made the slightest move or suggestive comment. He was my confidant, a kind of big brother who was privy to everything that happened to me; I would tell him about the people I hung around with, even the men I slept with. And he told me everything as well: secrets, minor worries and major anxieties, his plans, his love affairs. With Gilles I felt a sense of security that no man had ever provided before. He was a friend I could always rely on, no matter what the circumstances.

Once, for example, I went out to a club with a girlfriend, and toward the end of the night someone stole my handbag. It happened in the space of a few seconds. All of a sudden, there I was with no money, no credit card or debit card, no identification, and no key to get into my own house. Worst of all, I had no medication to control my epilepsy. I was in a total panic. But I knew I could call Gilles, even though it was two

in the morning. He was there within fifteen minutes. He found
a drugstore that was open twenty-four hours a day, and he
bought me some Epival along with some cosmetics for the next
morning. Then he took me home and dismantled the front
door to my apartment with the tools that he always kept
handy in his truck.

Besides providing a sense of security, Gilles was unfailingly
generous. At the time, I had moved with my brother into a
spacious two-bedroom on the second floor of an apartment
building on De Normanville Street, near Rosemont Boulevard.
The apartment was superbly located, not far from a metro
station, but was in dire need of a fix-up. Gilles specialized in
renovation, so he offered to help us. For a few weeks, he spent
several evenings after work helping me redecorate the bathroom – scraping out all the tile joints with a knife and putting
in new grout – redo the electrical wiring, install fans in some of
the rooms, and repaint the entire apartment. I would never
have managed without his help. At that point, we were still just
friends. He didn't want to be paid, and he asked for nothing in
return. The only pact we had was that every time he came over
to work on the renovations, he would find a hearty meal on
the dining room table.

Well before we officially became a couple, I sensed a kind of
wisdom in Gilles that I have rarely seen in a man, before or
since. It was on his advice that I reconciled with my father, who
I had hardly seen since my parents' divorce two years earlier.
Gilles made me realize that, for one reason or another, I missed
my father, and it would be good for me to reconnect with him.

I have described at length, earlier in this book, my father's
many shortcomings, chronic lack of responsibility, fickleness,

and lack of character. But undeniably, he also had plenty of human qualities. For instance, since their divorce, I had never heard him utter the slightest insult to my mother – who also had her faults, like anybody – or to anyone else, for that matter. Although he had been responsible for a great deal of chaos in our lives, he was a profoundly peaceful man, and in his way, he respected people. He was also an incredibly tolerant individual. When my brother had told him flat out that he didn't want to have anything more to do with him and that his life would be completely destabilized if he continued having a relationship with him, my father calmly answered, "If you think that's what you have to do, son, if you think that not talking to me ever again will improve your life, then go ahead and do it. I'll understand."

When I went to see my father again, on Gilles's advice, he was profoundly depressed. Before me was a completely shattered man, living alone in a cramped, shabby apartment above a garage, at the corner of Pie-IX Boulevard and Saint-Zotique Street, just north of the Olympic Stadium. He was a pitiful sight. He spent whole days in his tiny one-bedroom, with no money, alone with his demons and living on omelettes, canned noodles, and other junk food full of chemicals. Every once in a while, I would give him fifty or one hundred dollars and say, "Go buy yourself a steak. For God's sake, do something!"

Later, Gilles hired him a few times to help out with his renovation company, so he was able to earn a few dollars. But basically, my father remained a man utterly burned out by life, unable to take on the slightest responsibility. He would prove this to me several times in the years to come.

It was around this time that my relationship with Gilles began to change. One night, we went out dancing. It was a long evening, fuelled by a fair bit of alcohol, and by the time we left the club we were both pretty far gone. I have never had much of a tolerance for alcohol. It doesn't take very much to get me tipsy. Gilles wasn't a heavy drinker either, so his threshold was pretty low as well.

At the end of the night, he took me home, and as we stood on my doorstep, I asked for a kiss. He had full, sensual lips, and I guess that night – the alcohol having no doubt washed a good part of my inhibitions away – I wanted to find out what kissing them would feel like.

"Me? You want me to kiss you? Really?" he asked.

"Yes."

We went for it. It was like falling into an airbag or a downy pillow or some other incredibly comfortable surface. It wasn't even a French kiss, really, but I clearly recall a voice inside me going "Wow!" It felt like a scene in a movie, with two lovers sharing a languorous kiss and the woman voluptuously lifting one foot off the ground in a sign of pleasure and abandon.

We didn't take it any further, and I demurely opened the door and stepped into my apartment, alone. But I was overwhelmed by the sensation I had just experienced. The next morning, after the fog of the hangover had lifted, I thought to myself, "Come on, girl! It only happened because you were drunk. This guy's not your lover. He's your best friend, who just happens to be a guy. Don't mix things up. He's such a good friend, and that's the way it has to stay. It can't go any further."

When I think about it today, I realize my attitude was mostly one of denial. I obviously didn't want to admit to myself that I was falling in love, so I was trying to rationalize my feelings. I deeply valued that brother–sister closeness we had. I had never felt anything like it before, and I didn't want to risk losing it.

Besides the fact that I appreciated the kind of relationship we had, there were other factors keeping me from breaching the barrier between friendship and love. First of all, Gilles was much older than me; I was in my early twenties and he in his early forties. In fact, he was exactly nineteen years older than me. But the other thing that seriously put a damper on my feelings was the fact that he wasn't exactly unattached. He was living with a woman; they even had a son. Things weren't going very well between the two of them, and they led separate social lives. But still, these were hardly ideal circumstances for falling in love.

From time to time, Gilles would stay over at my place after we'd been out together – if he'd had too much to drink and didn't want to drive, say, or if the weather was bad. On those evenings, he slept next to me in my bed, and before falling asleep we would often lie there in the dark for hours on end, talking about anything and everything under the sun. We were like a couple of gossipy old ladies. Looking back, I realize it must have been terribly naive of me – not to mention cruel – to ask a healthy, normal man to share my bed without touching me. But he never complained about it, and never tried, either directly or in a roundabout way, to seduce me. Gilles was that much of a gentleman.

Nevertheless, it was on one of those nights that he slept over that our love affair really began. We got into bed, I turned out the light, and he started to tell me how, two or three days earlier, he'd been to see a fortune teller who had told him that he would soon meet the love of his life.

"Oh, yeah?" I said. "So is it someone you know?"

"Mm-hmm," he replied.

I waited for him to continue his story. I didn't suspect a thing. I don't think I was at all prepared for the next line. "Of

course I know her," he went on. "She's lying right beside me."
I burst out laughing, as if he'd just told a really good joke. But
just as quickly, I stopped and didn't say another word. It was
clear that my reaction had hurt him. A lot.

I have played back the events of that night many times since.
I think the reality is that, while I was really turned on by Gilles,
at the same time I was afraid, almost panicked at the thought
of losing our friendship and the sense of security that it brought
me. I felt that I would be running a huge risk if I agreed to
change the nature of our relationship. I turned the light back
on, looked him straight in the eye, and said, "Are you sure
that's what you want? I don't want us to lose our friendship
and the closeness that we have. Not for anything in the world.
I've never had anything like it before, and it's the thing that's
most precious to me. What if we decide to make love and it
doesn't go well?"

"Okay, but what about you?" he said. "How do you feel
about it? Do you think we can go further and do you think it
can work? Is it something *you* want?"

"Yes. But I'm afraid it might get awkward and then nothing
will ever be the same again."

"Okay," he said, "we'll make a deal. You and me. We'll try.
Right now. We see how it goes. We don't force the issue, and we
don't keep going just for the sake of it. If there are no sparks,
we put our clothes back on and we never talk about it again.
What do you say?"

"If you put it that way . . . I'm willing."

And that was how it started. The most enriching, serene,
and blissful relationship – on every level, not just romantic – of
my entire life.

14

In Pictures

"Gilles helped me heal childhood wounds that had been the source of a lot of suffering for a long time. He gave me self-confidence. With him at my side, I felt anything was possible."

By now, Patrick had started studying to be a police officer at Cégep de Maisonneuve. The main reason I had suggested that he come and stay with me was that I very much wanted him to finish his studies. My greatest fear was that he would do the same thing I had done a few years earlier: enter the job market and put off completing his schooling until later. It's quite rare for people who choose that avenue to find the strength and perseverance needed to see their plans through, because they find themselves caught up in the whirlwind of real life, with responsibilities, bills to pay, and so forth. I didn't want that to happen to my kid brother, with whom I've always been very close.

So I made a bargain with him: "I'm willing to support you financially as long as you continue your studies. But if you ever drop out of school, you're on your own. End of deal." Our arrangement worked well for a while, but after a few months

Patrick stopped attending his classes – only he didn't tell me about it and kept on living with me in the apartment as if nothing had changed.

My parents both knew what was going on, and my father told Patrick, "Son, you made a deal with your sister. What you're doing isn't right. She helped you out, and now you're lying to her. You have to tell her the truth." In the end, it was my father who told me that Patrick wasn't in school anymore. I felt somewhat betrayed, and it cast a bit of a chill over our relationship – which happily dissipated in fairly short order. But I did follow through on my warning to him; I was going to terminate our arrangement, and he would have to leave the apartment.

In the meantime, Gilles had officially separated from his partner. Since I was now living alone and Gilles and I spent almost all of our time together, he suggested that I move into his condo in Pointe-aux-Trembles, on the eastern tip of the Island of Montreal, which he had just started renting. I accepted and went to live with him.

Gilles's son, Pierre-Paul, was seven years old. He went to stay with his mother every other weekend, but otherwise Gilles had full custody. That was his ex's idea; I suspect she wanted to destroy our nascent relationship, believing that a young woman my age would run and hide at the prospect of living with a child who was not her own. On the contrary: things couldn't have gone better between Pierre-Paul and me. He wasn't at all a problem child; in fact, he was quite pleasant and endearing. In any case, I was so in love with his father that my affection for the boy was spontaneous. He also looked a lot like Gilles. Of course, he had to go through a period of adjustment, like any child whose parents separate. At first, when the three of us would leave the house to go and do something together, he would often say, "Why don't we ask Mommy to come too?"

The fact that Gilles had a new woman in his life didn't go down very well with his family, though. He had been with his ex for a dozen years or so. This led to some trying times. For instance, on Pierre-Paul's birthday, Gilles's entire family went to a party at his ex's place – unbeknownst to Gilles, of course. This was extremely insulting to him, and he felt obliged to set things straight. One evening, furious, he exploded at his mother: "I have someone new in my life, and that's that. Pierre-Paul's mother is no longer my wife, and never will be. So you'd better deal with it, simple as that." The situation eventually settled down, but things were still awkward for a while.

For every moment of the three years we spent together, Gilles was a friend, a brother, a lover, and a husband to me. He was a good man, gentle, always in a positive mood, and he had a calming and salutary influence on me. I must admit that when I first met him, I could be quite the grump, especially when I woke up in the morning. No doubt this stemmed from the tense atmosphere that had reigned at home throughout my teen years. It was Gilles who made me aware of it. One morning, when I was particularly snippy with him, he said, "Hey, you're not living with your parents anymore, you know. I'm not your mother. You're living with me now. I don't want to offend you or get into an argument with you, because I love you, and you know it." He said it in such a calm voice, I started to cry. I was ashamed and called myself all sorts of names. Gently, he came over to me, saying, "No, come on, don't take it that way. Just give yourself a little time, and it'll work itself out."

Gilles helped me heal childhood wounds that had been the

source of a lot of suffering for a long time. He gave me self-confidence. With him at my side, I felt anything was possible.

It was largely thanks to him that I put my modelling career back on track. It had pretty much been on ice since I came back from California. When I was younger, I never thought that I was particularly pretty. And when I went to interviews or auditions for modelling, acting, or extra work, I would walk in and see all the beautiful girls I was up against and think to myself that I didn't have a chance, that it would never work. Slowly but surely, though, my inferiority complex was fading.

I decided to get a firm foothold in the business while I still had my youth and my looks, as they say. I knew that a modelling career is almost always brief, but fairly lucrative while it lasts. One can easily earn between four hundred and five hundred dollars a day and amass a sizeable nest egg. I signed up for stage acting classes and jumped on every opportunity that arose, whether it was modelling or extra work or even speaking parts for TV or film productions. I didn't own a car at the time, so Gilles drove me to every audition. On the way, he kept up a constant pep talk: you can do it, you're the best, you're going to make it. He was my number one cheerleader.

Things went really well. I got all kinds of contracts and even had a number of regular clients, including the Canadelle lingerie company, for whom I was a fit model and posed for photos that were often shown in all the major department stores. I also acted in several films during that time, including *Highlander III,* which starred Christopher Lambert and was mostly shot in and around Montreal; I had a small part as a police officer in a bar.

I've lost count of the number of productions I acted in during those years, and forgotten their titles. Although I never had any serious ambitions in film and television acting and never won any lead roles, all in all I enjoyed the work enormously. The conditions could be difficult on occasion – I remember one shoot where we waited out two or three days of heavy rain in the woods near Rawdon, north of Montreal – but we were treated well and met lots of interesting people, and the pay was great.

Also during that time, in 1994, I had a role in the original miniseries on the life of René Lévesque, which aired on the TVA network with Denis Bouchard in the title role. I played one of his mistresses, seen getting out of bed while Lévesque sits meditatively, seeming to reflect on his past sins. I was apprehensive about the scene, because the script called for me to appear topless. I was worried that this would hurt my image and my prospects for more TV roles. I hesitated a long time before accepting, and discussed the scene at length with P.A. Morin, who was the most senior producer I knew at the network at that time. He urged me to agree to shoot it as written. "You don't have to feel judged," he argued. "It's not you on the screen, it's a character. And besides, the scene isn't at all in bad taste. We barely see part of your breast." I fully respected this man and his judgment, and in the end we shot the scene as planned. I have no regrets.

Around the same time, I was a hostess on the Loto-Québec game show *La Poule aux oeufs d'or*, which aired on TVA and was hosted by Guy Mongrain with France Beaudoin as co-host. My job was to chat briefly with Mongrain and then take either an egg or an envelope, depending on what the contestant had chosen, and deposit it on the display stand at the front of the studio.

In addition to a number of TV spots – including ads for the Cage aux sports restaurant chain – I also appeared in a few music videos. One was for a song by Roch Voisine, who was a superstar in those days. The tune was "Lost Without You," from his debut album in English, *I'll Always Be There*. The concept had Roch singing the song in a bar. I played a businesswoman – wearing a dark suit, hair tied in a prim chignon, looking a little stuck-up – who walks into the bar while he's performing, knocks back two Scotches, and notices a tall, blond, blue-eyed hunk playing pinball. They look at each other, and she walks over to him and motions for him to follow her to the washroom. They go in, she undoes her hair, and they kiss, then the washroom door swings shut behind them. It was the first time I had ever shot a scene where I had to kiss somebody – and pretty passionately at that. And, of course, there was a huge crew on the set, which made it even more uncomfortable.

After the shoot was over, I called Gilles and asked him to come pick me up. While I was waiting, Roch invited me to have dinner with some of the cast and crew. I declined, explaining that my boyfriend was coming to take me home. He was a good sport about it, and picked up his guitar and sang a song for me before I left.

The next day was a Saturday. I was at home with Gilles and his best friend, Robert Savard. Bob had stopped by for a cup of coffee, as he often did. He and Gilles were sitting at the kitchen table, and I was in the bathroom with a head full of hair treatment. All of a sudden, the phone rang. Gilles answered, then called out, "Julie! Phone's for you!"

"Who is it? Is it important? I've got all this stuff in my hair."

"Hold on a sec."

He popped his head in the bathroom door a few seconds later. "It's Roch Voisine."

"Okay, I'll take it."

I left the bathroom and went to pick up the bedroom extension. "Hello," I said.

"Julie? Roch Voisine here."

I wondered what he might want, on a Saturday afternoon.

"Would you like to have dinner with me tonight?"

"Um, I'm sorry, but I have other plans. With my boyfriend."

"Ah. So you have a boyfriend?"

"Mm-hmm. I thought I'd mentioned that on set yesterday," I said.

"I must have forgotten," he answered.

I suppose the idea was that, boyfriend or not, when Roch Voisine asks you out on a date, you say yes, no questions asked. But that's not what happened.

As I was hanging up the phone, I heard Bob haranguing Gilles angrily. "Man! What the fuck are you doing? She's the picture of beauty, and twenty years younger than you! You don't have a penny to your name; meanwhile, this guy's made of money and he's Mr. Handsome to boot! And you let her take the call? What were you thinking?! You're gonna lose her to him, for fuck's sake!"

As I have mentioned, Gilles was a man of infinite wisdom, and he proved it in the way he answered: "Bob, my man, let me explain something to you. If you pick up a handful of sand and clench your fist, all the sand will run out between your fingers. But if you keep your palm open, you won't lose a single grain." I have never forgotten those words.

15

The "Gangster"

"If Gilles's main source of revenue had been loansharking, then why would he have felt the need to get up every morning at six to go and do home renovations?"

With the media firestorm that has sprung up around me this year, I have once again been forced to see Gilles Giguère's name associated with epithets like *bandit*, *hoodlum*, *thug*, and other synonyms for *gangster*. When I read those words, I still get the impression that they describe a different man from the one I knew and loved with all my heart. True, Gilles was no angel. I was never blinded by love to the point that I believed otherwise. He broke the law more than once, spent time in prison, and was involved with people who weren't exactly reputable. That being said, he was never the kingpin that certain media outlets have made him out to be.

Back when we were still just friends, he was arrested – I no longer recall for what reason – and held for four days at the detention centre on Parthenais Street in Montreal. Eventually, he was released without any charges being laid. He didn't seem particularly upset by the episode, but it left me profoundly disconcerted. Later, when our relationship started to evolve, I brought up that episode and told him, "I'm not interested in living with somebody who could get busted by the cops at any time and be thrown into jail for six or seven years. That kind of life is too horrible." So I made a deal with him: never again must he run the risk of going to prison.

He then confessed to me that as a young man, at age nineteen, he had been sentenced to a prison term of two years less a day for aiding and abetting in a robbery. He had been driving the getaway car, and one of his accomplices, when later arrested, had informed against him. He also admitted to me that he had been involved in some shady dealings after that, but he didn't volunteer any details (and I didn't ask for any). "I was quite the bad boy for a while there," he told me. That was how he described his criminal period, which apparently corresponded to a good part of his youth. "But," he added, "I've stayed out of trouble for at least five years now." I didn't want to know any more. I was intelligent enough to know that if he wasn't inclined to give me any details, it was probably because it was best that I not know them.

Gilles was a man of principle. He wasn't someone who would do just anything for money. He never sold drugs and never had a firearm in our home. He believed profoundly that no person has the right to take another's life, and that if two men had a score to settle, they should do so with their fists.

After a while, I realized Gilles was a moneylender. But it was never anything more than a sideline for him. He was first and foremost a renovation contractor. He was never rolling in money and never led an extravagant life. He got up every morning with the sunrise and went to do an honest day's work just like everybody else.

I had noticed right from the start of our relationship that when winter came, he had fewer contracts, and his income suffered as a result. Of course, winter is a slack season in the construction industry, but on top of that, Gilles got almost all of his customers through referrals. If he wanted to find more work, he had to build up a reputation. And so I had what I thought, in all modesty, was an excellent idea. Back when I had worked briefly in real estate, I had found out about *Lovell's Directory*, which can be used to find a person's name by looking up their address. I bought a copy, and since my modelling work provided me with a lot of time off, I decided to do some cold calling on Gilles's behalf. When I knew he would be working in a particular area of the city, I would phone people who lived on neighbouring streets and offer them his services.

When I first told him about my idea, he wasn't all that confident in my marketing strategy. But I was a born salesperson, as I've said, and I knew it would work. Indeed, it worked so well that before long Gilles had to hire a sales manager, somebody who knew enough about the renovation business to be able to do estimates and draw up contracts rapidly. And because he could no longer keep up with the demand with the resources he had, Gilles soon had to put together work teams. He mostly hired people from the Gaspé region. He always said that one Gaspesian was worth two regular workers, because they were able to get the job done so well and so fast.

Within a year after I set up the telephone canvassing system, Gilles had doubled his sales. In fact, the growth was so strong that at one point he was worried he would be overwhelmed. I remember him once stopping by the house during his workday, and when he saw me on the phone trying to drum up even more business for him, he put his head in his hands, laughed, and said, "What are you doing? You're crazy! I can't believe how well your system's working. Just make sure we can meet the demand." His business success lasted until the end of his life.

When you're in a serious relationship with somebody, it's not long before you meet their friends. And since Robert Savard was Gilles's best friend, it wasn't very long after we met that he introduced me to him. Bob was a very friendly man, very pleasant, and had a great sense of humour. At least once a week, sometimes more often, he would come by the house to have a cup of coffee with Gilles. They had a lot of laughs together. Sometimes, we'd be invited to go and have dinner with Bob and his wife. Gilles and Bob were, above all, two great friends who loved to spend time together. Although I always made sure not to ask too many questions about what he did for a living, it soon became quite clear to me that Bob was a loanshark. Given what little I knew about the practice – and I have to admit that at the time, I was young and naive about such matters – it wasn't something that I found particularly shocking. People who had been refused loans by financial institutions simply went to see other people who were prepared to lend them money; that was the way I looked at it. It was just another way of doing business.

I knew that Gilles lent money too, probably through Bob Savard. I remember once accompanying him to a restaurant whose owner owed him money. "We're going to see one of my buddies, who runs a restaurant," he said. "We'll have dinner with him. His wife is nice, you'll see." Off we went. The place was an authentic greasy spoon that served submarine sandwiches and other fast food. We ate with the owner and his wife. At the end of the meal, just before we left, the guy slipped an envelope to Gilles and said, "That's for you." That was it. We left, as if nothing unusual had happened. It had been a very friendly meeting. Gilles and the restaurant owner seemed to know each other well and to like each other; the atmosphere was very cordial. Obviously, if I'd been forced to watch him beat up somebody who had missed a payment, or heard about him doing such a thing, I would have been extremely upset and would never have accepted it. But that wasn't Gilles's style. He wasn't a violent person.

I assume he knew perfectly well that what he was doing was illegal. I also imagine he was prepared to run the risks that were inherent to the practice; as for me, I felt that it was none of my business. More to the point, I preferred not to know. I was madly in love with him, and that was all that mattered to me.

But I also knew that Gilles didn't earn the bulk of his money from loansharking. He had a legitimate business to which he devoted the vast majority of his time and energy. If Gilles's main source of revenue had been loansharking, then why would he have felt the need to get up every morning at six to go and do home renovations? What would have been in it for him? When I read an article describing him as a mobster or kingpin, I want to laugh – even though, ultimately, it's sad as hell. Gilles never lived the life of a bum who gets up at noon, parties all day long, and goes to bed at three in the morning. He woke up every day at dawn and worked hard to earn a living, six days a week, usually. He would come home every night, his clothes dirtied with sawdust or plaster dust, get undressed in the laundry room – the only room in the house that had no carpeting – and chuck his clothes into the washing machine.

We weren't rich; we never lacked anything, but we never lived in luxury either. We drew up a budget every month, like most people. The entire time we were together, we never took any fancy trips or bought anything extravagant. The most expensive thing we ever did was take a fishing trip (Gilles loved fishing) one summer to Lake Magnan, north of La Tuque, in Quebec's Haute-Mauricie region.

When I met Gilles, the Hells Angels weren't yet taken seriously as a criminal organization. In my naive, little-girl-from-the-West-End worldview, the real gangsters were the Italians, not the bikers – who, while they were obviously involved in their share of illegal doings, seemed to me above all to be united by a shared passion for Harley-Davidson motorcycles. At the time, the infamous biker war – the ruthless conflict pitting the Hells Angels against the Rock Machine for control of the local drug trade – hadn't really begun, and Maurice "Mom" Boucher was nowhere near as notorious a figure as he was to become a few years later.

When I first started going out with him, Gilles had known Boucher for several years. You could even say they were friends. Their relationship went back to the days when Boucher had been released from prison and was looking for work. At the time, Gilles was a night foreman at the General Electric plant in Montreal. Boucher showed up one day to apply for a job and was forced to admit on the application form that he had a criminal record. Since Gilles had also done time, and was all too familiar with the prejudices that ex-detainees had to deal with, he decided Boucher deserved a break, so he helped him get hired. That was how they first met.

They stayed in touch after that, and Gilles eventually became Boucher's go-to guy for anything having to do with construction. If some repairs or renovations needed to be done at his home in Sorel, in one of the Hells Angels' clubhouses, or in some other meeting place, he entrusted the work to Gilles and to no one else. I remember Gilles spent a good part of one summer completely redoing the roof of Boucher's place in Sorel, along with some other repairs. In hindsight, it strikes me that Gilles must have been the only person Boucher trusted enough to be sure that after the work was done, the place wouldn't be teeming with hidden microphones placed there for the police or rival gangs. Despite his close ties to Boucher, however, Gilles never became, and never had any intention of becoming, a Hells Angel – a full-patch member, in the parlance of the organization. It simply wasn't something that interested him.

The first time I met Maurice Boucher was in a restaurant in Montreal. There were three couples there: Boucher and his partner, Bob Savard and his wife, and Gilles and me. Gilles had given me the lowdown on who "Mom" Boucher was: the figurehead of the Quebec Hells Angels, someone extremely important in the world of criminal biker gangs. I have a very clear memory of that first meeting with him. When we were introduced, he grabbed my hand hard and then began shaking it violently, which made my breasts start shaking as well. I thought it was uncalled-for behaviour, to say the least. But what struck me even more was the incredible void that I saw in his eyes – an utter lack of conscience. I was instantly afraid of him; his presence literally sent shivers down my spine. I remember that after we got home, I said to Gilles in no uncertain terms that I wasn't prepared to spend many evenings out with those sorts of people – if at all.

I saw Maurice Boucher only one other time while Gilles was alive. It was a few months later, at a corn roast that Boucher held on his Sorel property, and that Gilles was invited to. I wasn't really interested in attending. Without wanting to sound too pretentious, I found bikers, along with their girlfriends – most of whom were or had been strippers – to be rather vulgar.

But in every relationship, the partners have to make the occasional compromise.

There were around a hundred people there, and a majority of them were Hells Angels members, proudly displaying their colours and their buffed-up Harleys. There was a lot of loud music, plenty of things going on, and a large amount of alcohol flowing. But what struck me most about the evening was the sexist attitude of the bikers, who treated their female companions like dirt. I also noticed that Gilles was pretty much looked down upon by most of the guests. Sure, people said hello to him – but he was also made to feel that he wasn't one of them, that he wasn't a "brother," as full-patch members tend to refer to one another. As for me, it was clear that I wasn't at all in my element. I made no effort to talk to anyone, and besides, I had no idea what to talk to them about. I definitely wouldn't have won any public relations competitions that evening.

One incident in particular left a deep and lasting impression on me that night. On the grounds of the party there were two huge St. Bernards, a male and a female, locked up in a large wire-mesh cage. I've always loved animals, so naturally I walked up beside the cage to get a closer look. The male seemed friendly and playful, and came toward me – and then, in one blindingly fast move, tried to bite me. I yanked my hand back just in time and watched the huge dog's jaws snap against the wire mesh. I'd had enough. Not only was I bored to tears, but I'd almost lost a finger. Gilles and I left after that.

Luckily, "Mom" Boucher and the biker element were never part of our daily lives. If Gilles had hung out with them as often as he did with Bob Savard, there is no doubt that our relationship would have come to an end, and fast.

16

The Carnival of the Animals

"Two of the masked officers, who were standing in the doorframe separating the bedroom from the living room, bent down to stare between my legs, laughing and making lewd remarks. At that moment, I felt that the men before me weren't representatives of a supposedly civilized state, governed by the rule of law, but nothing more than savage animals, with more testosterone in their balls than grey matter in their heads."

Before 1995, I had never had the slightest run-in with the law. I'd never received so much as a speeding ticket or even a parking ticket. It turns out I had nothing to lose by waiting.

One evening in late winter of that year – February 22, to be precise – I came home from work to find the door to our condo yawning wide open. There were all kinds of people inside: five or six police officers looking around, searching for who knows what. After my initial shock wore off, I immediately called Gilles's lawyer, Gilles Daudelin. He asked to speak to the officer in charge of the operation, who told him that he had the requisite search warrant, which he then read to him and showed to me. The officer passed the phone back to me, and Daudelin said simply, "Everything's in order. Just let them do their job."

It all proceeded in a fairly civilized manner: no furniture turned upside down, no cushions sliced open, no violence. They found nothing and left. The problem was, that same day, the police also searched a six-unit apartment building that Gilles owned on Grande-Allée Street in Montreal East and found, in a storage room in the basement, four automatic weapons and twenty-five kilograms of marijuana. Based on that evidence, Gilles was formally charged with illegal possession of firearms and drugs.

He swore to me that the incriminating items weren't his, and that he had no idea how they had ended up in his building. We found out soon enough who the stash belonged to, though. It was Léo Lemieux, a former paramedic whom Gilles sometimes hired for renovation jobs. This man later became a police informant and the main source of the misfortune that was to befall Gilles in the final year of his life.

Gilles had met Lemieux earlier that year, and since he often worked with him, I got to know him fairly soon after that. He was a strange guy, fairly unstable emotionally, who showed all the classic symptoms of bipolar disorder. One day he would be depressed, on the verge of suicide, and the next day he would be upbeat and raring to go. He was a real motormouth, who could tell a story one day and then tell it again the next but with the details changed, clearly contradicting himself. He also continually asked all sorts of questions on all manner of topics, even the most trivial, like some kind of Columbo, permanently in detective mode. The more I got to know the guy, the more he got on my nerves, and the more I was convinced that he was a first class troublemaker. One evening, I shared my doubts with Gilles and Bob: "I can't believe this guy. I'm telling you, hc's got to be a police informant. He's going to be bad news for you guys someday."

"Hang on, Julie, you can't just say that about somebody," said Gilles. "That's a serious accusation to make without any proof to back it up."

"Well, I'm telling you, I'm sure about it."

One episode in particular set off alarm bells about Lemieux's nature and true intentions. He showed up at the house one morning proudly waving a handgun. "Check it out, man!" he kept saying to Gilles, offering to let him hold the weapon.

"Are you crazy?" Gilles answered. "Where'd you get that thing?"

"One of my buddies gave it to me."

"Yeah? And who's to know what he might have done with it, you idiot! And you're walking around with it in your pocket. Are you nuts? One thing's for sure, you're not coming into my house with a gun on you – I don't even want you coming near me with it. You better go home right now, 'cause you're not coming to work with me today carrying a weapon," Gilles cried.

And with that, he threw Lemieux out of the condo. He was furious.

There is no doubt in my mind that Lemieux was looking to incriminate Gilles that morning. If the gun had been used to kill someone and Gilles's fingerprints had been found on it, he could have faced a murder charge. It was obvious from Lemieux's behaviour that he wanted to take Gilles down.

The day after the police search in the building on Grande-Allée, Lemieux admitted to me that it was he who had hidden the weapons and drugs in the basement. Because he regularly worked with Gilles, he had a key to the storage room, and he kept his tools and materials there. I remember reading him the riot act when he told me. "What the hell were you thinking, stashing that stuff in his building?" I yelled. "You do realize you've gotten Gilles in deep shit, right?" He apologized and started crying, but I don't think he particularly regretted his actions; they had been carefully calculated and the goal was clearly to cause Gilles harm. Lemieux was to continue in the same vein in the coming months.

I was very upset by the two police searches, and I told Gilles how worried I was. He tried to convince me it wasn't a big deal, but I wasn't comforted. I pleaded with him again not to get himself into a situation that would put his freedom at risk and threaten to separate us for an extended period. We had a great life together; we were happy. I didn't want anything to jeopardize that happiness. He told me not to worry, that he was no longer involved in anything illegal and that he had long ago put those days behind him. He gave me his word. It was what I wanted to hear, and I decided to trust him. I didn't have many other options.

Several months later, on the morning of Monday, December 18, 1995, a Carcajou unit raided our condo.* I have never lived through such a violent event, before or since. It was six in the morning. Gilles and I were still asleep. As luck would have it, his son wasn't with us. The officers smashed through the door to our condo with a battering ram and burst in like a pack of rabid dogs, shouting, "Police! Police!" There were six or seven of them, dressed all in black, with military helmets extended down

---

* Created in September 1995 and eventually dismantled in 1999, Carcajou ("Wolverine") was an elite intervention unit comprising members of the Royal Canadian Mounted Police, the Sûreté du Québec, the Montreal Urban Community police department, and other municipal police forces. It was tasked with countering the activities of criminal biker gangs, specifically the Hells Angels and the Rock Machine.

over their foreheads, balaclavas shrouding their faces, and army boots. They rushed straight into the bedroom and tore the covers off the bed. Gilles threw himself on top of me, tightly wrapping his arms around me and gripping my shoulders. The officers couldn't pry him off me, so one of them suddenly jabbed a finger into each of Gilles's nostrils and viciously yanked upward. His nose was ripped open and blood spurted all over the sheets. Gilles had no choice but to let me go. They picked him up and, while holding his hands behind his back, shoved him against a commode that was right beside the bed. The impact was so violent that it made a huge hole along the length of the desk in the gypsum wallboard behind it. Then they threw him to the floor, and as he fell, I heard his head hit the doorframe, hard. They took advantage of his situation and handcuffed him.

Meanwhile, I tried to sit up, but one of the officers shoved me back down onto the bed. I was completely naked. While one of them held my hands above my head, two others spread my legs apart. Another began kicking Gilles repeatedly, even though his wrists were cuffed. Blood was streaming from his mouth. I screamed for them to stop. The only answer I got was, "You shut your mouth, bitch! Shut it, cow!" Another of the masked madmen, standing at the foot of the bed, looked at me and, with a laugh, said to Gilles, "Wow, congrats, Giguère. Life must be fun with this to look forward to in bed every night."

I kept struggling, wanting to stop the brute who was still beating Gilles, unrelentingly. I finally managed to wrest my hands free, and leapt out of bed and threw myself on Gilles to protect him, hoping they would stop. His face was bloodied. Out of the corner of my eye, I saw another of the barbarians, standing on top of the kitchen table, still yelling, "Police! Police!"

As soon as I reached Gilles, some of them rushed to try and pull me loose, but I wouldn't let go. When they finally separated us and threw me onto the bed, my back was full of scratches. After the riot gear–clad beasts finally finished their display, one of the members of the unit, whose face was uncovered, came up to me and asked, "Miss, you must have a dressing gown. Can you tell me where it is, please?" He was the only one who was polite, which made sense: he was also the only one I could identify. I told him my dressing gown was hanging behind the bathroom door. He went to get it and brought it to me. I barely had time to put it on and tie it loosely, and then he grabbed my arms, preparing to handcuff me as well. I'm claustrophobic, and I was afraid. "Is that really necessary?" I asked. "Could you at least leave my hands in front?" Nothing doing: he cuffed me with my hands behind my back, took me by the arm, led me into the living room, and made me sit on the couch.

When I sat down, my dressing gown fell open. I kept my legs closed, but two of the masked officers, who were standing in the doorframe separating the bedroom from the living room, bent down to stare between my legs, laughing and making lewd remarks. At that moment, I felt that the men before me weren't representatives of a supposedly civilized state, governed by the rule of law, but nothing more than savage animals, with more testosterone in their balls than grey matter in their heads.

Some plainclothes officers then came in, got Gilles dressed, put the cuffs back on him, and led him outside. They returned to tell me that they were taking me away as well, but didn't tell me where. They took me back to the bedroom and told me to get dressed, but they were rushing me so much that I didn't even have time to put socks on under my boots – and it was the middle of winter and quite cold out. They led me outside and into the back seat of a police car. They had taken off my handcuffs so that I could get dressed, and just before I got into the car, they were about to put them back on. I begged them not to.

"You're not going to make trouble?" one of them asked.

"No."

They didn't cuff me again, but they took me to the headquarters of the Sûreté du Québec on Parthenais Street. For eighteen hours, during which I wasn't allowed to sleep, eat, or smoke, in a tiny office measuring less than two metres square, officers grilled, intimidated, and threatened me, asking all kinds of questions, which mostly involved people I had never met in my life and knew nothing about – not even their names. They wanted to know if "Mom" Boucher had ever been to our house. No, I answered. Not surprisingly, they also asked me about Bob Savard. He had also been arrested that morning as part of the same operation. They told me Gilles had done so and so at such and such a time, and I countered that it couldn't be true because he had been with me on the day and at the time they mentioned. They were obviously looking to accuse him of some crime. They insinuated that he was part of a murder and extortion plot and that he had made a confession. Their game was to make me believe that Gilles was going to be brought up on some serious charges. "What? You're charging Gilles with murder?" I asked, incredulous.

"No, no. Nobody's dead. The charge is conspiracy to commit murder."

I didn't believe a word of it. "Bring him here," I told them. "You shouldn't have any qualms about that – you just said he's made a confession. Well, I want to hear it too." They refused.

(Not long after the raids, charges of extortion and conspiracy to murder Gérard Etcheverry, a former restaurant owner, and Loretta Lavallée, a real estate agent who herself had a criminal record a mile long, were laid against Bob Savard, Gilles Giguère, and Gilles Daudelin. But the Crown later withdrew the charges for lack of evidence. That wasn't surprising, because the accusations were based on the testimony of Léo Lemieux, who was eventually discredited as a manipulator and a liar in a Quebec Public Security Ministry report.)

Several times during the interrogation, knowing full well what my constitutional rights were, I asked to speak with a lawyer. "Is there one in particular you would like to talk to?" one of the investigators asked. I gave the name of the only lawyer I knew: Gilles Daudelin. The cop burst out laughing. "I don't think he would be much help to you today. See, he's in a little room just down the hall." Daudelin had been arrested as part of the same early-morning operation.

I tried to get the name of another lawyer, but the officers jerked me around. In the end, I never saw one. Sacred principles like citizens' rights are all very well in theory. But when the police are holding someone captive in a tiny room at headquarters, on their turf, and nobody knows about it, rights don't mean a thing.

The officer who was in charge of the interrogation knew everything about me. He told me that if he wanted, he could put an end to my modelling and acting career overnight, and have me blacklisted by every casting agency and TV station in town. All he would have to do was put my picture on the front page of the *Journal de Montréal* and it would be all over for me. He didn't follow through on that threat, but the next morning the Carcajou raid was front-page news in the *Journal de Montréal*, with an article saying, "*Un cadeau de Noël au ministre Ménard*" ("Christmas comes early for Minister Ménard"),* and there was a page 3 story headlined "*Carcajou frappe un grand coup*" ("Carcajou strikes major blow") that mentioned my name.

---

* Quebec's public security minister at the time, Serge Ménard.

The thing that disturbed me most during that long, intimidating interrogation session was that for several hours, the
investigators tried to make me believe that my life was in
danger. They said they wanted to take me to a condo in Saint-
Bruno, on Montreal's South Shore, a kind of safe house where
they hid people who needed police protection. Since I had just
witnessed their "protection" methods firsthand, I wasn't particularly interested in being protected by those people. I think
– although unfortunately I only understood this much later –
their strategy was to draw Gilles over to their side and make
him an informant, by leading him to believe that they were
going to keep me sequestered.

At one point, I asked for permission to go and use the bathroom. I ran into Gilles in the corridor. He was still handcuffed.
We weren't able to speak, but our eyes met. His seemed to be
telling me, with a slight twinkle, something like, "Yeah, we're
in a bit of a bind, but we'll get through it all right." My gaze
didn't tell him the same thing at all. My eyes unequivocally con-
veyed disbelief, worry, panic. I regretted that for years. Maybe
if I'd shown more control and confidence, he would have
behaved differently. He might have been stronger.

I found out later that his interrogation had lasted much longer
than mine, and that the police were able to force a number of
statements out of him, which he agreed to sign solely for the
purpose of protecting me – to make sure I would be released from
the hell I was being put through as soon as possible. Naturally, he
never intended to acknowledge those statements before a judge,
but I still believe they are the reason I lost him in the end.

After the eighteen hours of questioning, without being allowed
to speak to Gilles, I was released. It was two in the morning.

The police asked me where I wanted to be dropped off, but they refused to drive me home, claiming that my life would be endangered if they did. So I told them that I wanted to go to my father's place – the tiny apartment at the corner of Pie-IX Boulevard and Saint-Zotique Street. They ended up leaving me at the intersection of Pie-IX and Jean-Talon Street, about three blocks away. It was the middle of winter, and I was shivering in my bare feet and boots, with no handbag and not a penny on me. I went into the nearest café and, for the first and last time in my life, begged for a quarter so that I could use the phone. A woman gave me one. I called my father and asked him to come and get me.

As it turned out, my father had also been arrested that morning as part of the same Carcajou swoop. Like me, he had no prior record. But as I have mentioned, Gilles sometimes hired him to work for his renovation company, and no doubt that was the police motive for picking him up. He had been released almost immediately, though, after just a few hours in custody. He came and took me back to his place, and said, "Listen, you stay here for the night. In the morning, when it's light, we'll head over to your place."

When we ended up going back, in the early morning, there was still yellow "Police Line: Do Not Cross" tape across the door to the condo. We walked in, and you could have sworn the place had been hit by a tornado. Every last square inch of the floor was covered in bits of paper, clothing, and the spilled contents of drawers. It was a complete shambles. The mattresses had been overturned and thrown onto the floor, the pictures taken down from the walls, and the closets emptied of their contents. It looked like a scene from Beirut and Baghdad put together.

What was foremost in my mind at that point, however, was not the indescribable mess that Carcajou had so kindly left me. I wanted to know where Gilles was, what he was doing, and what state he was in. He finally called me around five that evening. I could tell from the sound of his voice that he was in a bad way – he was mumbling like someone who had just come from the dentist – and that he was worried. He wanted to make sure that I'd been released and that I was safe. He said that he was going to be held until he could go before a judge for his bail hearing, and he would probably spend the holidays behind bars – which is what happened.

Gilles's bail hearing took place in early January 1996. He was released immediately. As soon as he got out of prison, he told me that during his initial custody he had signed several sworn statements for the police, but that they had all been obtained through violence, intimidation, and threats involving me. He said he'd signed everything the police wanted him to sign in the hope that they would stop questioning me and release me as soon as possible. He also explained that he intended to deny everything he'd said in those sworn statements if the case ever went to court.

Life went on for us, but after the incidents of Christmas 1995, Gilles was never the same again. Since I'd known him he'd always been quick to laugh, animated, and unfailingly in great spirits – but no longer. He grew depressed, even aggressive. He had always been affectionate but was now cold and distant. I remember at one point trying to talk to him, to find out what was wrong, exactly. "I don't want to talk about it. Don't ask me any questions," he answered angrily.

In the days following the Carcajou raid on our home, I took steps to file a complaint with the provincial police ethics commissioner about the abusive behaviour of the officers. A lawyer, Pierre Goulet – the same one who had represented Richard Barnabé, a taxi driver who had been beaten in a police cell in 1993 and died of his injuries two years later – got in touch with me and said he was prepared to take on the case.

A few days later, I got a phone call from a man who didn't identify himself. All he said was, "You know, it would be a real drag if you were stopped for running a red light and the police happened to find a kilo of coke in your car." Then he hung up.

I don't want to speculate, a dozen years later, about who may have made that call. All I can say is that I got the message and immediately put a stop to the complaint procedure.

17

Death in Close-Up

"I turned on the TV. And I saw Gilles's body lying in a ditch, as if I were only a metre away from him. I recognized him right away. That's how I found out he was dead. Live, on television."

In late February of 1996, two months after filing charges of extortion and conspiracy to commit murder against Gilles Giguère, Bob Savard, and their lawyer, Gilles Daudelin, the Crown abandoned its case, acknowledging that it could provide no evidence to support it because the testimony of informant Léo Lemieux had been discredited.

And not long after he and Gilles had spent the holidays in jail following the December 18 raid, Bob said to me, "I gotta tell ya, sweetheart, you've got a good nose. You were right – you sized that guy up perfectly."

Gilles, however, still faced charges of illegal possession of the four automatic weapons and twenty-five kilograms of marijuana that had been found in the apartment building he owned in Montreal East – another "gift" from Lemieux. A trial date had been set for May.

*

After he was cleared of the extortion and conspiracy to murder charges, Gilles gradually got back on track and returned to his renovation work. He did a few jobs here and there as things got back to normal. Moreover, the previous summer, we had decided to get married. At first, we had set a date in June, but because of all the problems – the December 18 raid, his subsequent incarceration, and now the trial slated for May – we decided to put the wedding off until September. There was absolutely no reason for me to think that his life was in danger in any way, especially given the fact that there seemed to be a good chance that he would be acquitted of the weapons and drug possession charges, now that Lemieux had confessed to his involvement in the affair.

On Friday, April 26, 1996, we went out for dinner at an all-you-can-eat Chinese place in the east end of town; Gilles's son, Pierre-Paul, had said he wanted to eat Chinese food. We didn't get home very late. When we got back to the condo, Gilles realized we were out of cereal for Pierre-Paul's breakfast the next morning and said he was going to go buy some at the corner store. This must have been a little after nine o'clock. I wasn't really paying attention. I was watching TV. My favourite show, *The X-Files*, was just starting, and I was glued to the screen. Gilles said, "Okay, I'm off to the depanneur. Don't I get my kiss?"

"Mm? Yeah . . . Hang on just a sec," I said.

But the TV still held my full attention. So he called out, "Okay, then!" and walked out the door. Suddenly, for some reason, I decided it was incredibly important that I not let him leave without giving him a kiss. I got up, opened the door to the apartment, and looked out into the hallway; the elevator doors were sliding shut. I rushed down to the parking garage, only to see his truck pulling away. I went back upstairs and back to my TV show.

Three-quarters of an hour later, Gilles hadn't come back. That wasn't like him. Then, around ten to ten, I remember feeling a sharp pain in my stomach and suddenly feeling that maybe he was with another woman. I immediately chased the thought from my mind: that wasn't like him either. But strangely, as soon as I told myself, "No, it's impossible, he wouldn't do that to me," I was sure that something was wrong.

I tried to reach him on his pager but heard it vibrate on the dining room buffet. Then I dialled his cellular number and heard the handset ring from the same place. At that point, I began to be seriously worried. Pierre-Paul, who was usually in bed by ten-thirty, asked me if he could sleep in our bed until his dad came home and could tuck him in, as he did every night. Around eleven, I went to bed. The strange thing was that normally, in a situation like that, I wouldn't be able to get to sleep. But I was knocked out, as if I'd received a violent blow to the face. I fell asleep as soon as my head hit the pillow.

Around four in the morning, I woke up and instantly realized that Gilles wasn't there. He hadn't come back, and he hadn't called. At that moment, sheer panic set in. I got up and went to the bathroom. Now, I know that what I'm about to write must seem unbelievable, but it's exactly how I experienced it. Sitting on the toilet, my face buried in my hands, I said aloud, "Gilles, where are you? What are you doing? Why haven't you called? Why haven't you come back? Why are you making me worry like this?"

I looked up, and there he was. In the corner of the bathroom. Naked as the day he was born, standing, his arms hanging loosely at his sides, eyes closed. I could see him plain as day, but I sensed he was in a different dimension from mine, another world. "No, Gilles," I said to him. "You can't do this to me. It can't be true. Open your eyes." But he only smiled, shyly. At that moment – even though I would later go through various stages of denial until his body was found – I knew he was dead.

I covered my face with my hands again, and rubbed my eyes, willing myself back to reality. When I opened them, Gilles was gone – and a horrible ordeal began.

I rushed over to the phone. I tried to reach Bob Savard and every friend of Gilles that I knew. No one had heard anything or knew where he might be. Then, at eight o'clock on Saturday morning, I called Gilles's sister and asked her to come and pick up his son. I told Pierre-Paul that his dad had gone to work earlier than usual, and that he would be spending the day with his aunt. Then I called the police to report Gilles's disappearance. "I'm sorry, ma'am," the officer on duty said, "but we're talking about an adult here. He has to have been missing for at least twenty-four hours before we can do anything, unless he's mentally unstable and represents a danger to himself or to society."

"Fine, then," I said. "He's extremely suicidal, all right? And I wouldn't be surprised if he were extremely dangerous too. Are you going to start searching now?"

A police officer came round to take my statement, and then the endless hours of waiting began. My brother, Patrick, came to keep me company. I continued calling everyone I could think of and waiting for someone to call back. I was sick with worry, waiting for the slightest sign of hope that maybe the unthinkable hadn't happened. But with each passing hour, my confidence that Gilles would be found alive dwindled.

The next morning, I got a call saying that Gilles's truck, a GMC pickup, had been located in the parking lot of the O'Tooles bar/restaurant in Repentigny, off the eastern tip of the Island of Montreal. Patrick and I drove out there in my car to make arrangements to have the vehicle towed. But when we arrived, we found the police had seized the truck because I had reported Gilles missing. While we were there, I ran into Gilles's lawyer at the time, Michel Charlebois. As we were talking, a policeman came up to us and asked me if Gilles wore a partial denture. "Yes, why?" I answered.

"Because we've found someone," the policeman said, "and we're trying to establish his identity."

At that point I went into total denial. That Gilles was dead was not a conceivable option. It was impossible and unacceptable, period. I wouldn't hear of it. I even said to the policeman, naively, "Well, if you want to know whether it's Gilles, just ask him what his name is."

"If I could be a little more clear, ma'am . . . we've found a body. There's a possibility that it's him. We need someone to come to the scene and identify him."

My reaction was immediate: "No, no, no. I don't want to see him. If it's him, I don't want to see him like that." Patrick spoke up. "I'll go," he said.

"No," I answered firmly. "I don't want you to see him like that either. I don't want you to have to live with that image in your head."

I turned to Charlebois: "What about you; would you go? You've met him; you know what he looks like."

"All right, I'll go," he said.

I remained in utter denial, however, and convinced myself that it wasn't Gilles that they'd found. After Charlebois left to go and identify the body, Patrick and I got back in the car and he drove me home to the condo in Pointe-aux-Trembles.

As soon as I got back – it was just before five in the evening – I turned on the TV. And I saw Gilles's body lying in a ditch, as if I were only a metre away from him. I recognized him right away. That's how I found out he was dead. Live, on television. I hadn't wanted to go and identify the body, and now I had no choice but to see, in a grisly close-up, what had been done to him: six bullet wounds in a body bloated after being submerged for several hours in a watery ditch. A broad security perimeter had been set up around the scene, but a TV camera had managed to get a telephoto shot of my Gilles's body. I believe in freedom of the press and access to information, but when the braintrust at that TV network – the executives who decide, without consulting anyone, what ordinary viewers get to see, or not see – chose to air those pictures, did they think about Gilles's next of kin and everyone else who knew and loved him having to see his mutilated body that way, before they were even informed of his death through official channels? Did they have even the slightest notion of decency?

It's strange how your mind reacts in traumatic situations like that. I was so obsessed with the idea of finding Gilles that when I saw his body on television, my initial reaction was almost one of triumph. "Oh! It's him! They've found him!" I thought to myself. Then a fraction of a second later, reality struck me: "He's dead!" And I froze up. I went completely numb; I couldn't feel a thing. I disconnected from reality, which had suddenly become too heavy, too ugly.

My poor kid brother, who had always been very fond of Gilles, didn't take it well at all. He began sobbing uncontrollably, and cried, "Julie, I can't remember what he looks like! I can't remember his face when he was alive! What does he look like? I can't get these awful images out of my mind! What does he look like, Julie?"

I flew into the bedroom and yanked open a dresser drawer, rifled through some snapshots, and pulled out several. Patrick kept sobbing and moaning. I rushed back to him and showed him the pictures, pictures of him with Gilles, smiling huge smiles. We sat and looked at the photos together, crying.

All of a sudden, I felt I was going mad. I feared that my intellect was going to retreat into some far corner of my mind, where everything was pitch black, and from which I would never return. I held on tight to my brother and pleaded, "Patrick, I feel like I'm going insane. Hold me! Please, hold me tight . . . It's like I'm slipping away and I'll never be able to come back!"

At nine that evening, police officers from the Sûreté du Québec Crimes Against Persons squad knocked on the door, bearing the news I had already learned from the television. They confirmed that it was Gilles's body they had discovered. At that point, members of my family arrived as well: my mother, my father and his girlfriend, my sister with her newborn baby. I started crying all over again.

The police wanted to question me, despite the pain that was driving me insane. They asked me about Gilles's links with Bob Savard and other people. Did I know where Gilles was headed when he left the house? Who he was with? Who had he met in the preceding days? After three-quarters of an hour, my mother interceded. "I think she's been through enough for one day," she said to the officers, and showed them the door.

In a flash, I got up and went into the kitchen. Seized by uncontrollable, seething rage, I swept all the dishes off the counter with one swing of my arms; they flew onto the floor with a horrible crash. My sister started screaming, and my little niece burst out crying. Just as quickly, I calmed myself, not wanting to frighten the baby anymore.

18

Mourning

*"When I first saw Gilles in the casket, I felt my knees
buckle. 'Mom, they've made a mistake,' I said. 'It's not
him. It doesn't look like him.' Then my mother said softly,
'Look at his hands. You'll recognize him.'"*

My mother stayed overnight at the condo after my
emotional outburst. The next morning, I went to
the funeral parlour with Gilles's sister to choose a
casket and make the necessary arrangements for the viewing.
Because Gilles had been murdered, it was several days before
the body was released to his family. An autopsy had been
conducted, and since Gilles had lain dead in the water for two
days, the embalmers' task was more complicated than usual.
They had to work from a photograph that I gave them; I had
insisted on an open-casket ceremony, if at all possible. The
viewing, however, was not until the Thursday following Gilles's
death. The funeral service took place the next day, Friday,
May 3.

The viewing was at the funerary complex on Beaubien
Street East, just behind what was then known as the Cimetière
de l'Est-de-Montréal (today the Repos Saint-François-d'Assise).

When I first saw Gilles in the casket, I felt my knees buckle. "Mom, they've made a mistake," I said. "It's not him. It doesn't look like him." Then my mother said softly, "Look at his hands. You'll recognize him." Gilles had very big hands. There was no mistaking them. It was indeed him.

There was a huge crowd at the funeral parlour; in fact, they had to open up an unoccupied adjacent room to accommodate everyone. Many of Gilles's old acquaintances attended, including his fishing buddies and former co-workers from the General Electric plant, and of course members of his immediate and extended family as well as his former partner's family. I was thankful for the fact that there were two rooms, because this created a physical as well as a psychological demarcation between Gilles's former in-laws and me. Gilles's ex had a flair for the dramatic, and I feared most of all that she might treat us to a *mater dolorosa* scene beside the casket, after having done everything she could to poison Gilles's existence while he was alive. I didn't want to have to see that.

Several people connected to the Hells Angels were there as well. Eventually, "Mom" Boucher arrived, escorted by three or four other members. He chatted with Gilles's brother for a few minutes, and then he came over to me to offer his condolences. His presence at the funeral parlour was both revolting and disconcerting to me, because in those types of murder cases, one's first thought is to suspect somebody from the underworld milieu. I was fairly sure Gilles had been killed by one of his acquaintances, and there was a good chance that the Hells Angels had ordered the killing. Indeed, the police officer who had questioned me the previous Sunday had made no secret of the fact that the Hells Angels were among the possible suspects. He had asked me several questions aimed at ascertaining whether Gilles had been in contact with high-ranking Hells

Angels members in the weeks leading up to his death. I knew it was a possibility.

The rumour spread rapidly that Gilles had been killed because he had become a police informant. I knew that in underworld circles, all it takes is the merest sliver of doubt for the bosses to consider eliminating someone. They don't need to ask themselves whether the person might talk, only whether he knows something that might incriminate them. That's all that matters. That's how these decisions are made. In the opinion of many, therefore, Gilles's murder was clearly a gangland settling of accounts, as the saying goes. The question was raised during my brief conversation with "Mom" Boucher at the funeral parlour; I don't recall who brought it up first, but I clearly remember telling him, "It's terrible. They say Gilles had become an informant, that he was working with the police. It's not true, what people are saying. He wasn't talking to the police. If he had been, I'd have known about it."

"Don't worry about it," Boucher replied. "There's people who think I'm a snitch myself."

The way he responded was perfectly evasive, and it didn't clarify how he felt about Gilles in the slightest. But I at least had the satisfaction of getting a message through to him – essentially, "Gilles was never a snitch."

Gilles had nothing but contempt for informants. I remember clearly that in those days, all kinds of people with close ties to criminal bikers were going to the police. Informants were spreading like weeds. Gilles had never had anything good to say about them. He said it wasn't right to rat on your friends, that it simply wasn't done. "In life, if you make a mistake, you have to face the consequences," he'd always said. Informing was completely contrary to his principles. I knew it, and his friends should have known it too.

I also thought to myself that if the Hells Angels had indeed orchestrated the murder, if they had made the mistake of believing that Gilles was an informant, then they might very well have suspicions about me. I was afraid. Before Boucher left the funeral complex, I asked him to find the guilty party. "You have to find out who did this," I said. "I know you know that Gilles was against guns. He didn't deserve to die that way."

All day long, everyone had their theories about the murderers' identities and motives. Some people were sure it was Boucher; others thought it might've been Bob Savard. Still others believed it was a corrupt ex-cop. The entire gamut of possibilities was on the table. Everyone was playing amateur detective.

There was one other thing that really got on my nerves during that seemingly interminable day. Gilles's family was very religious, and Gilles himself had been a believer. Consequently, there was a priest at the funeral parlour, who periodically asked everyone to gather around the casket for a group prayer. I recall clearly that whenever the call to prayer was issued, I refused to join the group and remained seated. I was rebelling against all the deities of Earth, be they named God the Father, Allah, or Buddha. The priest was saying, "God has His reasons, which we can't begin to understand . . . The Lord works in mysterious ways" – the usual spiel. And I was saying, under my breath, "But God had nothing to do with this, you idiot! His life was taken by another man. Stop saying that God has come to take him!" The whole thing was ridiculous and unbearable.

The next day, a religious funeral was held in a huge church in the Hochelaga-Maisonneuve neighbourhood; I forget the name. It was Gilles's sister who had suggested the location, which had particular significance for their parents. After the ceremony, we went to bury him in the Cimetière de l'Est. He rests in peace there today, in Section 18A, Lot 258, just steps from the Beaubien Street entrance.

As anyone who has had to mourn a loved one knows, the experience takes you through many phases. First, you have to learn how to live through each day, feeling as though you have lost a limb. The months that followed Gilles's death were tinged with pain and a feeling of emptiness. For a long time, whenever I heard a truck outside that made the same engine noise as his, I would think for a fraction of a second that it was him. Wherever I went, I kept thinking I saw him. I was constantly caught up in a sort of fantasy that he wasn't really dead. Then reality would quickly wash over me. I would get up in the morning and make myself a cup of coffee; I would watch the sun come up, life going on outside, people going about their business, nothing having changed for them – while in my world, everything had come crashing down. There was a rage inside me.

When you lose your partner in such a violent manner, you also go through an intense phase of guilt. You sit and spend hours running the film of events through your mind, analyzing the most minute details. And you constantly second-guess yourself: "Why couldn't I see the danger coming? Why didn't I stop it? Couldn't I have done something?" It's enough to drive you insane. The reality was that I had never feared that Gilles's life might be in danger that way. I had worried he might have problems with the law, or at worst, be hit by a stray bullet in some gunfight. But not once did I suspect that he would be killed in such a cold, calculating manner.

It was several months before I went to his grave. I knew that his mother went almost every day, but that seemed to me to be twisting the knife in the wound. I think that, in a way, I had to put some distance between myself and his body, which had been so violently attacked. It was a matter of survival for me. "It's not him down in the ground," I said to myself. "It's his body, and the body is only a shell. Gilles's essence is gone. He's somewhere else."

So I went several months later, one afternoon in September, on what would have been our wedding day. It was cold out. I brought along a wool sweater and a bottle of champagne, which I almost finished even though I don't react well to alcohol.

I sat down next to his grave, talking to him while I drank the champagne that we would have shared that very day if he had still been alive. I was so upset with him. In fact, I was furious with him. When I had decided to go and live with Gilles, I knew he was no angel. I knew the people he kept company with weren't all reputable. But there were many things that I simply didn't suspect. At first, I didn't take his biker friends seriously, but as time went on I became increasingly aware of the danger until, eventually, I realized just how treacherous these people were, and how risky it was for Gilles to maintain ties with them. That was why I had made a deal with him: "You don't do anything else that will get you in trouble. You keep quiet," I had said. He had broken that agreement, and now I bitterly held it against him. I had lost him, I was suffering horribly because he was gone, and it was his fault.

I was afraid, as well. Very afraid. I didn't understand what had happened, and didn't know what might happen next. I kept thinking that if Gilles's murder had indeed been a criminal settling of accounts, whoever had ordered the killing might well suspect that I, too, knew things about them that I wasn't supposed to know. Not only that, but the media coverage of the murder had been completely out of proportion to Gilles's true standing in the world of organized crime. It was as if someone incredibly important had been killed. He was being described as a kingpin. The police as well as crime reporters had created a myth out of whole cloth. Moreover, the circumstances surrounding his murder remained murky. There were so many theories floating around, it was only natural that I felt my life was in danger.

I admit that for a few weeks immediately following Gilles's death, I went through a phase of intense paranoia. More than once, when I started the car in the morning, the thought crossed my mind that it might explode. I spent entire days in the condo, jumping at the slightest noise. For weeks, I slept with a knife under the pillow every night.

And yet, as contradictory as it may sound, there were often moments when the fear of being killed was swept aside by a desire to put an end to things by my own hand. During that time, I often thought of suicide. I might be driving on the highway and thinking of Gilles, saying to myself, "If only I could call him." All I wanted was to be by his side again. I missed him so much. I would think about slamming the car into the next concrete overpass pillar – and then, as it came into view, say to myself, "No, not this one. The next one." I think that just about the only thing that kept me from going through with it was the fact that I always had my little dog Tootsie with me – the last present Gilles had given me before he died. That suicidal phase was then followed by a period in which I was prepared to take all kinds of risks, because I didn't give a damn whether I lived or died. I wasn't afraid of anything, because life meant so little to me.

Not long after Gilles's murder, the well-known crime reporter and hostage negotiator Claude Poirier had begun to visit me. He was a good friend of one of my uncles – one of my mother's brothers who had been a policeman, a homicide investigator, in fact. Poirier thought it was unhealthy for me to be sequestered all day long, but he was also worried for my safety because of all the rumours surrounding Gilles's murder (to this day, the case has not been solved). He started coming to see me every morning, just to make sure I got out for some fresh air. I would accompany him while he worked, waiting in his car when he was busy, and at day's end he would drive me home. These daily outings lasted for a few weeks. They helped me reconnect with the world outside my windows, and I think they helped take my mind off my bereavement, at least to some degree.

19

Rebuilding

"I was sitting quietly in my living room when all of a sudden I heard what sounded like a maniac rapping madly on the patio door."

Two years before Gilles's death, a rule under the new Civil Code of Quebec, which had come into effect in 1994, required renovation contractors to hold a licence from the Régie du bâtiment, the province's construction board, which previously had been required only of general contractors. That led to all kinds of paperwork and extra fees, of course, but it also meant that one had to take courses and pass a theory exam to obtain the licence. Gilles was terrified by the prospect of having to "go back to school," as he put it. On one occasion, he even got into a shouting match with an inspector from the Commission de la construction du Québec. I was afraid that he would run into problems as a result of the incident, and he himself feared that he might have to shut down his company and find himself out of work. So I said, "Look, I'm good at learning things by heart. I'll study, write the exam, and get qualification for the company. You'll have your builder's licence and you'll be able to keep on working."

"But you don't even know how to frame a door with three two-by-fours," he said. "How are you going to pass the exam for a general contractor's licence?"

"That may be true," I said. "But if I have to learn a formula or anything like that, I can do it, no problem."

In the end, Gilles died before we were able to follow through with our plans. But the summer after his murder, the idea gradually came to me that the only way I could keep his memory alive was to honour my pledge to him. So I undertook the procedure for obtaining the licence. I signed up for a two-month course, which was given twice a week and every other Saturday by the Corporation des entrepreneurs spécialisés du Grand Montréal, or CESGM (Greater Montreal Specialized Contractors' Corporation). I sat the construction board exam and passed with flying colours.

By passing the exam, I killed two birds with one stone. First, I kept my word to Gilles, and second, I found a way to be gainfully employed again. Not surprisingly, in the wake of the December 18, 1995, police raid, Gilles's murder, and the news spreading that I had been his common-law wife, my modelling and acting jobs had dried up almost completely. I had lost my contract with Canadelle, my biggest source of work, and I knew full well that it would be extremely difficult to build up a new client base. And besides, I now suffered from horrible bouts of stage fright on the rare occasions when I did get a modelling or acting gig. They were a constant source of stress. So I decided to abandon that career and go into business as a general contractor. I had all the legal documents I needed to proceed, I had learned a lot about the construction industry in my years spent with Gilles, and though I wouldn't be able to take on the physical part of the job myself, I knew that I could handle the project management side effectively.

I founded a company, GPJ (for Gilles, Pierre-Paul, and Julie) Construction, and had it incorporated. I purchased vehicles and materials, took out the necessary civil liability insurance, and set about looking for contracts. I decided to work exclusively with subcontractors, which freed me of several responsibilities and a lot of paperwork (because when a general contractor hires sub-contractors in Quebec, it merely has to ensure that they have a valid construction board permit and civil liability insurance).

My first contract involved reducing the grade of the driveway leading to the underground parking garage of an apartment building in downtown Montreal, on Bishop Street between Sherbrooke Street and Doctor Penfield Avenue. I went to see a property manager who had been one of Gilles's customers, and offered my company's services. He didn't seem to take me all that seriously at first, but I made the lowest bid, so I was awarded the contract. And since I had started building up a good network of contacts during my courses at the Specialized Contractors' Corporation, I was able to hire a site manager immediately, as well as other specialized subcontractors, and we were ready to go.

It was a fairly complex job: the driveway had to be almost entirely redone, from the sidewalk all the way to six metres or so beyond the garage doors. We would even have to divert traffic for a few days so that the cement mixers and gravel trucks could access the site properly. Things got even more complicated once the work actually started, though. The very first day, the excavator I'd hired started to break up the concrete driveway with a jackhammer. All of a sudden, I heard a thunderous noise and saw the ground collapse, taking the worker and his jackhammer with it. Thankfully, the man wasn't hurt, but the jackhammer was damaged. Only then did we realize that just below where he had started working, there was a crawlspace that hadn't been on the plans, and a huge sewer pipe that had burst from the impact. Needless to say, the smell was awful.

Worst of all, this unforeseen event would probably lead to a significant delay in completing the work; not only would we have to fix the damage, we would also have to ensure that everything complied with the as-built plans and with municipal code. We would also have to build a concrete gabion with a steel armature around the sewer pipe, to ensure easy access for maintenance and in case of a break. All of this was extra work that hadn't been planned for. Of course, building contracts always stipulate that if the contractor cannot complete the work in the allotted time, it has to pay a fine. So the property manager reviewed the budget and the completion timetable, and promised me a bonus if the work was finished on time. In the end, we finished five days ahead of schedule. On my first job as a building contractor, I had not only managed to see the work through to completion despite difficult conditions, but I had also saved the building owners from having to pay what could have been very hefty fines. I was proud of myself. And every once in a while, I still pass by that building and see that the driveway remains in great shape.

Shifting from modelling to the construction industry in such a short time wasn't easy. I was getting up at five in the morning, calling my subcontractors at six to make sure their crews would be on-site in time, and by seven I would be on the premises myself. I was leading the same life as Gilles had, and in a way it brought me closer to him. I came to know why he had loved his work so much. And for my part, I had the satisfaction of rising to a difficult challenge.

A few weeks later, the same property manager called on me again. He had another project in the same building on Bishop Street. This time he wanted to convert the garage roof into a patio. To make sure this kind of structure is sturdy enough, you have to lay what is known as a hot-mop membrane onto the roof surface. In this instance, however, we first had to install a roof drain to carry rainwater down below the garage. It was a fairly simple job, so I hired a plumber, an Italian I didn't know. I made it clear to him that we were going to hot-mop the roof afterward, so he would have to use different, heat-resistant materials for the drain. Later, when the crew arrived to work on the roof, they immediately saw that the plumber hadn't used the right materials when installing the drain. "I can't do hot-mopping on top of that," the foreman told me. "The drain will collapse into the garage and smash the cars parked inside."

I immediately called the plumber to get him to come and redo the job, but he said he wouldn't be available until four days later. Now, I had already paid him half his fee up-front. That was how I worked: "I pay you half now, and half when the job is finished." It was a good way to earn the trust of a subcontractor I didn't know and was working with for the first time. But when this guy told me he wouldn't be able to come back until several days later, I said, "Look, if you can't redo the work within two days, I'm going to have to hire somebody else. And by the way, you're going to come by and reimburse me for the money I paid you, because you did a shit job."

A week or two later, on a Sunday evening, I was sitting quietly in my living room when all of a sudden I heard what sounded like a maniac rapping madly on the patio door. I looked outside. It was my incompetent Italian plumber. I was less than thrilled. You don't disturb people at home like that, least of all on a Sunday night. I slid the patio door open and asked what he wanted. "I want you to pay me the balance of what you owe me. You only paid me for half the job," he said.

"I don't owe you a thing," I retorted. "You're the one who owes me, because I had to have your amateur job redone by someone who knew what they were doing."

"You listen to me," he said. "Maybe you don't realize who you're dealing with. If you keep on like this, things are gonna turn out bad for you. I'm going to call a meeting with some pretty heavy people, and you'd better show up. They're going to decide how to settle this."

"You do whatever the hell you want. Call the Pope, for all I care. But I know I'm right. It's *you* who's trying to rip *me* off. Tell me when and where. I'll go to your meeting," I said.

As I mentioned, in those days I pretty much didn't give a damn about anything. I wasn't afraid of anything, and I had started taking risks I never would have taken under normal circumstances. I don't think I would act the same way today. So I went to the meeting, armed with a copy of the contract, the plumber's estimate, my invoices, copies of the cheques I'd made out to him – and most important of all, my side of the story. And I laid it all on the table.

Three men were there with the plumber, all of a certain age, and all with undeniably Italian accents. One of them seemed to be in a particular position of authority. I'd never seen them before in my life. They read through the documents and asked a few questions. One of them asked the plumber, "Why did you do the job that way?"

"She didn't tell me to do otherwise."

But none of them believed him. You can tell when someone is in hot water, and lying. After a few minutes, the leader of the triumvirate decided I was in the right. He apologized for having put me through all that trouble for nothing, and ordered the con-man plumber to reimburse what I had already paid. He also warned the man never to trouble him and his cronies again for such a trifling matter, nor to ask them to "represent" him in a situation where he knew he was wrong.

I gained more than I had anticipated by showing up for that strange tribunal: not only had I managed to get rid of a crank who had tried to intimidate me and could have become dangerous, but on top of that, I had recovered an amount of money that I thought I would never see again. There was no way I would have moved heaven and earth to try to get a few hundred dollars back, but at the same time, I wasn't about to let myself be duped any more than I already had.

I never tried to find out the identities of the three men who attended the "arbitration hearing," despite the fact that it was obviously highly unorthodox. I don't think it would have been a good idea for me to go down that road. All I knew was that they had found in my favour. I didn't need to know any more.

My company went on to win several renovation contracts over the next few months for the same property manager, in the same building. Then one day my banker called to say he wanted to meet with me. We made an appointment and I went to see him. He explained that the property manager who had provided GPJ Construction with all those contracts was in serious financial difficulty and owed the bank a lot of money. More importantly, the manager had withdrawn all the assets from his company and transferred them to another one that he had just set up – and, naturally, opened an account for that second firm with another financial institution. "If you have any accounts receivable from him," my banker told me, "I'd suggest that you not cut him too much slack, because this doesn't look good at all."

As it happened, the client owed me nearly forty-five thousand dollars. I wasted no time and went directly to his office and asked him when he intended to pay me. "Take it easy," he said, "your invoice is still less than thirty days old. We're not late."

"True," I said. "But it's not like you to wait thirty days. We've never worked like that. Usually, I have your cheque in my hands within a week."

At that point he got the feeling I was hounding him, so he brought out the bluster: "Well, how about this, then. Things aren't going the way I'd like. So if you're not happy, you can just go ahead and bankrupt me."

"What?!"

"You heard me. Sue me, that's all. Come and get me. Anyway, the company no longer has any assets."

He said it with a laugh, as if he couldn't care less.

Meanwhile, my credit line with the bank was at its limit, and I owed money to suppliers as well as subcontractors. Suddenly, I started to panic. I put some of my own money into the company. I continued to take on small contracts and put all the profits into paying off the credit line.

At that point, I realized my interest in a career as a general contractor was waning. First there had been the business of the incompetent plumber, and now there was this dishonest client. Although the company had been fairly successful, I found the job to be quite demanding and time-consuming. After spending the day at the work site, I would go home, eat in a hurry, and spend the evening doing administration, paperwork, and accounting. And as everyone knows, the construction industry is tough, especially for a woman. It's a hardball world where the language of business is more likely to consist of "fuck yous" rather than "pleases" and "thank yous." To be taken seriously, I often had to raise my voice, argue, and berate people who were usually twice my size. It was starting to wear me out.

And I had to face the fact that I hadn't embarked on this venture out of love for the building trade, but on a whim, motivated above all by emotion: I had had the feeling that by doing this job, I could keep Gilles closer to my heart.

But enough was enough. I had cleared my debts and didn't owe a penny to anyone, so I decided to simply wind up the company, liquidate its assets, and do something else with my life. It was the summer of 1997.

Meanwhile, I still hadn't digested the fact that the property manager still owed me a fair chunk of money, forty-five thousand dollars, which I had no legal way of recovering. At the time, I had already met Stéphane Sirois – whom I will write about a great deal in the next few chapters – and had told him the story. He said to me, simply, "Don't worry about it. I'll go and collect."

Then Stéphane said to the property manager, "I'm telling you right now, you may be declaring bankruptcy, but you're not going to drag her down with you. You have to pay her what you owe her. So you'd better play ball."

He got the message. It took him a while – two thousand dollars here, three thousand dollars there – but in the end he paid me every last cent of what he owed me.

20

Stéphane

"At one point, he even said, straight out, 'I want to switch gears. I'm fed up living this life. And now with this war on . . . It's getting pretty heavy. It's not just business anymore. So I have to ask myself, you know, do I really like this life enough to want to risk getting shot or even killed?'

In those days, I was still going through survivor's guilt. I was finding it very difficult to accept the fact that I hadn't seen Gilles's murder coming. At that point, I thought to myself, If I hadn't been able to save Gilles, maybe I could at least save this guy Stéphane."

Even before I undertook the procedures to wind up my company, around the spring of 1997 I had started earning money from my savings by acquiring property, gradually putting together a modest real estate portfolio (I liked to call it "playing Monopoly"). Since I had experience in both construction and real estate, I knew what was involved in buying homes, hiring competent people to renovate them, and then reselling them after allowing their value to increase. This was how I planned to earn my living, at least in part.

By then it had been about a year since Gilles's death, and I was still very much in mourning. It was difficult to get used to life without him. I was shaken, revolted, troubled. Emotionally and psychologically, I was still very fragile. Except for Friday night, which was girls' night out at the Jardins du Ritz, the outdoor terrace of the Montreal Ritz-Carlton hotel, I remained confined to my apartment. I didn't feel like going out or seeing anybody at all – and anyway, my work left me very little free time. It was at this time, when I was exceedingly vulnerable, that I met Stéphane Sirois.

One day Hélène, one of my best friends, said to me, "Julie, this is getting to be ridiculous. Eventually you're going to have to start going out again. It's about time you met somebody. You're not even thirty yet. He's the one who died, not you. You have to do something."

So that evening, I went out with her and some other girl-friends to a bar that was very trendy at the time, the Cocktail Disco Club on Saint-Michel Boulevard in east-end Montreal.* As soon as we sat down, someone anonymously ordered us a bottle of champagne, which we sent back. After a few minutes, a stranger came up to us to offer us the bottle of champagne in person. He wasn't too tall, fairly handsome, with close-cropped black hair, and he was clean-shaven and wearing jeans, a button-down shirt, and a small sleeveless leather jacket. He introduced himself as Stéphane Sirois. I'd never heard the name

---

* In an article in the June 6, 2008, issue of the *Globe and Mail*, to which I will refer several times in these pages, Stéphane Sirois claims that the site of our first meeting was a bar "known to be a biker hangout." How could I have known this, seeing as I didn't spend my time with bikers (even back when I had been living with Gilles Giguère)? Indeed, if memory serves, there didn't seem to be all that many bikers there that night.

in my life, but since he'd just stepped away from a few guys who were obviously bikers, I didn't have to ask myself too many questions about what kind of guy he was. And it wasn't very long before I learned that he was a full-patch member of the Rockers, the Hells Angels' "puppet club."

"I'm Gilles Giguère's widow," I told him straight out. "So you'll understand if I say I don't have much sympathy for your kind."

"My condolences," he replied, adding, "Of course I understand."

But he didn't leave. He stayed put and tried to smooth things over. He wasn't without his charms – on the contrary. He was a smooth talker. Something about his easygoing attitude was attractive to me. It changed the dynamics of my emotions and, to a certain extent, helped me forget the drama and the grief that I was still wallowing in. He was also very persuasive; as the saying goes, he could have sold a refrigerator to an Eskimo. Later, I had a hard time figuring out why this man had never done anything better with his life. He had a lot of talent, he was a people person, he was a great salesman, and he had a knack for marketing. It later became clear to me, however, that all those qualities were negated by a seemingly incurable laziness.

We chatted for a few minutes and danced a little, and then I went back to my girlfriends and finished the evening with them. I was sure I'd never hear anything about Stéphane Sirois again for the rest of my life. There is no doubt that had it turned out that way, I would have been much better off.

A few days later, I went out again with the same group of girlfriends, this time to the Action Disco Club, another nightspot that was very popular at the time and was located next to the Metropolitan Expressway, near Lacordaire Boulevard. We were seated at a table on the outdoor terrace when a big truck, a Ford

Expedition, rolled into the adjacent parking lot. And who should step out but the same guy I'd met the previous week, at the other club. He saw me and shouted, "Well, well, well! Look who's here!"

I didn't believe for a minute that he had just happened to arrive while we were there. He went up to the bar, ordered a drink, and came and sat down beside me. "You *no comprendo* very well, do you?" I said to him right away. "Seems to me I was pretty clear last week. I'm not interested in dating a biker."

"Bah – you know, it doesn't mean that's what I want to do with the rest of my life. Doesn't mean I won't have other ambitions," he answered.

At one point, he even said, straight out, "I want to switch gears. I'm fed up living this life. And now with this war on . . . it's getting pretty heavy. It's not just business anymore. So I have to ask myself, you know, do I really like this life enough to want to risk getting shot or even killed?"*

In those days, I was still going through survivor's guilt. I was finding it very difficult to accept the fact that I hadn't seen Gilles's murder coming. At that point, I thought to myself, If I hadn't been able to save Gilles, maybe I could at least save this guy Stéphane. I basically gave myself the mission of pulling him out of the life he was living and helping him build a better one. It would be a way of making up for having been so blind when it came to Gilles. I don't expect anyone to understand this, necessarily. I only mean to explain what was going through my mind when I agreed to embark on a relationship that was so obviously doomed to fail.

Right from the start, I made it crystal clear that if Stéphane

* He was referring to the biker war between the Hells Angels and Rock Machine.

wanted me to be part of his life, he had to quit the biker scene. He complied almost immediately, handing back all the insignia that showed he was a member of the Rockers and, of course, giving up all the "privileges" that came with membership.

But that wasn't all; I also told him quite clearly and honestly that I wasn't in love with him, and that my heart still belonged to Gilles. "I know this can't be easy for you," I said, "but I don't want you to have any illusions about us. If you can accept the fact that I still have a long way to go before I'll be finished mourning Gilles, so much the better. But if you can't live with the idea that he's still the love of my life, I'll understand. But you'll have one consolation, at least: I'll never be able to cheat on you with him."

"No problem," he said. "I can understand that."

But there was a problem in the end. Stéphane Sirois never understood me. In the short time I was with him, he was continually tormented by pathological, borderline violent jealousy – of the living, and of the dead as well.

Not long after I started going out with him, I left (for obvious reasons) the condo I had lived in with Gilles and rented another one in a new building, in a nice neighbourhood in Rivière-des-Prairies, on the eastern tip of the Island of Montreal. I had a ground-floor unit and soon made friends with a guy who lived immediately above, and who started flirting with me. One day, I was having a quiet conversation with him in my kitchen, when Stéphane arrived unexpectedly – and flew into a rage. He intimidated the neighbour, who quickly retreated to his apartment. When I saw the poor guy again a few days later, he said, "Listen, I don't want any trouble with guys like that." I never saw him again, except by chance.

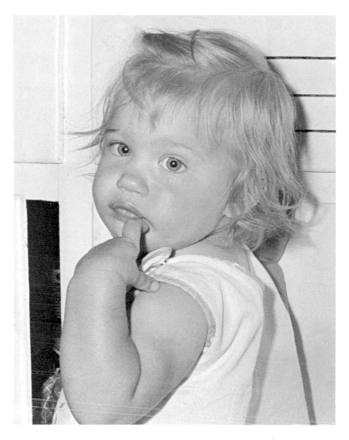

At ten months.

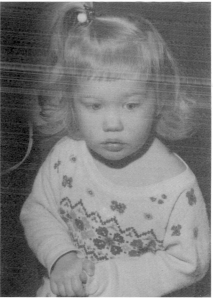

At age two.

Age nine, with my brother, Patrick, age four at the time.

With my parents at my high school graduation ball, 1986.

Visiting California as a
young adult,

With Patrick, New Year's
Eve 1992.

With Gilles, the love of my life, in 1993.

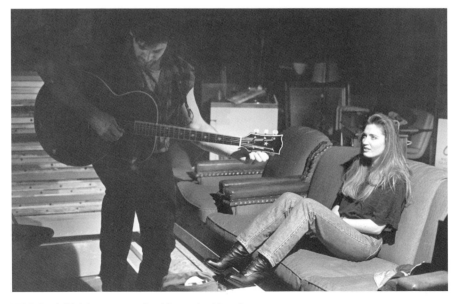

With Roch Voisine, on set after his music video shoot.

Fishing at Lac Magnan, 1993.

At Le Carrousel de la
Rive-Sud riding school, 1993.

At my sister Johanne's wedding, in 1994.

© Jean Blais

© James St-Laurent

Photos from my modelling career, age seventeen to twenty-six.

Arriving at the church for my wedding.

Under the watchful eyes of my admirers . . . the RCMP? The Wolverine Squad? The Sûreté du Québec?

My wedding to Stéphane Sirois, 1997.

Honeymooning in the Bahamas.

Stéphane, alias Steve,
whom I would divorce
fifteen months later.

With Patrick, my best
friend and confidant.

In 1998, on the birthday of a most kind and serene soul, my grandmother Simone.

"One last shoot, just for fun."

Holidaying in Aruba, August 2007.

At Maxime Bernier's swearing in,
August 2007.

To Julie Couillard
With best wishes,

With George W. Bush on the occasion of the opening of the 62nd session of the UN General Assembly, September 2007.

With Laura Bush.

With Mrs. Kerim, wife
of the president of
the 62nd session of the
UN General Assembly,
Srgjan Kerim.

With Madam Yoo (Ban)
Soon-taek, wife of
UN Secretary-General
Ban Ki-moon.

At a Christmas reception at the Canadian Museum of Civilization, December 2007.

When I first got to know Stéphane, he gave the impression that, while he was no millionaire, he was far from being in the poorhouse. He lived in a luxurious house on La Périère Street, in the Saint-François neighbourhood of Laval. He drove a high-end, late-model four-by-four. And of course, like any self-respecting biker, he was the proud owner of a Harley. He was also the co-owner of a tanning salon, a legitimate business that was also located in Laval. So in my mind, the two of us were pretty much on an equal financial footing. Over the next few months, I would soon realize that nothing could have been further from the truth.

The truth was that he was riddled with debt when he left the biker scene. He owed huge amounts of money to a lot of people. I eventually learned that he had a reputation for living far beyond his means, and that when the time came to hand over the profits of his biker activities, he was always short of money.

As I have mentioned, by the time I met Stéphane, I had started buying properties and reselling them after they went up in value. Stéphane was good friends with a real estate agent, Rick,* who offered him a sure-fire deal: a shopping centre in Laval, which had been repossessed by the bank and promised a considerable return on investment, with prestige tenants and outstanding profit potential. Stéphane was not a qualified buyer because of his poor credit rating, however, so he asked me to be his partner. When Rick showed me the numbers, I could see that it was indeed an excellent deal. We started putting together a plan to submit to a financial institution. That allowed Stéphane to get a close-up look at my entire financial situation: my account balances, RRSPs, market investments – everything. He was able to see that while I wasn't extremely

---

* Not his real name.

rich, I had considerable manoeuvring room. He wasted no time taking advantage of the situation; within days, he had borrowed five thousand dollars from me, the first in a long series of loans that he never repaid and that practically ruined me.

A short time later, Rick, the real estate agent, informed me that the shopping-centre deal we were working on had mysteriously fallen through; he told me an improbable story involving another buyer who had made a better offer and pipped us at the post. In the months that followed, though, I continued working with him on certain transactions, this time in the residential market.

For Better and for Worse

"Minutes later, I was walking down the aisle on my father's arm, when suddenly, for the merest fraction of a second, I saw Gilles waiting at the altar in a tuxedo. Then I blinked and realized that it was Stéphane. For a second or two, I stopped in my tracks, and thought about turning around and putting an end to this unfolding comedy of errors. But the guests were all in their pews, the limousines were waiting, and the caterers were busy preparing the meal. The pressure was too great. There was no turning back."

Stéphane Sirois and I had known each other for barely three months when he asked me to marry him. It happened on a summer afternoon. Rick, Stéphane, and I had gone to visit a property for sale near Lachute, northwest of Montreal. At one point we stopped to get a bite to eat at a hot dog stand in the middle of nowhere. And it was there, next to a rundown shack with the smell of fried food heavy in the air, that he popped the question. "Julie, will you marry me?" he asked.

Needless to say, it wasn't the most romantic setting a girl could imagine. Worse, we weren't even alone together. I was sure he'd said it as a joke, and I told him to quit fooling around. Then Rick turned to me and said, "Don't laugh, Julie. I think he's being serious."

I tilted my head back ever so slightly and looked at him for a few seconds. I know I had to be more than a little messed up to be thinking this way, but what flashed through my mind right away was that when Gilles had been killed, we had been about to get married. Everything was ready. I had reached that point in my life. After losing Gilles in that sudden and violent way, I had gone through different stages, fear and extreme anger, to name a few. After that, I'd developed a kind of obsession with the idea that I could die today or tomorrow, who's to say? What I had just gone through made me feel that no matter how much you plan your life, control is just an illusion. So I was in a hurry to live. It was like it was between me and marriage – it didn't matter who was asking. I remember looking at Stéphane and thinking to myself, "Why not? No, you're not in love with him. No, you don't know him well enough. But it could work out. Who knows? You wanted to get married. You wanted a big wedding. Well, here's your chance! And if it doesn't work out, you'll just get a divorce, that's all." That was my cold, detached assessment of the situation.

Three months isn't a long time. But it was enough for me to get a good idea of the kind of person I was dealing with. Stéphane Sirois wasn't necessarily a bad sort, but he was obviously irresponsible, an eternal adolescent who took nothing seriously and whose sole focus when he got up every day was to party it up that night. He fantasized about buying all kinds of things, but was never prepared to put in the effort required to achieve those dreams. He had no discipline whatsoever. And this was the kind of person I said "Yes" to. I took the whole thing far too lightly, and in the end I paid a heavy price.

After I accepted, things happened quickly. Less than two months later, we were married. Stéphane wanted to do it in grand style. He wanted a huge, Italian-style wedding, with two Rolls-Royces (the same ones that Céline Dion and René Angélil had used for their wedding), a seven-course meal, an orgiastic buffet with sculpted food, and a five-person band. Nothing was too good for him. As the plans for the celebration went on, I started to realize just how frivolous and irresponsible my future husband was.

We went to a jeweller he knew to pick out and order our rings. We didn't skimp; mine had a one-carat diamond and was worth something like $12,000, while his, more modest, was going to cost me $3,500. Two days before the wedding, when we went to pick up the rings, my fiancé was flat broke. He had been expecting to be paid for some transaction or other – probably imaginary. I had to pay for both rings, and I'm still waiting for Stéphane to pay me back the cost of mine. By this point, things were starting to smell less than rosy. But that was only the beginning.

We were married at the Église Saint-Jean-Baptiste on Rachel Street, a church that for many years was Montreal's second largest, after the Notre-Dame Basilica. There was no religious service, only the wedding celebration, which was quite brief. The celebrant, whose name I have long since forgotten, was the chaplain of a detention centre and an acquaintance of Stéphane's. There were few guests from my family. My mother and sister had refused to attend because they were against my marrying Stéphane, but my aunt and uncle on my mother's side came with their families. My father and brother were also there, as well as one of my cousins and a few friends. Stéphane, meanwhile, had invited around two hundred people – including a lot of his biker friends – but in the end, fewer than half of them showed up.

When I arrived at the church, I was extremely nervous – but it wasn't the normal jitters that a person feels just before embarking on such an important life journey. Rather, I felt an unease, a feeling that I was making a colossal mistake. In the car on the way to the church, my father sensed my discomfort and did his best to reassure me: "Don't worry, sweetheart. I have a good feeling about this. I'm sure things are going to go well between you and Stéphane."

Minutes later, I was walking down the aisle on my father's arm, when suddenly, for the merest fraction of a second, I saw Gilles waiting at the altar in a tuxedo. Then I blinked and realized that it was Stéphane. For a second or two, I stopped in my tracks, and thought about turning around and putting an end to this unfolding comedy of errors. But the guests were all in their pews, the limousines were waiting, and the caterers were busy preparing the meal. The pressure was too great. There was no turning back.

Immediately after the ceremony, everyone headed for the Buffet Christina, on Jarry Street East, for the reception. Stéphane knew the owners, and they had outdone themselves to impress the guests. It was way over the top. There was an ice sculpture covered in a massive assortment of fruit, a fruit-and-vegetable replica of the Brooklyn Bridge, and a polar scene with a troupe of penguins on a huge spread of blue Jell-O representing a vast expanse of ice. The musicians he had hired were no less impressive. Besides a tenor and soprano singing famous opera themes, there was an extremely talented and versatile band, including several multi-instrumentalists, who covered a wide range of musical genres.

There was only one minor problem: Stéphane, who was supposed to take care of the caterers as well as the musicians, never paid anyone a penny. Ever. I remember paying part of the band's fee myself later that night, but they never received the balance.

For our honeymoon, Stéphane and I went to the Sandals Royal Bahamian Spa Resort in Nassau, considered one of the most elegant resorts in the whole of the Caribbean. It was magnificent: beautiful white sand beaches, blue water as far as the eye could see blending into a cloudless sky, comfortable rooms, superb meals at the restaurant, and all the amenities one could imagine for a dream vacation. Given the nature of my travelling companion, however, I should have had some inkling that the nirvana was to be short-lived. We had only been there for a few days when the magnetic hotel room key stopped working. We went down to the administrative office to find out what was wrong, and they told us there was a problem with the credit card. This was another Stéphane Sirois special; people like him rarely owned credit cards (in his "line of work," you paid people, and were paid, in cash), so one of his acquaintances, who apparently owed him a favour, had lent him his. Except that now, in the middle of our honeymoon, we suddenly couldn't get into our hotel room.

Stéphane behaved like a complete idiot with the hotel's administrative staff. He ranted at them vehemently, threatened them, and treated them like dirt. He screamed at them like a lunatic, throwing out gems like "Do you have any idea who you're dealing with here?" "You're going to be sorry," and "I'm not about to be humiliated like this in front of my wife," as if he were a man of the world and not the small-time bum he'd always been. He was so out of control that I worried the staff might call the police, and I remember telling him, "Calm down! Do you want them to arrest you and lock you up? The prisons here aren't exactly four-star hotels, you know."

After I finally managed to bring him down to Earth, he called the credit card holder in Montreal, who made the necessary arrangements to unblock the account. Embarrassed, the hotel staff offered to let us stay an extra week at no charge. But I wasn't exactly thrilled to hear that. Not only was I getting fed up with having Stéphane on my heels twenty-four hours a day, but I was nearly out of epilepsy pills. The ones I had to take weren't available in the Bahamas, so I had to see a doctor and a pharmacist locally and find an equivalent medication.

After the honeymoon, we returned to Stéphane's house on La Périère Street in Laval. There were a few surprises in store for me. In the mailbox was a notice from the caisse populaire warning that Stéphane had sixty days to sort out his mortgage payments, otherwise seizure and eviction procedures would be undertaken. Not only that, but the phone and electricity had been cut off. "Well, uh, I was a bit tight there, you know?" was his explanation. "And then there was the wedding and all . . ."

"A bit tight." He hadn't been able to pay for my wedding ring, the reception, or the musicians. He'd cooked up who knows what scheme to cover the cost of our honeymoon, and now he had the gall to say that it was because of the wedding that he hadn't been able to face up to his obligations.

I had to transfer the phone and electricity services to my name to have them reconnected. The house was another matter. We had to find a solution. He was already four or five months behind on his payments, which were about two thousand dollars a month, and on top of that, the heating bill was huge. We had no choice but to move. We found a small bungalow not far away on De Tilly Street. I bought it, and since the owners were looking for something bigger, Stéphane sold them his house.

Not long after that, an acquaintance of Stéphane's came to us – Stéphane, Rick, and me, that is – with a deal whereby we would take over a Cantel cellular phone franchise. At the time,

Cantel was a subsidiary of Rogers Communications. The partner sold his stake in the business to Stéphane's friend for one dollar, supposedly to honour a debt. We would be managing two stores, one in the Saint-François neighbourhood of Laval, and another in Trois-Rivières. (He wanted us as partners to invest in the Laval location.) On the face of it, it was a great business opportunity; at the time, cellular telephony was really starting to take off, and the revenues from line activations and customer airtime were very attractive. There was only one problem: the partner who sold Stéphane's friend his share for one dollar had overdrawn the company's credit line by fifty thousand dollars without authorization from the head office. Cantel had approved the management transfer on the express condition that the deficit be reimbursed soon.

We got to work quickly, and committed ourselves fully to the company – two of us, that is: Rick handled finance and administration, while I was in charge of sales. Stéphane, meanwhile, was depressed. Strangely, his bouts of depression tended to come on whenever it was time to work. In an article published in the *Globe and Mail* on June 6, 2008, he told the journalist who interviewed him that he had "picked up his lunchbox" again, but that "[c]lean businessmen that I knew wanted nothing to do with me because of my biker days." * The truth is that he now had a legitimate job, he was a partner in a business, and he had a real opportunity to put his life back together, but he never made the slightest effort to get up in the morning and go to work. He would roll out of bed around noon and spend his entire day lying around, watching TV, smoking, drinking, and composing incredible cocktails of pills that he washed down with huge gulps of cognac. When I came home in

---

* *Globe and Mail*, June 6, 2008, page A14.

the evening, I would find him sitting in a corner, dishevelled, drunk, and high. And when I left for work in the morning, he would sometimes open one eye and the corner of his mouth to say, "Don't forget to leave me my twenty dollars for cigarettes."

On the rare occasions when he showed some signs of energy, it was to fly into a jealous rage in front of me. It was like a disease with him. In a closet in the basement of the house, I had stored some boxes in which I had kept most of the mementoes I had of Gilles: pictures, a few miscellaneous items, and the romantic notes that he had left me every day before going to work. For some reason, Stéphane had managed to get his hands on them. He ranted and raved, tearing the photos and notes to shreds and trampling all over them, and told me that he was my new husband, and holding on to these memories of another man was indecent.

Not long after we had bought the Cantel franchise, I was out at a hardware store with a contractor, buying materials to renovate one of the stores, when my cellphone rang. It was Stéphane. "What'd you do with my gun?" he asked. "I want to end it all."

At one point, he had kept a .22-calibre revolver in the house, without my knowledge, but one of his friends, knowing that Stéphane was depressive, had surreptitiously taken it from him, fearing he might "do something stupid." Stéphane had been threatening to commit suicide for a while by that point. The first time, I had felt completely overwhelmed, but after a while I realized that it was all just an act.

One day, I said to him, "Listen, if you're this depressed, you should go to the hospital and get help. I don't know what your problem is, exactly, but it's pretty serious, that's for sure. I'm not a psychologist or a psychiatrist. I don't have the tools to help you."

Shortly thereafter, Stéphane was hospitalized for the first

time, and spent a week or two in the psychiatric ward of the Cité de la santé in Laval. He saw a psychiatrist and was prescribed medication, but his attitude didn't improve. Later, one of his uncles told me that Stéphane had been mentally troubled since his childhood; he had always been a liar and a manipulator, and was depressive. "And you never felt like sharing this information with me before?" I asked.

As time went on, the emotional blackmail tactics grew increasingly malicious. He started saying things like "You've already lost one guy. Be careful you don't do anything that would make you lose another." There was more than one message in that manipulative threat. He clearly meant: "Don't push me. I'm fragile and if you go too far I'm going to blow my brains out." But after a while I realized there was another connotation: "If you don't pay off my outstanding debts, my old biker friends are going to come and kill me, and it'll be your fault." In fact, it often happened that people would knock on the door asking for money that Stéphane owed them. One of them once told me with a smile, "You married him for better or for worse. You must be looking forward to the 'better' part!"

I can't begin to count the number of debts I paid on his behalf. When Stéphane claimed, in the *Globe and Mail* article cited earlier, that I was "attracted to people with money and power," he somehow failed to realize that he was a glaring example of just the opposite.

At one point, he even started dropping all kinds of hints that I was in danger of being taken out by a biker hit squad. He would sometimes say, "You know, Julie, they spared your life once, but if they decide to come back for me, I'm not sure they'll let you live this time round."

Stéphane Sirois was a master liar and manipulator. He made up a demented story – which he recently recycled for the journalist from the *Globe and Mail* – about my life being in danger. "You know," he said one day, "'Mom' still holds a grudge against you. He suspects that you went to the cops."

"That's bullshit," I shot back. "If I'd worked with the police, people would have found out about it. There would have been consequences."

In the *Globe and Mail* article, Stéphane claims that he had several conversations with "Mom" Boucher about me. I doubt very much that these exchanges ever took place. As far as I know, the biker gangs have an extremely well developed hierarchy. Why would the top boss of the elite Hells Angels club have been in regular contact with a small-timer in a puppet club – let alone admit to him that he had ordered a hit (in this case, the murder of Gilles Giguère)? It doesn't make any sense. If "Mom" Boucher had had the slightest doubt about me, I wouldn't be here today, according to a journalist who covers crime. Also according to him, not only that, "Mom" Boucher wouldn't have waited over a year to eliminate me. That much is quite clear to me and to anyone with even rudimentary knowledge of how biker gangs work.

The reality is that Stéphane Sirois was playing these mind games with me because he knew I was starting to be fed up with his depressive episodes, his fits of jealousy, and his laziness. He also knew I was sick and tired of supporting him and paying his debts. He was looking for a way to hold on to me because I knew I wanted out of the marriage, and he wanted to squeeze as much money out of me while he still could.

I knew by then that he was a pathological liar and I feared that he might tell his biker friends ridiculous, made-up stories about me that would create a serious safety risk. So, fed up with his threats and his manipulative tactics, I did go to see Bob Savard, as Stéphane claims in the *Globe and Mail* story.

Stéphane's version is that my visit to Savard was what prompted him to decide to become an informant – supposedly, he was afraid that I'd said too much to Bob.* In fact, all I had wanted to know from Bob was whether the Hells Angels, and specifically Boucher, had anything against me. "No," Bob told me. "Why?"

"Because my marriage is on the skids and I want a divorce."

Bob burst out laughing and said, "Well, sorry, honey, I'm not a marriage counsellor!"

"So you guys don't give a damn whether I get divorced?" I asked.

"Not at all! Why do you think we care?"

"Because the fact that I asked Stéphane to quit the Rockers might have upset them."

"Nah. You said it: he's not part of the gang anymore. The rest is none of our business," Bob said.

I never said anything to Bob Savard about the delusional allegations that Stéphane Sirois had made, in particular his fantasy that "Mom" Boucher had admitted to him that he had ordered Gilles's murder. Had I done so, there is no doubt that he would not be alive today. Moreover, if Stéphane had really felt that he was in danger to the extent that he claimed at the time, he would certainly not have tried to rejoin his former biker gang a few weeks later.

After speaking to Bob, I went home and told Stéphane that nobody gave a damn about us or our marriage, because he was no longer a gang member. That is what I said to him.

The same newspaper article insinuates that I had some sort of involvement with a drug trafficker: "Through the patio

---

* "In my eyes, I'm fucked," Mr. Sirois said. "This is going to get back to Mom. I've got days to live." Op. cit.

window, [Sirois] says, he saw his wife with a man he recognized as a low-level drug dealer associated with the Hells Angels."* My only response is, that is completely untrue. I have never had any contact whatsoever with any drug dealers, be they "low-level" or any level, and regardless of their affiliation. That passage, like many others in the *Globe and Mail* story, says much more about Stéphane Sirois's fertile imagination than about what really happened.

Stéphane Sirois's claim that he cut a deal with "Mom" Boucher to save my life is unmitigated nonsense. As events would soon demonstrate, Stéphane Sirois never meant to protect anyone but himself – and to that end, he would eventually go so far as to betray his friends.

---

* Op. cit.

22

Divorce

"Stéphane had smashed the side door in and ripped out the doorframe. He had stolen all my underwear and my agenda, and had called all my business contacts, telling them that I was his wife and that if any of them tried to approach me, he would kill them."

The Cantel franchise venture, in which Rick and I invested so much time and effort, went sour in the end. As soon as we had paid back the fifty-thousand-dollar credit line overdraft, the Rogers head office decided to cut off all further credit. Anything we had to buy from then on would have to be cash on delivery, including demonstration handsets and our sales representatives' airtime, which had been free up to that point. Since we didn't have enough working capital to operate that way, Rick and I decided to fight the Rogers decision. Armed with our contract, we hired some lawyers. We had barely begun when they started bickering about whether our case should be heard in a Quebec or an Ontario court. We very quickly realized that if we were going to pursue legal action, it would be long, complicated, and more important, costly. Did we really want to go after Rogers? Play David against Goliath? After less than a year in operation, we decided to liquidate all of our assets.

Three or four years later, that business failure came back to haunt me. Our partner – the one who had bought out his associate's stake for one dollar – had taken out a twenty-five-thousand-dollar loan for the company, which I had endorsed, and had now defaulted on it. The bank wasn't able to track him down – but they did find me. With the help of a friend who knew his way around such things, I was able to settle out of court, but it cost me a fair amount of money.

Near the end of our relationship, Stéphane, hoping to get back on his feet financially, persuaded my father to work for him in a plan that, to my mind at least, was clearly doomed to fail. He wanted to start a marijuana grow op in the basement of the house where my father lived on Mylène Street, not far from our house in Saint-François. They set up a hydroponic system and started growing several pot plants, intending to sell them. I knew all about the scheme and I was firmly against it. I remember very clearly warning them, right from the start, "I've got a bad feeling about this, guys. Don't do this – you're going to wind up in deep shit."

It didn't take a fortune teller to predict that the plan wasn't going to work. First of all, its two masterminds weren't exactly gifted in the organization department. Second, people usually get caught, sooner or later, trying to pull off this kind of enterprise. Moreover, although I have nothing against people who like to smoke a joint every once in a while, I have always been opposed to the idea of trafficking in marijuana, because I believe that the profits are dirty money.

As it turned out, it wasn't long before the police busted the operation. In fact, they had help. Stéphane had wanted to set up a second grow op in another house, but had got into an argument with the prospective "tenant," who promptly called the police and tipped them off about the plants in the house on Mylène Street.

My father, who by then was in his fifties, learned at his expense that a life of crime – like plenty of other trades – can't be learned late. He was arrested and, ignoring the advice of his lawyer, pleaded guilty to a charge of possession of a banned substance. In the end, he got off with a suspended sentence. The police were none too thrilled. "We weren't after you," an officer told him. "It was Stéphane Sirois we wanted." Had my father told the police that the pot plants belonged to Stéphane, they wouldn't have been able to charge him with anything. My father has plenty of faults, but he's not a snitch. Unfortunately, not all the men in my life can make the same claim.

In the meantime, I was seriously thinking about separating from Stéphane, who was still sponging off me, and was becoming more unstable than ever. I couldn't take it any longer. One day, I told him, "I've had it. It's over. I want you out of here."

He refused to grant me a divorce. He would hear nothing of it. He immediately threatened to kill himself, but by then I was used to his dramatics and I wasn't about to be sucked in.

I suppose by that time – since they have ways of finding such things out – the police had figured out that Stéphane was extremely vulnerable. One day, two officers showed up at the front door, asking to speak with him. Needless to say, ever since the Carcajou raid in December 1995, the police hadn't ranked very high on my list of favourite people. I warned Stéphane, "You want to talk to them, fine. But this is my house. My turf. I don't want any of you three conversing here. There's a cornfield

out behind the house – you can go do your business there."
Stéphane accompanied the two officers and spoke with them for
a few minutes. Before they left, they handed him a card, which
he kept. But I guess he wasn't yet in enough trouble to accept
their offer. It wouldn't be very long, however, before he was.

I couldn't live in the same house with him any longer. I went
to see a lawyer to start divorce proceedings, and decided to
have a bailiff serve the papers in my absence. I called a travel
agent I knew and asked her to find me a vacation package –
anything, as long as it was nice and cheap and the flight left
the same week. She found me something in Cuba. I left on
a Wednesday and made arrangements for the divorce papers
to be served to Stéphane Sirois while I was relaxing in the
Caribbean sun.

When I came back a week later, I discovered he had again
found a way to get back at me. Before going on holiday, I had
left him the keys to my car in case he needed to move it; my
brother, Patrick, who was living in the basement, also parked
his car in the driveway. For some reason – unpaid traffic tickets
or too many demerit points, I forget which – Stéphane no
longer had a valid driver's licence. While I was away, he had
taken my car and managed to get arrested by the police, probably on purpose. My car had been seized, and I had to pay
nearly five hundred dollars to get it back from the pound. I was
furious. This time, I told Stéphane straight out, "I want you
out of here. Get out, now."

He left the house, again threatening to commit suicide, not
surprisingly, and went to rent a room in a small motel in Laval,
along the Boulevard des Laurentides. He called me that night
from the motel, in tears, still playing the suicide blackmail card,
among other incoherent ramblings. He was high; that much
was obvious from his voice. He pleaded with me to go and see

him. I called the police instead. "I've just officially separated from this man," I told them. "He's mentally unstable and threatening to commit suicide. He's been hospitalized twice recently, in the psych ward at Cité de la santé. An extended stay there may well be what he needs, so that he can get proper treatment once and for all. So go and pick him up, send an ambulance, do whatever you want. I can't stand it anymore. I'm not his mother."

Stéphane didn't take the news very well. Not only had I not reacted to his cry for help, but now I was handing him over to "the system." He realized he no longer had any hold over me, and in desperation repeated his earlier threats about my real estate deals, more seriously this time. "You won't get rid of me that easy," he shouted over the phone. "I'm going to report you. You're going to be in some major shit."

"Do whatever you want, Stéphane. Go ahead and call the police. I haven't done anything illegal. I pay my bills, and my mortgages. You're the one who won't pay your debts, everywhere you go."

A few days later, I came home after work to find the house had been broken into. Stéphane had smashed the side door in and ripped out the doorframe. He had stolen all my underwear and my agenda, and had called all my business contacts, telling them that I was his wife and that if any of them tried to approach me, he would kill them. Needless to say, the phone started ringing off the hook. It was my clients calling to say, "This guy's completely insane!" Then Stéphane phoned: "Nobody else but me is ever going to see you wearing these bras and panties, understand? You bought them to please *me*!"

I immediately filed a complaint with the Laval police department and obtained a restraining order; Stéphane had to refrain from contacting me and was barred from coming within a certain radius of the house. After his latest escapade, I was more determined than ever to divorce him as soon as possible. The law, however, doesn't provide many grounds for divorce if a couple has been separated for less than a year. Basically, the grounds are adultery, mental cruelty, or irreconcilable differences between the parties. I had invoked the latter. But Stéphane had hired a lawyer, who had informed my lawyer that he outright refused to divorce me. My lawyer then told me, "Julie, you have no choice. You'll have to wait until you've been officially separated for one year. At that point, we'll be able to go before a judge again, and he'll have no choice but to grant you the divorce." I started to panic. There was no way I was going to stay married to that idiot any longer. So I started thinking about another way to get a divorce without having to wait a year.

After the Cantel franchise had gone under, I had gone to work for Rick, who in the meantime had never given up his real estate business. One day, at his office, I had met a guy named Bruno.* He was a friend of Rick's, who had just sold his house and was looking to buy a new one. He knew Stéphane too, and the two of them didn't get along at all. Bruno was a very good-looking guy, around my age, with amazing blue eyes and an imposing elegance. We clicked right away. During the time I was trying to arrange a shotgun divorce by any means possible, I ran into Bruno again at Rick's office. He asked me out to dinner, and I accepted. We spent a very nice evening at a fine restaurant. During the meal, we spoke briefly about my having filed for divorce, and about Stéphane's refusal. Only half-jokingly, Bruno said, "You know, we could give him a very good reason to grant you that divorce." Needless to say, the

---

* Not his real name.

hint didn't fall on deaf ears, especially given the fact that Stéphane and I hadn't slept in the same bed for several months and my sex life had dried up completely. Bruno and I spent the night together.

The next morning, I said to him, "You know what? Why wait until Stéphane starts to suspect something? We should just tell him what happened last night." I picked up the phone and dialled Stéphane's number. He picked up. I didn't say hello. I simply said, "As far as I know, I'm still technically your wife, right?"

"Yeah, why?"

"Because I'm about to give you a good reason not to be."

I passed the phone to Bruno, who, unable to hide his satisfaction, said, "Hey, what's up, asshole? You should have taken better care of her!" Then he hung up.

A few days later, Stéphane himself informed me that he was ready to agree to a divorce. He began the procedure, citing adultery, and I was served the papers within a few days. To say I was glad to hear the news would be an understatement. There was a problem, though: we hadn't made any pre-nuptial agreement, and family property legislation in Quebec stipulates that all property accumulated during a marriage must be split fifty-fifty in case of dissolution.

The judge, however, soon realized that my fifteen-month marriage to Stéphane Sirois hadn't been very profitable for me. When I had first met him, I owned a company, with assets, and had a fairly substantial bank account, investments, and RRSPs. Now, as we were about to be divorced, not only did I not have any cash, but my accounting books stated I had sixty thousand dollars in accumulated debt. The judge looked straight at Stéphane and told him, "You may consider yourself fortunate, Mr. Sirois, that your sole possession at the moment is the shirt on your back. Otherwise, I would have decreed a much fairer sharing of assets. It is quite obvious in the eyes of the court that Madam was in far better financial shape before she met you." In spite of it all, though, I was finally rid of him.

I moved in with Bruno shortly after that. Six or seven months later, early one morning, I had just stepped out of the shower when the telephone rang. "Ms. Couillard, this is Sergeant Bilodeau.* I'm in front of your residence with a colleague, and we are in the company of Mr. Stéphane Sirois. We'd like to meet with you, and Mr. Sirois would also like to speak with you." My answer wasn't long in coming: "I have nothing to say to him, and I have nothing to say to you either. If you have something to say to me, I'm listening. But it's going to be by phone."

"Listen, Madam. It's important that we meet in person."

"Why?" I asked.

"Because you are part of the conditions of the contract that we have with Mr. Sirois," the sergeant replied.

"Contract? What contract?"

"Mr. Sirois is now working with us, and he has demanded that we ensure your protection."

"My protection? From whom?"

At that moment, I realized what was going on: Stéphane had become a police informant. So I said to the sergeant, "Sir, are you aware that this gentleman lies as often as he breathes, is seriously mentally unstable, has been interned twice, and

---

* Not his real name.

threatens to kill himself every time the wind changes direction? And you've entered into a contract with him? If I were you, I wouldn't invest too much money in it."

"Maybe so, but he has helped us gather a great deal of valid information," the officer said.

"Look, under those conditions, that's all the more reason for me not to say a word to you. I don't want to have anything to do with him, or the police, or the underworld. Is that clear?" And I hung up.

Several years later – in 2004, to be precise – my phone rang, around seven-thirty in the morning. As soon as I picked it up, I recognized the voice on the other end.

"Hi. How's it going?"

I didn't answer.

"You know who this is?"

"I've had a few boyfriends in my life, but there was only one I made the mistake of marrying," I said.

"Listen, I'm calling because things are going really well for me. I'm settled, I'm living in the States now, and making all kinds of money. And I want you to come and live with me. I'd like for us to pick up where we left off."

It wasn't a particularly comforting prospect, needless to say. "What are you talking about?" I answered. "You do know I have a life here, right? And a good job. And I haven't run away from anyone. I've paid all my debts, I've settled everything, I don't need to be on the run. Everyone knows where I live, I can look everyone straight in the eye, and I don't need to look down at the sidewalk when I go out."

"There's good jobs everywhere. It's not a problem."

His tone was condescending, pretentious – as if he'd

metamorphosed into a man of the world, when he was still nothing more than a bum, with no stature. A lowly snitch, forced to live under witness protection. It would have been funny, if it weren't so sordid. I couldn't believe his nerve.

"Look, Stéphane, I'm happy things are going well for you, really," I said. "But if you want me to even begin to think about maybe considering your offer, you can start by sending me a cheque for $150,000. If you're as rich as you say you are now, you should have no problem paying me back what you owe me. If not, don't waste your time calling again."

I heard the line go dead almost immediately.

23

A Painful Decision

"I had zero financial security, I had no idea what the future held, and I had no one to help me. There was no way I would be able to work and raise a child at the same time. . . . In the end, I decided to have an abortion."

My first night with Bruno had more serious consequences than I would have liked. It helped me be rid of Stéphane Sirois, but it also forced me into making one of the most wrenching decisions of my entire life.

I had stopped taking the pill about a week earlier, after having been on it for about twelve years, non-stop. And although Bruno and I were careful that night, I got pregnant. It couldn't have happened at a worse time. I was in debt up to my ears. I was practically destitute. I had zero financial security, I had no idea what the future held, and I had no one to help me. There was no way I would be able to work and raise a child at the same time.

I was already four weeks pregnant when I found out, and it took me another two to finally make a decision. One day, I would want to keep the baby; the next, I would tell myself I was crazy for thinking that, because the child would live in misery. Struggling with the decision was all the more painful because I had a clear feeling that if I didn't carry the baby to term, I would probably never have another chance to become a mother. In the end, I decided to have an abortion. My father came with me to the Cité de la santé hospital, and to this day I am grateful for what he did. He is a man of many faults, as I have said elsewhere in these pages. But in that one situation, in that extremely difficult and emotionally trying time for me, he displayed a profound openness and humanity. "Whatever decision you make," he said, "I'll be there for you." And he kept his word.

That episode in my life was deeply upsetting, and remains firmly embedded in my memory. I don't regret what I did. I think that, given the circumstances, I didn't have a choice. But I often think of the child I never had, how old he or she would have been today, and the bond that would have been forged between us.

As I said, my financial situation was extremely precarious. At one point, to try and get back on track, I worked three jobs at the same time. I was still working for Rick during the day, I served breakfast from five to nine in the morning at the Brasserie Don Quichotte in Laval, and in the evening – albeit only for a short time – I was an assistant sommelier at the LeBlanc Restaurant Lounge, which had just opened on Saint-Lawrence Boulevard in Montreal.

Not long after my divorce from Stéphane Sirois went through, I moved into Bruno's house, which was in Repentigny, east of the Island of Montreal. We had a very clear idea of the nature of our relationship. There was no question of getting married. We knew we weren't going to spend the rest of our lives together, but we got along great and had decided to simply play it by ear. I do admit that in large part, Bruno was doing me the favour of taking me in, to ease my financial burden and help me get back on my feet.

In the meantime, a fairly attractive business opportunity presented itself. Bruno had a friend, Simon,* who was a mechanic. He specialized in large trucks, and he told me there was strong demand for maintenance of refrigerated trucks. It was a promising niche, he said, because there weren't really any garages specializing in it. I didn't know the first thing about auto mechanics, but I sensed this was a vein worth tapping, with excellent potential for development. I did some groundwork, feeling out potential suppliers and customers and learning as much as I could about that industry segment: what it entailed, the regulatory context, and so on. I studied the market potential. It looked promising, so I started the necessary procedures to set up a company, rented an industrial condo just off the Metropolitan Expressway in Pointe aux Trembles, in east-end Montreal, and secured a commercial loan for $250,000 from the caisse populaire.

There was just one hitch: before long, I began to suspect that this Simon, who had put me on to this business opportunity, wasn't exactly a paragon of honesty. He tried to con me out of fifteen thousand dollars in short order. As a result, with the memory of my nightmarish relationship with Stéphane Sirois still so fresh, and fearing I might be ripped off again, I decided to back out of the whole thing. I didn't want to have to spend my time watching my business partner's every move, or fighting with him. At the same time, I couldn't embark on

---

* Not his real name.

this venture alone, without a trustworthy partner who knew the ins and outs of the industry. So I called the caisse populaire branch manager and told him I didn't want the loan after all. I never went to sign the credit agreement. The manager said he'd never seen anything like it.

Around this time, Bruno and I ended our relationship, and I moved out. We parted on perfectly amicable terms and have remained good friends ever since. At that point, I decided to go back to live in Laval, in the small basement apartment of my duplex on De Tilly Street, where I still live today (although three years ago I moved to the main floor).

The main-floor apartment was still occupied by the family who had been living there when I bought the house. The basement tenant was an older man who lived there alone, with a big dog. His apartment was revoltingly filthy, and it absolutely reeked of dog urine. In addition, collecting the rent every month was always a problem. The tenant in the main-floor apartment told me that there were people coming and going downstairs at all hours. I asked around, and everyone I spoke to said it was obvious that the man was a drug dealer. Since I had no wish to start long-winded eviction procedures with the rental board, I asked Bruno to come to my rescue. He paid the undesirable tenant a visit and told him he had forty-eight hours to vacate the premises, or else he would call the police. Problem solved! I could move in.

The apartment was in such a sorry state, however, that it had to be entirely renovated. I had to have the floors redone, because they were encrusted with dried dog urine, and the bathroom and the kitchen needed work too. But I was eventually able to settle down in surroundings that I had decorated according to my taste. I had my own place, and I felt comfortable there.

After the abortive company start-up in Pointe-aux-Trembles and my breakup with Bruno, I got a steady job as a sales representative for a radio station, COOL-FM, whose studios were located in the same building as CKVL and CKOI, on Gordon Street in Verdun. The station, which broadcast at 98.5 MHz and had previously been known as CIEL-FM, had recently changed ownership and location. The new managers had decided to change its format to alternative rock (which, incidentally, didn't work out very well). I didn't like the job very much; it wasn't so much the fact that I had to sell advertising, but rather the obligations that went along with the position. For instance, if a program or a promotional activity required a live broadcast on an advertiser's premises – more often than not, this was in a bar, in the evening – I had to be there. But I was still expected to be in to work at the station by nine the next morning. On top of that, the daily commute between Laval and Verdun took forever. I held the job for less than a year, and I left with no regrets.

24

Sylvain

"To him, just about anything was worth buying; what mattered most was the price he paid and the profit he stood to make."

I met Sylvain* in 1998, during my brief spell – it lasted barely a month – as an assistant sommelier at the LeBlanc Restaurant Lounge. He was a businessman and a regular at the establishment.

One evening, he came to have dinner at the restaurant with his lawyer. As I was uncorking a bottle of wine for them, I could hear that they were discussing a technicality related to real estate law. They disagreed on how to interpret a particular statute. I realize, of course, that eavesdropping isn't normally acceptable behaviour, but Sylvain was a patron I knew quite well, and since I had some expertise in real estate, I took the liberty of interrupting. "I'm sorry, but I couldn't help overhearing," I said to Sylvain, "and I'm pretty sure your lawyer is right."

---

* Not his real name.

That was how Sylvain found out that I knew about real estate. We continued chatting briefly about the issue at hand. Then, a few days later, he said to me, matter-of-factly, "Why don't you come and work for me?"

I didn't really answer, and we didn't touch on the matter again – until he asked me out to dinner. I suspected, of course, that his interest was not strictly professional. But I also knew that he had a wife and children, so I told him straight out that I didn't want to date a married man.

As any woman will tell you, however, such considerations rarely get in the way of a man who has decided what he wants. Sylvain reiterated his offer of employment, telling me he wanted to build up a real estate portfolio; it would focus on bank repossessions, because at the time the market wasn't particularly thriving. The banks were saddled with many mortgage repossessions, and municipalities faced similar problems because of unpaid taxes. Sylvain saw this as a chance to snap up properties at bargain prices and hold on to them until the market rebounded.

Sylvain had made a lot of money as the owner of a car dealership, but he was above all a first-rate negotiator who always succeeded in making the most of whatever opportunity came his way. To him, just about anything was worth buying, what mattered most was the price he paid and the profit he stood to make.

I was hesitant, probably because I was fairly sure that sooner or later I would succumb to his charms. By that time I had been working at COOL-FM for a while, and I was already fed up with the demands of the job and the long commute by car. So eventually, I called Sylvain back to ask him if his offer still stood. We agreed on a salary and a commission scale. My agent's licence was no longer valid, so we agreed that the best way to proceed was for me to set up a real estate–consulting firm that would negotiate on behalf of his company. It was less complicated that way.

Our first transaction wasn't concluded in the most orthodox of circumstances, and it proved to me, right off the bat, just how seasoned a businessman Sylvain was. He knew of a property manager who handled mortgage repossessions across the province of Quebec on behalf of a financial institution. He assigned me the task of contacting this gentleman and asking for access to his registers, so that we could choose properties with the best possible return on investment. This wasn't at all standard procedure; normally, financial institutions liquidate their repossessed properties through real estate agents they know well, and don't negotiate directly with potential buyers.

It was a tricky assignment. If I had asked to meet with the manager, explaining exactly what I wanted, I probably never would have got an appointment. So I snuck into the office, knocked on the door, and asked if I could bother him to have a coffee with me. I sat down and started explaining that I was there on Sylvain's behalf, that we were interested in acquiring repossessed properties, and that we wanted to explore what possibilities might be open to us. He accepted.

Eventually, I found the needle in our real estate haystack: a fifty-four-unit apartment building in Quebec City, in a fairly rundown neighbourhood. When the bank had repossessed it, the building was mortgaged for $875,000; Sylvain managed to negotiate the purchase for $500,000, financed at 100 per cent. It was the deal of the century; with those terms, the rental profits on the building would be $100,000 per year.

The way the transaction was concluded demonstrated to me why Sylvain was a millionaire several times over. As usual, the purchase offer was conditional upon the building inspection.

We went to Quebec City for the weekend and proceeded with the inspection. After we came back, Sylvain deployed a stalling tactic. He didn't call the banker to tell him how the inspection had gone; he waited for the banker to call him. "So, where are we at with this deal?" he asked. "Are we ready to close or what? Everything's approved. All that's missing is your signature."

"Mmm . . . yeah, I was just mulling it over," Sylvain said. "I've got the inspection report right here, and you know, we're going to need to put a lot of money into this building. The plumbing's not so hot, and don't even get me started on the electrical. It all has to be redone. It's going to cost huge amounts of money. This really doesn't look like such a great deal after all. I have to say, I'm not all that interested anymore – and besides, Julie and I are already looking into another project that's a lot more attractive."

"What do you mean?" the banker said. "I thought we had a deal."

"Okay, listen. I'm going to make you an offer here, totally off the cuff. You can take it or leave it, I don't really care. I'm prepared to give you $250,000, cash. That's my final offer."

The banker agreed. I couldn't believe it. Less than a month later, Sylvain went to another financial institution and lined up a $650,000 mortgage on the same building. He really was a big-league player.

The problem was that, in return for the effort I'd put in, he paid me a commission of ten thousand dollars – around the same amount I would have received on the sale of a modest residential property. It really wasn't very much, considering the return on investment he'd achieved with the purchase of the apartment building. But Sylvain and I had become lovers in the meantime, and I didn't want him to think I was going out with him for purely material reasons.

Before long, though, I came to one inescapable conclusion: Sylvain was easily the stingiest man I had ever met in my life. He proved it on several occasions during the five years we were together (more or less; we broke up and reconciled several times). I had a very hard time understanding that, but I eventually decided his behaviour must have been motivated by guilt about his wife and children. It was as if he'd said to himself, "It's bad enough that I have a mistress, I'm not about to spoil her as well!" And since I was not only his mistress but also, in a manner of speaking, his employee, by maintaining me in a relatively precarious financial situation he could be sure I remained dependent on him. It gave him a degree of control over me that he otherwise wouldn't have had.

Like, I would imagine, the majority of women who have been in an extended relationship with a married man, it was very difficult for me to rationalize after the fact why I would put up with that kind of situation for so long. On top of it all, Sylvain wasn't even my type; far from it. He wasn't bad looking, but he was fairly slender, and shorter than me – certainly not your typical Don Juan. He was funny, though, and warm-hearted, and exuded an almost childlike enthusiasm toward everything he undertook. There was also a fair share of admiration in the love I felt for him. He had made something of himself. He had undeniable qualities as a businessman. It was really something to watch him negotiate, analyze a situation, and make a decision (almost always the right one) in no time. We made a great team when we worked together on transactions, and I learned a lot from him. I was impressed by his intelligence, his quick wit, and his self-confidence. I was also very much seduced by his daring and his spontaneity. We had some truly extraordinary adventures together that I will not soon forget.

25

Promises, Promises

"I lost count of the number of homes we visited, ostensibly to move in together. The last one was not very far from Lorraine, the town where I'd spent so much of my childhood. It was a magnificent, luxurious house, fully furnished, in a posh neighbourhood.

Sylvain asked me, 'Do you like it?'

'Yes.'

'Okay. I'll buy it,' he said.

He did buy that house. Last I heard, he was still living there with his wife."

Almost every married man who wants to attract a potential mistress trots out the same old story. "It's like my wife and I just don't have anything in common any more." "Our marriage is in a shambles." "It's only a matter of time before I leave her." Sylvain was no exception to that truism. As for me, like almost every mistress, I let myself believe for a long time that he would finally keep his promise.

Life as the Other Woman is never pleasant, and it was particularly difficult in my case; I've always been forthright and have never had more than one lover at a time. On weekdays

Sylvain and I were a couple, but come the weekend, I was alone. Holidays were especially hard. In a love triangle, the cuckolded woman isn't always the married one.

After a while, everyone Sylvain knew – friends, family, and eventually even his wife and children – was aware of my existence. But it made no difference. Of course, from time to time, when he sensed I was at the end of my rope, he would make some gesture designed to convince me that he was finally going to go through with it and leave his wife. I lost count of the number of homes we visited, ostensibly to move in together. The last one was not very far from Lorraine, the town where I'd spent so much of my childhood. It was a magnificent, luxurious house, fully furnished, in a posh neighbourhood.

Sylvain asked me, "Do you like it?"

"Yes."

"Okay. I'll buy it," he said.

He did buy that house. Last I heard, he was still living there with his wife.

About a year and a half after Sylvain and I started seeing each other, my father declared bankruptcy. The problem was, he had lost his home as well, and had nowhere to live. Despite all his faults, I couldn't accept that my father no longer had a roof over his head, and I wanted to help.

In the meantime, I had rented a house Sylvain had bought – a brand new bungalow in a new development in the Saint-François neighbourhood, not far from where I lived. He had asked me to sign a one-year lease and move in right away, promising that he would soon come and live there with me – "as soon as I can sort things out," he said. He had also promised to buy or maybe build us something more permanent, and even encouraged me to sell the house on De Tilly Street. Thankfully, I hadn't followed his advice.

So I moved into the bungalow and told my father he could stay in the basement apartment on De Tilly. But my brother, who was still the owner of the house in name, didn't like the idea at all. "Unless you vouch for him," he said, "he's not moving in here." I complied with his request, and signed a document stating I was responsible for my father.

I moved into the new house to wait for my "Prince Charming" to come and join me. Months went by, though, and nothing changed. I was beginning to tire of waiting for him. I wasn't living in my own space anymore, and every month I was paying rent to a stranger – an amount equivalent to twice the mortgage payments I was making on my house. Worse, it was money that I would never see again. Something was becoming increasingly clear to me: my Prince Charming was, to put it bluntly, jerking me around.

Not long before that one-year lease was due to expire, I took a week's holiday in the Caribbean. When I came back, I went out and bought some new clothes from a boutique that belonged to a man I had briefly gone out with just before Sylvain and I started seeing each other. That evening, Sylvain came over, and I proudly showed off my new acquisitions. But instead of sharing my happiness, he went into a violent, jealous rage. "So you went to see your ex-boyfriend again, is that it? And I'm supposed to be happy about that? As soon as my back is turned, you're off to see someone else!" he screamed, and then stormed out, slamming the door. It really took some nerve – but that wasn't beyond him at all. Sylvain was pathologically, morbidly jealous.

A few days later, I went to spend the weekend in Ottawa, at the home of a female friend. Sylvain kept trying to call me on my cellphone, but I wouldn't answer. When I got back home on the

Sunday, he wasted no time making another scene, rattling off a new litany of accusations: I'd spent the weekend with another man, I'd never loved him, he couldn't trust me. At that point I completely lost it. I really let him have it: "Fuck you, asshole. You drag me out of my house and completely mess up my life, and a year and a half later, I'm still waiting for you to quit dicking around. And you've got the gall to accuse me like that?! Get out of my sight. I never want to have anything to do with you again."

This time I was really in a bind. No job, no money, no house. No choice but to go and live with my father and his girl-friend in the basement apartment on De Tilly. I slept on the living-room couch. I was living like a vagrant.

As if that wasn't enough, a few months later another wrench was thrown into the works. My brother got a notice from the City of Laval saying that the house was going to be seized because the property taxes hadn't been paid. The unpaid balance was several thousand dollars. We realized that my father, who had agreed to pay the taxes in lieu of rent, hadn't sent the city a penny in nearly two years. We went to talk to him about it, but his only answer was that he didn't have any money. Worse, he behaved as if it was none of his business, and the least of his worries. To boot, I had vouched for him. This was the last straw. My father couldn't manage a measly four hundred dollars a month in rent, and once again was foisting his responsibilities on his children. It was too much.

Luckily, I had made him sign a lease in due form. Patrick and I went to the rental board to obtain an eviction order and force my father to pay the several months' rent he owed. Instead, the people at the rental board decided we were a pair of unworthy, heartless children bent on harassing their father. In the end, they handed down a compromise ruling: my father had to leave, but he wouldn't have to pay anything. On the morning he was due to vacate the apartment, however, he refused to go. My brother had to call the police to have the rental board's ruling enforced. The police arrived and warned my father that if he wasn't gone by the end of the day, they would return to forcibly evict him, and simply throw his belongings out into the street.

I felt utterly betrayed by my father. I flashed back to all the times that I'd helped him out of trouble – and how, when I was living with Stéphane Sirois, I had twice paid to have my father released from the Laval Detention Centre. He had been jailed for unpaid traffic tickets. It had cost me seven thousand dollars the first time and three thousand the second time. On both occasions, I had done it because I couldn't stand the thought of my father rotting in prison. Then, when he had been completely destitute, I had let him have my apartment, and vouched for him, and now he didn't have the fortitude to honour his promises. He had really gone too far this time.

I haven't seen or spoken to him since.

Since when it rains it pours, it was also at this time – the end of 2002 – that I was forced to declare personal bankruptcy. A few years earlier, I had incorporated a business that had remained dormant since its creation. Having no particular project with this company, I sold it to Rick for the price of the incorporation, because he wanted to get into real estate. We signed the necessary documents to transfer the business and nothing more happened, until a few months later when I received from the Canada Revenue Agency a notice of contributions owing on the business of approximately one hundred thousand dollars.

Flabbergasted, I wrote to the CRA to explain that the ownership of the company had been transferred to another person, that I was no longer the owner, and that I would prove it. Unfortunately, the problem didn't lie here, but in the fact that an administrative error had ended up in the document advising the agency of the transfer of ownership. There was nothing to be done.

I met with a tax agent to try and negotiate a repayment of the debt over three years, but I met with a categoric refusal. It was one year or nothing. I said to the agent, "Do you understand that you are forcing me into bankruptcy? Instead of being repaid the full amount, with interest, you won't even recuperate 10 per cent of what you are asking of me."

He looked at me from head to toe, and with disdain in his expression and tone, replied, "If I go by how you are dressed, Madam, I would doubt that you are in danger of declaring bankruptcy." But you can't expect a bureaucrat with job security and a generous pension to show any level of intelligence greater than that.

In the meantime, Sylvain had been trying to get back together with me. I had been forced into an untenable financial situation – I needed work, and fast – so I swallowed my pride and accepted his offer to resume our professional partnership. I was then able to settle the municipal tax bill and keep the house from being seized. Around the same time, my brother and I went to a notary and transferred ownership of the house back to me. I was officially back home again. And since no equity was now linked to the house, I could keep it, despite my bankruptcy, largely thanks to my bank, who put their trust in me.

Predictably, once I resumed working with Sylvain, it wasn't long before our personal relationship picked up where it had left off. Of course, nothing had changed in terms of his commitment (or lack thereof). He was still married, and I was still the Other Woman. Over the next few months, though, we would have some passionate, harmonious times together, at work as well as in love. Not to mention some memorable, adventurous holidays.

26

Adventures in Paradise

"Some of the swells had reached over twenty feet. Inside,
everything that had been stowed was thrown to the bottom
of the boat. The solid wood door leading to the bunk room
was split from top to bottom, and the entire contents of
a 250-gallon drum of drinking water had spilled onto
the floor. . . .

I made my way to the bridge, picked up the transceiver,
and said: 'Could you repeat, please?'

'This is NASA. We are about to proceed with the test
launch of a missile. You're going to have to hold your
position.'"

There was one thing that went a long way toward making
up for all the frustrations I felt as the companion of a
married man: life with Sylvain was almost never boring.
He was addicted to glitz, glamour, and play-acting. He was in
love with the James Bond aesthetic: the fast cars, the luxurious
seaside villas, and the impossibly beautiful girls sunning on the
beach who would slip between the sheets with the super spy as
soon as the sun went down – or even before. One of his
favourite movies was the remake of *The Thomas Crown*

Affair, with Pierce Brosnan as the idle millionaire who moonlights as an art thief, as much to chase away boredom as to taste danger. Sometimes, when we worked together on particularly lucrative real estate deals, he would fancy himself a brilliant, athletic, and invincible movie hero teaming up with his sexy mistress on some kind of caper. He lived his life in a kind of Hollywood bubble.

When the urge struck him to buy something extravagant, he was like a child who wanted a toy: he had to have it right away, and he would do anything to get it. One night, we went out to the movies to see *Exit Wounds,* starring Steven Seagal and rap star DMX. In one scene, DMX's character goes to a luxury automobile dealership to buy a Lamborghini Diablo. Sylvain decided he had to have one. "That's the car for me," he said. "I've got to find one in time for summer. It's going to be awesome!" At the time, there were only a handful available in North America, and each one sold for the tidy sum of $380,000 Canadian. He eventually tracked one down somewhere in the U.S., and bought it. The day he took delivery, I had told him I would be having lunch at Restaurant Calvi, on Saint-Martin Boulevard in Laval. When he drove up in his new toy, revving the motor, he was happy as a kid at Christmas and proud as a peacock. It created quite the commotion among the other restaurant patrons.

One day, in the same spirit of investment diversification, Sylvain decided he was going to start buying and reselling boats. His plan was to send me down to Florida – a prime location for this type of transaction, of course. The idea was inspired by our real estate business: I would scope out good deals on yachts that had been repossessed and put up for auction by sheriff departments (a common occurrence). But since I didn't know anything about boats, before my first assignment he asked me to sail down to Florida with him while he delivered his own yacht – a fifty-five-footer that he kept docked at the marina in the Old Port of Montreal – to its new owner. He had sold it to an American so that he could purchase a bigger one. The trip would be an opportunity for me to learn about sailing, and about how to go about buying a boat.

He had his yacht trucked to Atlantic City, so that we could sail from there and deliver it to the buyer at his marina at a place called North Fork, near Port Sainte-Lucie, Florida. We would be at sea for four days. Sylvain and I flew to New Jersey and set sail. After a full day, we put in at a marina for the night. The thing about travelling by sea is that the itinerary is never set in stone – far from it. The next day dawned cold and grey, and the weather forecast was for storms and strong swells. Signs warning NO SAILING TODAY had been posted all over the marina. But when Sylvain put his mind to something, there was no stopping him. He'd promised to deliver the yacht by a certain date, and he was intent on keeping his word. As soon as we were out of port, ten-foot waves began pounding against the hull – and we hadn't seen anything yet.

Few things are more intimidating than the ocean unleashing its fury. Before long we were in the middle of a fierce storm, and the yacht was being tossed back and forth. I was below deck, trying my best to make some sandwiches, when the boat lurched violently, smashing my head against a cupboard above the counter. I was bleeding, but thankfully it stopped after a few minutes. Some of the swells had reached over twenty feet. Inside, everything that had been stowed was thrown to the bottom of the boat. The solid wood door leading to the bunk room was split from top to bottom, and the entire contents of a 250-gallon drum of drinking water had spilled onto the floor.

In the midst of all this, something happened that was so

bizarre that, had I not experienced it myself, I wouldn't have believed it. Suddenly, through all the chaos and confusion, I heard Sylvain calling me from the bridge: "Hey, Julie, there's someone on the radio! It's some woman and I can't understand a word she's saying. All I could make out was that she's with NASA. But that can't be."

"You must have misunderstood," I shouted back. "We're not on a moon mission, we're sailing."

I made my way to the bridge, picked up the transceiver, and said: "Could you repeat, please?"

"This is NASA. We are about to proceed with the test launch of a missile. You're going to have to hold your position." Then she explained that they couldn't locate the beacon for their missile. I couldn't help but answer, "Make sure it's not under the boat!"

The woman then asked what our position was and, after recording it, ordered us to sail in a circle and remain within a certain perimeter until she gave us the all-clear. We complied, and about an hour later the missile suddenly shot up and over the sea, maybe two thousand or three thousand feet away from us, and back down into the water. In spite of the poor visibility, we saw everything: a kind of explosion without any flame, the missile arcing through the sky, and a sort of mushroom of water at the point of impact. Almost an hour later, the NASA officer radioed back, gave the all-clear, and told us we could proceed. I remember thanking the woman on the radio for the free entertainment. "It's not my tax dollar at work, but still it was a hell of a show!" I said. "Thank you!" And with that, we headed back to shore as fast as we could.

The weather didn't improve during the rest of the trip, and when we finally put in at North Fork a couple of days later, the yacht was only a shadow of its former self. The captain's chair had been ripped from its base, the cabin windshield wipers no longer worked, and several of the tables were in pretty bad shape. The damage was in the thousands of dollars. By that point, all Sylvain wanted to do was scuttle the damn thing and go home. But in the end, we waited for the three days it took to have the yacht repaired, and then went and delivered it to the buyer.

As I mentioned, when Sylvain yearned after some material prize – a car, a boat, or a piece of jewellery – he had to have it right away. One day, he decided he needed a watch. Not just any watch, but a particular Cartier model. It was diamond-encrusted but, for a Cartier, fairly discreet. Still, it cost a pretty penny: forty-five thousand dollars Canadian. After looking around, he located one for sale in a jewellery store in the Cayman Islands. Before long, he'd concocted a plan. He was going to fly to the Bahamas for a quick holiday with his wife and son. I would then catch a plane to Miami, where we would meet and travel to the Caymans together to buy the watch of his dreams.

He asked me to rent a room in the most beautiful hotel in South Beach. "I want something really sharp," he said. I found a brand new luxury hotel on Collins Avenue, built in the Art Deco style that had made the area famous. It was worth the visit for the outdoor design and landscaping alone. Everything was painstakingly groomed. On either side of the steps leading to the entrance, rows of palm trees had been planted such that their height perfectly matched the slope of the land. Their fronds were so green and so perfect, you had to touch them to be sure they were real. At the rear of the hotel, marble steps led down to a private beach. I had booked a luxury suite; the room rate was a mere $7,500. I settled in to wait for Sylvain, who was due to arrive the day after next.

I quickly made friends with another woman staying at the hotel; she was a doctor in town for a conference. We went out for a walk, to do some window-shopping and generally see the sights. As we chatted, she asked whether I'd noticed that Gabriel Byrne, the actor, was staying at the hotel. I said no, I hadn't. Then, as we arrived back in the lobby of the hotel, we spotted him. I remembered him from the Arnold Schwarzenegger film *End of Days*. Good-looking man, very tall, casually chic and wearing little round blue-tinted glasses. As he passed us, he looked at us both and said, "Good day, ladies," in a charming Irish accent that I could have sat and listened to for hours. Then he went on his way.

The next day, I went down for a poolside breakfast and Byrne was there, reading the morning paper. A few minutes later, a mimosa arrived at my table. The waiter – who happened to be from Quebec, and with whom I had chatted briefly earlier – whispered in my ear: "Mr. Byrne was wondering if you were alone."

"At the moment, yes," I said. "But my boyfriend is coming to meet me tomorrow."

The movie star and I raised our glasses in a silent toast across the patio, and it went no further than that.

The next morning, there was a knock on my door. It was a delivery boy. He handed me two dozen roses – the most magnificent bouquet I had ever seen: tiny, delicate white flowers with the stems intertwined. And there was a card with a note: "*From a secret admirer.*" I was sure it was a romantic gesture courtesy of Sylvain, who was due to arrive in the late afternoon. The day went by, and around four o'clock, as planned, I went to pick him up at the airport. Just as we arrived back at the hotel, I said, "Mm, I almost forgot! Thank you for the flowers!"

"What flowers?" he replied.

"You didn't send me flowers?"

"No."

Normally, he would have been jealous. In this case, it must have been tempered by guilt.

We went downstairs for a drink and settled into some chairs by the pool. Shortly thereafter, Gabriel Byrne came over. "Hello, miss! I gather it smells very good in your room today."

"So I guess you're my secret admirer."

"Indeed."

Before I had time to say thank you, Sylvain blurted out, in his broken English, something about the fact that he had ruined Byrne's weekend. To which Byrne replied, with a little mocking smile, "Well, you both have a good weekend then," and left.

Sylvain was silent for a while. Then he asked, "That's who sent you flowers?"

"That's the man who was kind enough to think of doing that, yes," I said.

I have to admit I felt a tinge of regret as I watched Byrne leave our table. I had travelled alone so often, and this time, with a charming gentleman courting me, it just so happened that I was accompanied. And, what's more, by a married man who gave every indication of wanting to stay married.

We stayed in South Beach for a few days before flying to the Cayman Islands so Sylvain could buy his watch. From the airport, we went to the Ritz, on Grand Cayman, where Sylvain had booked us into a suite even more lavish than the one we'd just left in South Beach. The next morning, we went to the jewellery store to have the watch fitted to his wrist size, and then went back to pick it up in the afternoon. Forty-five thousand dollars later, the bauble was his. You might think, since we were at a jeweller's, he would have splurged on a little something for his beloved Julie . . . But he didn't, of course. Ever the tightwad.

How Sad Venice Can Be

*"At midnight he got out of bed, took a hundred-dollar bill
out of his wallet and set it down on the bedside table, and
said, 'I'm going down to pay for the room.' Then he left."*

Sylvain and I had been seeing each other for more than
four years. By then, everyone around him knew I was his
mistress. The relationship was no longer secret, and it
hadn't been for months. I'd met his brothers, and knew his
friends well. Even his family, including his wife and children,
knew about me. We went out to restaurants all over town
without trying to hide from anyone.

At one point during our stay in South Beach, we were in our
hotel room when his wife called me on my cellphone. "Julie, I
know my husband is there with you. I'd like to speak with
him." I was stunned that she was calling, and I did my best to
cover for Sylvain: "Well, he is here in Florida, but he's not with
me. I'm in my room. I can go get him for you."

"Don't screw around with me, all right? I know he's with
you." She was screaming at me. I tried my best to calm her
down. A mistress, however, rarely succeeds in comforting
her lover's wife.

In the meantime, Sylvain had figured out who was calling. "It's my wife, right?" he said. "Give me the phone."

He took the phone and he didn't pull any punches: "You listen, and listen good. I've got nothing to say to you, okay? I'll talk to you when I get home. And I don't want you calling here again, is that clear?" It wasn't the first time I'd heard him speak to her in that tone of voice. It was something I never would have stood for.

At regular intervals, Sylvain would tell me that his mind was made up, and that he was on the verge of dumping his wife. A few times, he even went so far as to leave his wife and children and move into an apartment. But on the rare occasions he did so, he always went back within days.

Some of those false alarms could have spelled disaster for me. As I have mentioned, the first time Sylvain had promised me he was about to leave his wife, he had managed to persuade me to sell my own house and rent a brand new one. It was sheer luck that I had been able to move back to my place, after he had contrived an argument with me so that he wouldn't have to fulfill the pledge he'd made. His manipulating ways could easily have cost me my home.

He would often say to me, "Just give me a little while to get my things in order. If ever she flies off the handle, I don't want it to cost me an arm and a leg, you understand?" Then one day, to my great surprise, he told me: "It's done. I've decided. I'm leaving my wife, and you and I are going to move in together. I'm fed up with all the responsibility. I'm wasting my life working and giving my all to other people." That was the way he saw it: he was living for others. Today, from a different perspective, I realize that in reality, he was consumed by ambition and a love for money – and especially the things money could buy. He was also incredibly full of himself, and cared very little about the effect his actions had on my life, or that of his wife.

But he seemed serious this time. Everything was settled, he said. He'd come to an amicable arrangement with his wife, with no lawyers involved, and he was now free to strike out on his own. He'd even cooked up a script for the start of our new life together, right out of a Hollywood love story. "I want you to put together an itinerary for us," he said. "We're going to spend two months in Europe, starting in Venice."

Then he told me that he'd been to Venice before, but hadn't gone on a gondola ride because he had always meant to save that ultimate romantic moment for the woman he truly loved. What a performance. And it went on; he was more and more enthused with every word: "You'll go first. You'll fly to Venice, and when you get there, I want you to check in to the most beautiful hotel in town. We'll stay there for four days. 'Cause after four days in Venice, you've had enough."

Then, he explained, we were going to rent a car – a Mercedes convertible, no less – and, from Venice, we would drive across northern Italy and down to Monaco. "And," he went on, "I don't want you to take any luggage with you. Just a carry-on bag with your toiletries. We'll buy all our clothes as we go." I nearly fell out of my chair. Could it be for real this time?

On the appointed day, I flew Air France from Montreal to Charles-de-Gaulle airport in Paris. From there I was going to take an Alitalia flight to Venice. For once, Sylvain – skinflint Sylvain – had told me to book my seat in first class, and this bolstered the idea, in my mind, that this time he really was going to go through with it. As he'd asked, I travelled in a simple summer dress, with only an overnight bag. The Air France flight was delayed, as it turned out, and I missed the connecting flight to Venice. I had to book a seat on another plane. While waiting, I got a bite to eat and checked out some of the airport boutiques. When the boarding call came over the intercom, I realized that the departure had been moved to another terminal and, since Charles-de-Gaulle is so huge, I missed that flight, too. So when I finally got to Venice, late in the day, I was completely wiped out. But despite my advanced state of fatigue, I was truly impressed by the city, which I had never visited before. As I beheld this marvel, built entirely on the water, with its squares, its famous canals, its splendid architecture, and all its faded grandeur, I felt like I had arrived on another planet.

But I had to find a hotel, and I didn't want to spend too much time looking. From Marco Polo airport, I hired a water taxi and asked the driver for the name of the finest hotel in Venice. "The Danieli," he said immediately.

"Fine, the Danieli it is." As soon as I stepped off the water taxi, I realized I couldn't go far wrong. The Danieli was a late-fourteenth-century gem, with monumental doors, pink marble, gilded columns, and Murano glass chandeliers. It is hard to imagine such sheer opulence if you have never seen it. But what struck me most was the huge pedestal mirror in my suite, framed in finely sculpted wood, darkened by time. As I stared at my reflection in the glass, I had an eerie feeling, as if I could sense the souls of all the myriad guests who had paraded before it over the centuries.

The next morning, I went to the airport to pick up Sylvain. As soon as I saw him, I could tell something was up. He looked weird, and he was in a bad mood. He had travelled as lightly as possible, like me, and we went to the hotel to drop off what little luggage he had.

"Okay, time for the gondola ride," he said without further ado, as if it was some formality that absolutely had to be concluded.

"Uh, hello? I've been here for two whole days, and I'd like a change of clothes. Could we maybe go shopping first?" I had done some laundry the day before in the hotel room's sink, but I didn't want to repeat the chore that evening.

"No, no. The gondola first."

As we drifted along the canal, he began telling me a desultory tale about having hired some artist to paint a portrait of his wife, and the guy had said he couldn't do it because she was too pretty. What he was saying was obviously insensitive, and he knew it, but I had no idea what he was getting at. He'd always told me his wife was boring and emotionless, and now all of a sudden she was the Mona Lisa and Helen of Troy put together. I didn't appreciate this in the slightest, and I told him so: "First you tell me you've been saving this gondola ride for the one woman you truly love, and now you're going on about how wonderful your wife is? Where is this coming from, all of a sudden? Have you lost your mind?"

Just as we stepped off the gondola, Sylvain's cellphone rang. It was his brother, a partner in one of his car dealerships, calling from Montreal to say that Sylvain's wife had flipped out and that their separation arrangement was off. She had apparently got her hands on an article in some magazine in which Stéphane Sirois – him again – had ranted on about me. He'd said, among other things, that I had ruined his life, and that if he had to do it all over again, he would never have married me – the whole nine yards. Sylvain's wife had told his brother there was no way she was going to let her family be destroyed by a woman like me, who would obviously leave her husband sooner or later. So she had decided to renege on the agreement she'd made with Sylvain. If he wanted to leave her, he was going to have to pay a huge price. "You're in deep shit, Sylvain. If I were you I'd get back here, and fast," his brother said.

The truth was, Sylvain's entire family was basically sponging off him, and their worst fear was that if he got divorced, his wife would wind up with a huge piece of the pie. Let's just say not many of Sylvain's family members were on my side.

We strolled around Venice and saw a few of the sights, but I soon realized his mind was probably made up. He stayed inside his bubble, not saying a word. When he did open his mouth to speak, it was only to ramble on about the same subject, and to say he was seriously thinking about flying back to Montreal. I was incredulous and shocked, and I let him know it. "It can't be . . . You're joking, right? You can't do this to me, Sylvain! You can't go back to your wife. Not again, not after all the other times. I believed your story this time. I trusted you! I won't stand for this. Snap out of it!"

A pall of anguish and insecurity hung over us the rest of the day. We went back to the hotel. Sylvain was feeling really down. At that point, I sensed he had made up his mind to go back to Montreal. I realized that, after four long years of waiting, my dream of having the man I loved all to myself was once again slipping through my fingers.

At midnight he got out of bed, took a hundred-dollar bill out of his wallet and set it down on the bedside table, and said, "I'm going down to pay for the room." Then he left.

The second the door closed behind him, I felt my heart leap into my mouth. I ran to the bathroom and threw up. The rest of the night was hell, probably one of the worst nights of my life. Once again, I couldn't believe it. I felt like I was in a nightmare. But it was real. I was shattered, helpless. I really loved that man.

I called my sister and one of my best friends, and then I booked a seat on the next available flight to Montreal. The plane left a few hours later, and I arrived back home in the afternoon. One of my friends was waiting for me. We fell into each other's arms. She was crying, and so was I.

Suddenly, I felt a light tap on my shoulder. Believe it or not, it was him. Looking sheepish and unshaven. "Julie," he said, "I just came from the garage. I went to get the Winnebago. I want you to come down to Florida with me, to Walt Disney World."

I think I was even more stunned than when he'd left me the night before. "What?! Are you insane, or what?" Then he took me by the arm and said, "No, listen . . ."

"Let go of me," I said, my voice rising fast. "You just left me on the other side of the world, alone, with a hundred dollars in my pocket. If you know what's good for you, you're going to turn right around and leave. If you don't, you're going to get my fist in your face. That clear enough for you? I wouldn't trust you as far as I could throw you, you bastard!"

Then my friend went one better; she was yelling even louder than me. "You insensitive asshole! You dumped her in Venice?! What the hell did you think you were doing?"

Sylvain walked out of the arrivals lounge, and that was the end of our story. As he had done countless times before, he had tried to win me back. But this time, I stood firm. We were done.

28

Robert

"Among the guests seated at the same table as me was one Robert Pépin, whom I didn't know from Adam. We got to talking, and he mentioned that his father had recently founded a company that specialized in security solutions."

The breakup with Sylvain was very painful indeed, but I didn't have much time to wallow in my sorrows. I had lost my job as well as the man I loved. But I had to roll up my sleeves and find work as soon as possible. I saw a job offer in the newspaper that I thought might be right for me: a group of construction contractors was seeking a sales manager for a development in Lachenaie, a suburban town northeast of Montreal. A hospital complex was being built there, and this had led to a bit of a construction boom in the area.

I landed the position without much difficulty. The project was a residential development near the new hospital, managed by three partners. Unfortunately, I can't say it was the most fruitful business experience of my life. Relations between the partners became strained quite quickly, and disagreements over how to interpret the shareholder agreement only added to the confusion. As a result, the project was dead in the water less than a year later. After that, I teamed up with one of the three partners and tried to put together another project – a commercial development this time – but it was no more successful because the owner of a part of the land we wanted to build on demanded a ridiculous sum, and our financing fell through as well. It was a shame, because it was a fine-looking project, and we had worked like beavers to get it off the ground. But you have to move fast in that line of business, especially when the competition is fierce – and we wasted a lot of time on pointless squabbling.

Around this time, something rather extraordinary happened: I was given a horse as a present. I'd loved horses since I was a little girl and had always dreamed of owning one. The gift came from a most improbable source: Sylvain.

When I first met him, Sylvain had bought a large stable in Mascouche, northeast of Montreal, and had wanted to buy a horse as well. Naturally, though, in keeping with his obsession with the movies, not just any old mare would do. He wanted nothing less than Zorro's mount: a purebred black stallion, young and sound.

We found the gem he was looking for: a splendid beast with rippling muscles under a coal-black coat, impeccably groomed. Its grandsire had been a famous racehorse that won several prestige events in the United States. It was truly a magnificent horse. At the same time, the owner also showed me the horse's sire, Bernie, who was ten years old at the time. It was love at first sight. He was the most beautiful animal I'd ever seen in my life. But never in my wildest dreams did I think that I might one day own him.

More than a year after our breakup, Sylvain called. I'm convinced it was mainly a way for him to try to reconnect with me, because he knew that I'd always wanted to own a horse. "You remember Bernie, that horse you loved so much?" he said. "The owner's selling him for eighteen thousand dollars. At that price, he's a steal."

"You know very well I can't afford that," I answered.

"Well, how about I loan you the money, then? Zero interest."

Even with the terms Sylvain was offering, it would have been a huge investment. Plus I would have had to board Bernie, feed him, and pray that he remained in good health – because veterinary care for a horse costs a fortune. I told Sylvain that I would think about it for a few days and get back to him.

"So, have you decided?" he asked me a few days later.

"Well, you know I've dreamed about owning a horse since I was a little girl . . . but I have to be reasonable. I just can't afford it. So the answer's no."

He didn't say anything for several seconds, as if he was thinking. Then he said, "Ah, listen. I'll give him to you. I owe you that much."

"You're kidding me."

"No, no, I swear. He's yours. I want you to have him."

How could I refuse?

It was the start of a wonderful adventure. I remember my mother, her husband, and my brother, as well as my sister and her husband, all coming out to the stables to admire Bernie the day I officially became his owner.

On weekends, and on evenings after work in summer when there was still plenty of light out, I would go to the stables, saddle Bernie, and go riding for hours. I would ride on the well-kept trails in the woods behind the stables, together with a group of women who were all excellent riders and with whom I got along very well. We would pack lunches and head out at an easy trot, enjoying the outdoors, without a care in the world. After a while, we would take a break at one of the rest stops along the trail, where there were cabins equipped with simple wooden stoves. We would get a fire going and warm up, and then have our snacks, accompanied by a glass of wine, while our mounts rested outside, tied to a tree. I would sit back and think: life doesn't often get any better than this.

On one of these horseback rides, I struck up a friendship with a woman named Monique.* Her horse was boarded at the same stables as Bernie, and she would go riding often, either alone or with her partner, Lise.† Monique was a great lover of horses, and she seemed to have a way with them. After two and half years or so, I ended up selling Bernie to Monique, for much less than he was worth. At any rate, I no longer had as much time to take care of him, so Monique had already begun to do so and had formed a bond with him, and I knew he would be well treated. Monique was a controller for a large company. In the course of our conversations, she often mentioned that she no longer found her job very motivating, and that she felt she needed a new challenge.

In early 2005, not long after the failed real estate venture in Lachenaie, I attended a birthday party with a group of business people. We were in a private room at a restaurant in Laval, and among the guests seated at the same table as me was one

---

* Not her real name.
† Not her real name.

Robert Pépin, whom I didn't know from Adam. We got to talking, and he mentioned that he and his father had recently founded a company that specialized in security solutions. He went on to explain that, at the moment, business wasn't going particularly well.

"I've had salaried employees for six months but we haven't won a single contract yet. So I'm fifty-five thousand dollars in the red," he said.

When he started asking me about my professional experience, prior jobs and such, I said, "My expertise is mostly in real estate and construction."

"So you know all about managing employees and work crews, right?" he said.

"Oh, sure. But see, I don't know the first thing about the security business. I've never done that kind of work. I mean, I have an alarm system at home and I don't even know how it works," I said, laughing.

"Not a problem," Robert said. "You'll learn. You'd have all the tech support you'd need from the suppliers. We want to work the integration side of things. I'm looking for somebody to manage all that."

And so a few days later, I met with Robert Pépin again, this time at the offices of his company, DRP, in a brand new building on Saint-Martin Boulevard in Laval. I was very impressed by the office layout, the quality of the furniture, and the huge conference room. Everything about the place projected a slick image. They seemed like a serious outfit.

Robert outlined the structure and operations of his company for me. Among other things, he explained that his father, a retired police officer, was the licenced owner of the company – because in order for a security firm to be granted an operating permit, the law requires that its top management include at least one person with the skills and abilities relevant to that industry. Then he made me a serious offer: "If you're interested in running the company, becoming the manager, I'm prepared to bring you in as a full partner, on an equal footing with my father and me."

It was certainly an attractive proposition, especially given that I had always been self-employed and this arrangement would allow me to continue working that way. The other major selling point was the company's growth potential. In the post–September 11 world, with companies everywhere becoming acutely aware of the importance of safeguarding their data and their intellectual property, it wasn't hard to see that the security industry was on the verge of a major boom, comparable to that of the telecommunications field during the 1990s.

As part of the media frenzy around the so-called Bernier-Couillard Affair, several people have insinuated that I claimed to be a security "expert" during this period. I have never made any claim to anyone that I had in-depth knowledge of the security and surveillance business. DRP didn't need that type of expertise to operate as a security systems integrator; all that was required was to understand our customers' needs, partner with competent suppliers and subcontractors who knew what they were doing, and coordinate the work of all these people in the achievement of our business goals. We were simply business people exploiting an industry niche that promised excellent growth. Nothing more, nothing less. I therefore accepted Robert Pépin's offer to become the general manager of DRP.

29

Security

"We knew that if we were able to win the contract, which was worth several million dollars, we would be recognized as a major player. DRP's credibility and prosperity would be ensured for years to come."

When I was first hired at DRP, the person in charge of the company's accounting was a young woman in her early twenties who clearly lacked the necessary skills for the task. Moreover, she was using accounting software that was designed for individuals and therefore unsuited to a large company's needs. I explained to Robert that we would be better off hiring a bona fide controller, someone who could set up the appropriate systems and properly manage the company's financial operations – and I told him that I knew somebody who was competent, experienced, and could be trusted to properly administer DRP's finances. I was thinking of Monique, whom I saw regularly during our weekend horseback riding sessions. She was feeling more and more fed up with her current job, so I took the opportunity to ask her if she was interested in coming to work for us.

"At this point, obviously, we can't offer you as much as you're earning now," I said. "But as the company continues to grow, we'll be able to increase your salary accordingly."

She said she was interested.

Robert and I met with Monique formally and made her a firm offer, which she accepted. She was hired as DRP's controller, and right away she told me she found her new responsibilities very stimulating. For my part, I was extremely happy that I could count on a person of honesty and integrity, in whom I had complete trust, to occupy such a key position in the company.

DRP's operations focussed on four major areas: security guard services (which, while not particularly lucrative, provided a certain degree of visibility that made for good marketing), private investigation, alarm systems installation, and security systems integration.

Our first contract was for the installation of security systems in a 120-unit apartment development in Lachine. At the time, the industry was really starting to take off. More and more builders were delivering properties with security systems included. As part of my business development strategy, I approached a number of people I knew in the construction industry to offer them our services. One of them was a representative for a construction firm in Lachine that specialized in redeveloping disused factories into condominiums, whom I called to offer a quote. One of DRP's suppliers sent over a sales rep, and we went to meet with the builder to demo the security system. The equipment included motion sensors, door and window contacts, and individual alarm systems for each condo unit, all connected to a central station. The builder signed on.

After that initial contract, things moved very quickly. We became a key client for that supplier, with monthly orders of around three thousand to four thousand dollars. After a while, their regional sales manager called me to arrange a meeting. He came to my office, and we discussed the outlook for the security industry in general and DRP in particular.

"We now have a solid customer base in the private sector," I told him, "and we're happy about that. But to really grow our reputation, we need to start getting public-sector contracts – at the federal and provincial levels, as well as at the municipal. For a security company, that's the key to building true credibility. It's a kind of quality guarantee."

The sales manager opened up a bit, and he eventually said to me, "Listen, there's someone I'd like for you to meet, an inventor. He's come up with a new technology that's completely revolutionary, and incredibly efficient. So much so that I've been seriously thinking of setting up a company with him, because I'm convinced that his product is that far ahead of anything else that's currently available in the field."

We met with the inventor in question. His product was indeed very impressive: a fully integrated management system that handled every aspect of a security and alarm system while being fully customizable to individual customers' needs. It was self-programming and self-diagnostic, and it automatically detected and reported weaknesses in specific zones. It also featured time-management functionality for employees assigned to security, making it exceptionally cost-effective. The core of the system was housed in a device the size of a pack of cigarettes. In addition, it was fully wireless and compatible with WiFi technology.

When I saw the system at work and grasped its potential, I was immediately convinced that nothing else on the market could match its performance. It was going to make us into a major-league player, well-positioned to bid on public-sector contracts. We began drawing up a list of organizations likely to be interested in our system, and seeing whether any of us knew any people connected to them. At that point, Robert had a flash: one of his father's acquaintances, a childhood friend in fact, knew Jacques Duchesneau, the former Montreal urban community police chief, who in 2002 had been appointed president and CEO of the Canadian Air Transport Security Authority (CATSA).

Robert got in touch with Duchesneau, who agreed to set up a meeting so that we could give a presentation on the benefits of our new technology. At the time, CATSA was about to issue a call for tenders for the procurement of a high-tech system to streamline and improve time management in the security departments of Canada's airports. We knew our system was a good fit for their needs.

As Duchesneau had promised, CATSA officials got in touch with us to set up an appointment. Before things could reach that stage, however, we had to comply with a very thorough screening process – which was normal, given the nature of the project. Every person who wanted to attend the meeting had to fill out an elaborate form, disclosing their social insurance and driver's licence numbers along with a host of other personal details. Each of us was also required to sign a document empowering the competent authorities to conduct in-depth background checks and collect any information they deemed appropriate. It was also clearly stated that CATSA had complete discretion to grant or bar anyone's access to the meeting without providing a reason. We all complied with those conditions, including Robert, who at the time did not have a criminal record.

We travelled to Ottawa to meet with Jacques Duchesneau and other CATSA officials and give our presentation. I was fairly sure they were impressed by the technology we demonstrated, although that didn't mean they were going to award us the contract, of course. Public-sector tendering almost always involves lengthy and complex procedures, and there were still many steps to follow before we would be anywhere near our goal.

We knew that if we were able to win the contract, which was worth several million dollars, we would be recognized as a major player. DRP's credibility and prosperity would be ensured for years to come. So we rolled up our sleeves and got to work: we hired a professional who specialized in writing proposals for federal government contracts, and we set about responding to the requests for clarification that CATSA had sent regarding our proposed system's features and performance. All of this took several months. Though DRP was not awarded the contract in the end, it certainly wasn't for a lack of trying.

Certain observers have made much of the fact that Robert Pépin and I supposedly had access to sensitive information in the form of the specifications for the CATSA contract, and have in turn insinuated that we could easily have provided that information to members of criminal organizations so that they could infiltrate Canadian airport security. That's as good a conspiracy theory as any other, but I must unfortunately inform its proponents that it is nothing less than absurd. I'm not at all familiar with the infiltration methods employed by members of criminal organizations, but I highly doubt that such people would have needed us to carry out such an exercise.

In bidding on the CATSA contract, DRP was not setting out to jeopardize national security, nor to open the doors of Canada's airports to organized crime. Our motivations were, quite simply, the same as those of any other company interested in making a profit: to secure an extremely lucrative contract with a reliable customer who was highly unlikely to bounce the cheque. I don't know of many business people who would turn up their noses at the opportunity to deal with a public body of that scale, with rock-solid credit and a signature on memorandums of understanding that would guarantee instant financing from any bank in the country.

I should add that, during those few months, we didn't devote our time solely to the CATSA tender. We were awarded several other contracts in both residential and commercial buildings, be it to provide guard services or install security systems. Business was going very well, and if I may say so myself, I felt like I was a significant asset to the company. When I'd been hired, DRP was $55,000 in debt; a few months later, we had contracts for the next three years, worth a sum in excess of $1.2 million. Let's just say I've seen worse sales records.

All that time, however, I hadn't done very much in response to the equal partnership that Robert had offered me. I had asked my lawyer to prepare one or two draft shareholder agreements, but I was always so caught up in the various aspects of my work, from business development to bidding on contracts, that I hadn't gone any further than that. Obviously, with every new contract that DRP was awarded, it was increasingly in my interest to formalize my full partnership. But Robert Pépin didn't seem to be in any hurry.

And I must admit that, in the meantime, I had made a serious mistake, one for which I would eventually have to pay very dearly: I had mixed business with pleasure.

30

Locked Out

"I arrived at work the next morning to find a security guard seated at a little table in front of my office door. He wasn't wearing a DRP uniform. As I approached, he stood up and asked, 'Are you Julie Couillard?'

'Yes,' I said.

'I'm sorry, but you no longer have access to this office.'

'Excuse me?!'

He handed me a business card. On it was the name and telephone number of a lawyer. 'Contact this gentleman. He'll explain everything.'"

When I started working for DRP, Robert Pépin had been living with the same woman for several years – a woman who, in fact, worked in the office with us. He confided to me that they had only been friends at first, but had gradually grown closer and become romantically involved, and that, although their relationship had its ups, it had more downs, and now it was back to being more of a friendship.

I could understand why there would be tension from time to time, because although Robert wasn't a bad person, he had one major flaw: he was a very heavy drinker. He told me that when he was younger, he had also been heavily into cocaine, and that his brother had died of an overdose. He had sworn off the coke after that, but hadn't stopped drinking. I've never met anyone who drank as much as he did in my entire life. He didn't seem to enjoy it very much, either. Alcohol made him depressed – and aggressive.

One night, quite late, my doorbell rang. It was Robert. He was in an advanced state of intoxication, and he was holding a green garbage bag that had a few articles of clothing hanging out of it. He'd had an argument with his girlfriend and left her. "I got nowhere to go," he said. "Can I stay with you until I straighten things out?"

I let him in, of course. And some days later, the inevitable happened. I was single, and I didn't owe anybody anything. I made it clear from the start, however, that it was to be a temporary arrangement – a week or two at most – after which he would have to start looking for somewhere else to live. Several months passed, however, and he didn't seem at all interested in leaving. On the contrary, he was starting to become part of the furniture. And he drank all the time. Once, he even went into a jealous tantrum after discovering the photo album of my honeymoon with Stéphane Sirois. He had obviously gone through my things, because I never kept that album out in the open. From that point on, I was increasingly unable to tolerate his presence in my house, and finally I told him, "Look, Robert, I can't take it any more. I want you to leave and find yourself an apartment."

But he stubbornly refused. He kept trying to convince me that he and I could make things work, that we just needed some more time to adjust to each other the whole bit. So I gave him some slack. But a few days later, at the office Christmas party, he went over the line in a big way.

Together, we had decided to organize a big holiday reception at the Piccolo Mondo restaurant on Curé-Labelle Boulevard in Laval. The company was doing extremely well, and a party would provide the perfect opportunity not only to acknowledge the hard work of all our employees, but also to motivate them to rise to the challenges of the coming months. We invited all the staff and their spouses, as well as a few of our suppliers. An office party, of course, equals plenty of alcohol. So I had taken pains to warn Robert: "Just make sure you don't overdo it. This isn't the time. You're the boss. You embody the image of the company. All our employees are going to be here tonight, along with some of our suppliers. You can't afford to make a fool of yourself."

My advice to him went in one ear and straight out the other. Robert went on a serious bender that night. At the end of the meal, I gave a very short speech thanking our staff and suppliers for their part in the success we'd enjoyed during the year gone by, and emphasizing the potential for expansion during the next. Not to be outdone, Robert decided he had to speak to the assembled guests as well. Not surprisingly, given his condition, the results were pitiful: he spoke incoherently and was constantly at a loss for words, and his diction clearly revealed his drunken state. He rambled on and on until, finally, I kicked him in the shin under the table, signalling to him that he'd best wrap up his "closing remarks." He had left no doubt in the mind of anyone present that he was in a drunken stupor. As if that wasn't enough, a little while later he tripped and fell to the floor of the restaurant before stumbling outside, where he threw up. I was furious.

During the party, Robert had spent a lot of time talking to Monique's girlfriend, Lise, who remained perfectly sober throughout. I should mention here that Robert was quite a gullible person, and it was fairly easy to make him believe just about anything. For some reason, Lise had decided to convince him that the reason Monique spent so much time at the office was probably that she was having an affair with me. His reaction was quite predictable given the fact that, on top of his natural propensity to extreme jealousy, he was now completely soused.

We went home after the party, and practically as soon as he set foot in the house, he exploded. "So, Lise tells me she's positive that you're sleeping with Monique. Well, I won't stand for it, that's for damn sure."

He was still drunk, and by now extremely aggressive. Robert was a very big guy: he was six foot two and must have weighed around two hundred and twenty-five pounds. He grabbed the cellphone I was holding in my hand, threw it to the floor, and started stamping on it with both feet. I was scared out of my wits. I didn't even take the time to put on a pair of boots. I grabbed my coat and ran out of the house as soon as I could.

I was frightened, but also as angry as I've ever been in my life. I jumped into my car and, though it was past midnight, drove straight to Monique's. I hammered on her front door. She came down and opened it, stunned to see me there. "What's going on?" she cried.

"Where's your girlfriend?" I demanded.

"Lise? She's asleep in bed. What's the problem?"

"I need to speak with her. Now."

My head was swirling with questions. Why would Lise try to convince someone that I was a lesbian, when I had never shown the slightest desire for a woman in my life? Worse, why had she said it to somebody who everyone at DRP knew had a tendency to become very aggressive as soon as he'd had a few drinks? Surely she knew that by making up a story like that, she was putting my safety at risk? The answer was obvious: jealousy.

I went upstairs and really let her have it: "You stupid cow, what's the deal with this bullshit story? You realize that he could have killed me? Why'd you do that?!"

"Let me sleep . . . I want to go back to sleep" was all she said.

"You wanted a six-foot-two, 225-pound beast to beat me up, you crazy bitch? Next time you want to send me a message, you come to me; you don't go through him. Got it?"

It had been a rough night, to say the least, and one that didn't augur well for my future with DRP. Needless to say, after that episode Robert moved out of my place, and fast. Right away I sensed that the shareholder agreement with him and his father was doomed. After that, Robert came to the office to try and convince me to get back together with him. I tried to soften the blow, explaining as gently as possible that we were probably meant to be friends and business partners but that we would never be happy together as a couple. Despite my efforts, he wouldn't hear of it, and soon he only rarely came into the office. When he did, he held small meetings in secret with people he was close to, and had virtually no contact with me. Some days later, Monique – who in the meantime had broken up with Lise – advised me in no uncertain terms to prepare for the worst: "It doesn't look good, Julie. If I were you, I'd incorporate my own security company right away. You'd be able to recover some clients. If he's as good as he thinks he is, let him do all the development, go knocking on doors and getting contracts." I followed her advice and founded Itek Global Solutions (IGS), a company that I still own today, although it is no longer active in the same line of business.

The writing was on the wall, but I still tried to push through the shareholder agreement, believing I had played a significant role in DRP's growth and deserved to be rewarded for it financially. We held a meeting at the office, and I laid the numbers on the table. Robert was there along with his father, his lawyer, and one of his close associates. I felt like I was in front of a tribunal rather than attending a meeting amongst equals. Robert's father was particularly antagonistic toward me. In hindsight, I can understand why. His son had suffered a great deal because of our breakup, had lost weight, and I was the guilty party – the man-eater who had caused his poor boy such grief.

The meeting was unproductive, to say the least. Like more than one man before him, Robert had made up his mind that if he couldn't have me, he was going to try to destroy me. At the end of the meeting, he said, "You'll never be a partner in this company."

I arrived at work the next morning to find a security guard seated at a little table in front of my office door. He wasn't wearing a DRP uniform. As I approached, he stood up and asked, "Are you Julie Couillard?"

"Yes," I said.

"I'm sorry, but you no longer have access to this office."

"Excuse me?!"

He handed me a business card. On it was the name and telephone number of a lawyer. "Contact this gentleman. He'll explain everything."

I didn't need some lawyer to explain what had been crystal-clear for several weeks already. Instead, I called my own lawyer. "There's a way out for you, Julie," he said. "We can get an injunction and put everything on hold, because you have proof that you were in negotiations to sign a shareholder agreement, and you were active on the business development side of things in addition to managing the execution of contracts. We'll get an injunction to freeze all the bank accounts, and if they want to continue operating, they'll have to sit down and talk to you. They won't have any choice."

There was just one minor detail: my lawyer told me that in order to proceed, I'd have to deposit twenty-five thousand dollars into a trust account. I didn't have that kind of money lying around, of course. And besides, I thought, did I really want to force these people into a partnership agreement with me now that they were my enemies? The best thing to do was cut and run.

As I was to learn later, Robert had been forced to get rid of me, in a way. He had apparently accrued a large debt to an individual who, realizing that DRP was a profitable company, had forced his way in as a partner in an attempt to recover the money he was owed. Robert had obviously seized upon the opportunity to kill two birds with one stone: he settled a debt that was hanging over his head, and he got revenge on me for having supposedly dumped him.

This was at the very beginning of 2006. I never exchanged so much as a word with Robert Pépin after that. Truth be told, I couldn't forgive him for what he'd done, and I held a grudge against him for a long time. When I learned nearly two years later that he had committed suicide, however, I must admit that I was quite taken aback by the news. Not long before then, I had met someone who knew him well and who said he was doing very well financially, had an attractive new girlfriend, and seemed confident about what the future held in store.

31

Square One

"Finally, on January 15, 2007, I threw in the towel. I got out of the security business and decided to reactivate my real estate agent's licence."

Robert Pépin's underhanded tactics led to three casualties in the DRP ranks: myself, my closest ally, Monique, and a man named Marc* who ran a vehicle leasing company that belonged to Robert and that had offices on the same premises. The three of us found ourselves high and dry, and we needed work. We decided to start another vehicle leasing company, which would allow us to generate enough short-term revenue to at least pay ourselves a decent salary. In the meantime, I forged ahead on my own in the security business with IGS, the company that I had set up shortly after it had become obvious that my days with DRP were numbered.

Monique, Marc, and I still had to find a financial backer for our leasing company. Marc knew someone who said he

---

* Not his real name.

might be prepared to help us out. We sent him our business plan, and he agreed to provide us with a line of credit. The business involved granting loans to individuals experiencing cash-flow problems, based on the value of their vehicles. For example, if a customer arrived with a car that was worth ten thousand dollars, we would lend him half the value of the vehicle for a period of one year, and he would then repay the sum in the form of a monthly rental fee.

It wasn't a particularly enjoyable commercial venture for me, even though my relationship with the company was conducted from a distance while I concentrated on my security firm. And right from the start, I had moral qualms about the nature of the operation. Obviously, all of the people who used the service did so because they had money problems. Some of them weren't able to pay back the loan, so the vehicle they had put up as collateral was seized. If it was a junkie who spent the entire day getting high, that seemed to me to be a lesser evil. But it could also be, say, a single mother, and I wasn't at all comfortable with that. In fact, it was downright depressing. Yes, it was something I should have thought of in the first place, but I had never stopped to consider that with that kind of business, it was quite likely that those kinds of scenarios would be commonplace.

There was another reason why I soon grew disinterested in the company: Marc had started living the high life with our financial backer. They were going out together, hitting the trendiest nightspots in town. The problem was, Marc realized he didn't have the means to keep up with his friend's expensive lifestyle, so he decided to start stealing from the company. More than once, he tried to break into the safe, which was in my office. He was often in the company office at night, when customers sometimes came to make their monthly payments in cash. When they did, he would pocket the money without declaring it.

Of course, I tried to get it through our financial backer's head that our partner was embezzling company funds, but he didn't seem particularly moved. So I told him straight out, "I have been entrusted with the responsibility of managing a firm that you are financing. I come to you and tell you to your face that our partner is trying to rip us off, and you cover for him? And afterward, you're going to come point a finger at me because there's money missing? No, thank you! I'm out of here."

I transferred all my assets in the company and left, with no regrets.

By this time I was devoting the bulk of my time and energy to my security firm, IGS. When I was forced out of DRP, the CATSA contract, which Monique and I had worked so hard on, had still not been awarded. Robert Pépin thought that my departure wouldn't change anything as far as the tendering process went, but our technology provider soon forced him to take a reality check. When the provider learned that I was no longer with DRP and, overnight, found himself dealing with someone new, he told Robert, "Look, we've been working with Julie on this bid for four months. We're not about to start all over with somebody new, and show them the ropes. Forget it."

Eventually a three-way deal was reached, whereby a commission in an amount negotiated in advance would be paid directly to my company by the supplier if ever the CATSA contract was awarded to DRP. So, if DRP ended up winning the contract – which, as we now know, it didn't – at least the time and effort I'd put into the project wouldn't have been a total waste.

In the meantime, I had continued to work with that same supplier on my own security system installation projects. In fact, I had been awarded an initial contract, with that supplier on board, to provide such a system for the City of Laval's detention centre, located on the Boulevard des Laurentides.

I was also dealing with another supplier that specialized in fingerprint access systems, and still another that marketed other biometrics ID systems. I had even begun talks with some public-sector companies regarding the installation of these types of systems. But the competition was fierce – especially from DRP. They had put together huge sales teams and had many employees. Their size was a big asset compared to the much smaller scale of my firm. It enabled them to attract more and better suppliers, for example, and they even threw out ultimatums: "You're either with her or with us," and so forth. I couldn't help but notice that the dynamics of my relationships with IGS's main technology providers were changing as the months went by. A few of them had even tried going behind my back and doing business directly with my clients, while others chose to deal with bigger integrator firms that had a higher visibility.

The last battle was a difficult one, and I was exhausted by the struggle. Finally, on January 15, 2007, I threw in the towel. I got out of the security business and decided to reactivate my real estate agent's licence. That meant I would have to take the sixteen-week course from the Quebec Association of Real Estate Brokers and Agents all over again, a condition imposed on anyone whose licence had lapsed for more than two years.

A few weeks earlier, around the end of 2006, I had been forced to break off all ties with Monique. By then we had come to know each other very well over a couple of years, and our friendship meant a lot to me. After we both left DRP, we had continued working closely together, for the vehicle leasing company as well as IGS. Meanwhile, in the wake of that infamous holiday office party, she had broken up with her partner, Lise, and we had started to spend a lot of time together, both in and out of the office. We would often go for a drink after work or go out to dinner later in the evening, talk about everything and nothing and have a good laugh over a glass of wine.

But our relationship was becoming complicated. I could sense impatience in Monique, at times even aggressiveness – until, after a while, it was plain to see that she had basically fallen in love with me. Even our co-workers had noticed. She would often tell me, especially after a drink or two, that she found me pretty, that I was the woman of her dreams, and so on. It made me extremely uncomfortable and distressed. It's one thing to be in a bar with a woman and use the "Sorry, I'm with my girlfriend" excuse to ward off the advances of some creep, but it's quite another to be confronted with another woman's desire, when one has never doubted one's heterosexual identity. Like many gays and lesbians I had met, Monique believed every person has latent homosexual tendencies. That may be true for some people, but it certainly isn't in my case. At one point, it all came to a head. I was fed up with her advances, which I felt were now bordering on harassment, and I told her, "Monique, look into my eyes and listen to me once and for all: homosexuality is not the measles – you can't catch it! Why can't you respect me for who I am the way I respect you? If, at my age, I've never been attracted to a woman, it's because it's just not in my nature. Can you understand that?"

Inevitably, she grew more and more frustrated and, no doubt, hurt by it all. Our relations became increasingly strained. When I eventually transferred my share of the vehicle leasing agency, I also gave up the office space, moved all my furniture and files into my house, and started running IGS from there. Monique and I never saw each other after that. It broke my heart, but there really wasn't any other way. I miss our friendship very much.

32

Kevlar

"Philippe explained that the federal government had issued a call for tenders to procure land for the construction of a federal building in Quebec City, and that Kevlar owned a property there that was currently being used as a parking lot. Then he asked me, 'How would you like to represent Kevlar in this dossier?'"

One evening in the winter of 2007 – it must have been sometime in February – I made a date with a friend at the bar of the Hôtel Sofitel in downtown Montreal. I arrived before her, and was sitting at a table when she called to say she wouldn't be coming; her daughter was running a fever. She told me to go ahead and enjoy my evening without her, optimistically adding, "Finish your drink. You never know, girl. You might get lucky and meet somebody interesting."

Sure enough, while we were chatting, I noticed a man sitting alone at the bar, a bottle of wine in front of him. He was typing idly on his laptop and kept turning around to glance in my direction. He was good-looking, in his late thirties, had blond hair and blue eyes, and was slightly dark-complexioned and very sharply dressed. I could tell he had heard every word I'd said on the phone. Not long after I hung up, he stood and walked over to my table. "Excuse me," he said. "Are you alone? Are you waiting for somebody?"

"Well, I was waiting for a friend. But – and I think you guessed it – she won't be able to make it."

"In that case, do you mind if I join you?" he asked.

"Not at all," I said.

He introduced himself. His name was Philippe Morin. We made the usual small talk, and he asked me what I did for a living. I told him I was in the midst of my real estate agent training. "No kidding?" he said. "Well, I run Kevlar."

"Oh, really? How about that!" I said.

The name of his company meant absolutely nothing to me, and I could see he was a bit upset. He went on: "You should google it sometime. Kevlar. K-E-V-L-A-R."

Then he told me that his company had an impressive real estate portfolio, and was in fact the second largest property owner in all of Quebec City. He was obviously out to impress me.

We didn't have dinner, but he ordered a few side dishes, which we ate with a glass of wine. After an hour or two, he asked me whether I'd like to go and have a drink somewhere else nearby. I wanted to head closer to Laval, so I said, "I know a little resto-bar in Rosemere, right beside the river. It's a really nice place and the music is good."

To my surprise, he accepted, and he followed me up to Rosemere. We had a few drinks, and I noticed that that night he had an amazingly high tolerance for alcohol; he didn't appear to be the slightest bit intoxicated. He was coherent the whole time, in control of himself, and never said anything out of line. The evening flew by. Suddenly, it was three in the morning and the bar was closing. But Philippe didn't feel at all like calling it a night. I made it clear to him that he wasn't coming back to my place, so he said, "Okay, let's go dancing, then."

"Go dancing? Everything's closed."

"What, there's nowhere around here that stays open late?"

I remembered an after-hours club in Laval that I hadn't been to in years, and we went there. The crowd was almost exclusively young people, eighteen-to-twenty-year-olds, and we danced until four-thirty in the morning. It's going to take me a week to recover, I thought to myself. Then we said goodbye, after exchanging phone numbers. I could tell he was disappointed that I hadn't invited him back to my place. But he didn't push it. All in all, it had been a very pleasant evening. I knew I'd made an impression on him – and the reverse was also true. At one point, I had asked him straight out whether he was single.

"Separated," he had said. "I just bought a condo and I'm having it renovated. Meantime, I'm living at the hotel. Weekends I go back to my house on Nun's Island, but it's just to see the kids. My wife and I sleep in separate beds."

It wasn't long before he called me. The following week we went out to dinner several times. The chemistry was still there, and we soon took things to the next level.

There was only one thing that bothered me, of course: he was still married. So I laid my cards on the table right away: "Philippe, if you still have issues, if you still have to live the life of a husband and you can't see me on weekends, I'll understand – but I won't be able to see you anymore. That whole 'it's over between her and me but I just need a little more time' routine? Been there, done that."

"Relax, it's not like that at all," he said. "The kids are in bed by eight, and after that I'm a free man."

The next two weekends he wasn't available. But during the week he was an absolute angel. I had caught a really nasty cold, and he took care of me, attentive as could be. I remember twice in the same week he went to get some takeout pasta at my favourite restaurant, Da Emma in Old Montreal, and brought it all the way back to Laval for me.

Despite his generous ways, though, I began to sense very clearly that Philippe hadn't made a clean break from his wife. There was obviously still something between them. And one night he sighed and admitted to me, "You know, I've been getting these guilty feelings. Maybe there's still a chance I can save my family after all."

I wasn't about to put myself through the same hell again. I was already extremely fond of him, and I didn't want it to go any further and risk an even more painful breakup. I told Philippe that it was over between him and me, but that I hoped we could remain good friends.

A few days later, I stopped in at the LeBlanc Restaurant on Saint-Lawrence Boulevard to have a drink. There was a guy sitting not far away who was more or less flirting with me. He bought me a drink and we got to chatting. He said he was waiting for a friend who'd asked to meet him there. After a while, the friend in question arrived and introduced himself. His name was Bernard Côté. He had a great sense of humour and we hit it off right away. He told me he worked in the office of the federal minister of public works, Michael Fortier. As I wasn't particularly interested in politics, I didn't make a big deal of it. I told him I was finishing up my real estate agent's course and that I was thinking of going to work outside the country. A friend of mine had recently told me she owned a condo in the Turks and Caicos Islands, that a lot of real estate agents from Quebec worked there, and there was good money to be made. I mentioned to Bernard that I'd been thinking of moving there. "Funny you should say that," he replied. "I happen to know a lawyer who specializes in securing overseas work permits, and just the other day he told me how he'd helped someone get a permit for the Turks and Caicos. If you're interested, I could ask him to forward me some information, and I'll email it to you." We exchanged business cards and email addresses. Then he went and sat down to eat with his dinner companion, and I left the restaurant.

A few days later, I went to meet Philippe and his business partner, René Bellerive, for happy-hour cocktails at the Hôtel Germain in downtown Montreal. As I was chatting with Philippe, my cellphone rang. It was Bernard, calling me back with the name of the lawyer he'd told me about. Eventually, Philippe realized that the man I was talking to was named Bernard Côté. As soon as I got off the phone, he asked me, "You know Bernard Côté? The Bernard Côté who works for Public Works Canada?"

"Well, I wouldn't go so far as to say I 'know' him. We've spoken to each other once or twice," I said.

"Well, next time you see him, put in a good word about my land in Quebec City."

"What land in Quebec City?" I asked.

Philippe explained that the federal government had issued a call for tenders to procure land for the construction of a federal building in Quebec City, and that Kevlar owned a property there that was currently being used as a parking lot. Then he asked me, "How would you like to represent Kevlar in this dossier?"

"What do you mean, exactly?" I asked.

"Well, there's a whole procedure that needs to be followed when tendering for government land procurement: requests for information, clarifications to be provided, explanations to be given, all that stuff. Bernard Côté is the guy who handles all that. His department, Public Works, manages all federal government properties. So it would be great for us to have someone who's on good terms with a guy like him." I got the distinct impression that relations between Bernard Côté and Kevlar management weren't what you'd call cordial.

It was only a few weeks until I would be finished with my course, and here I had an excellent opportunity to get back into the real estate business. Not only that, but this would be a commercial deal, and I'd never been all that happy working in the residential market. Plus, in my time at DRP I'd gained more than my share of experience with the long and complicated procedures involved in public-sector contracts. I was pretty sure I could take on this project. So I accepted Philippe's offer, and he agreed I would be a Kevlar affiliate agent.*

We then drew up two separate contracts: one under which I was to represent Kevlar in the competition for the land in Quebec City, and another stipulating that I would conduct prospecting for sites that would be a good fit for Kevlar Jazz, a division that specialized in retirement home development. They also had two hundred and fifty Kevlar business cards printed up, with my name and the title *Agente au Développement des Affaires* (business development officer). I have to admit that I don't understand why Philippe Morin and René

---

* In Quebec, real estate agents are considered self-employed workers – a regulatory nuance that later allowed Kevlar management to claim that I had never been an employee of the firm – but any transactions they conclude must be sanctioned by a brokerage firm.

Bellerive later denied that I had ever worked for Kevlar, although it is true that I never had an office on the company's premises; I worked from home. There is no denying that we were bound by those two contracts. I did business development for them, conducted research for them, and introduced them to senior municipal officials with whom they held talks regarding planned seniors' residences to be built on their territory. Kevlar was a major client of mine.

33

Politics

"A few weeks later, Philippe called me. 'Listen, I've set up a cinq à sept *and a dinner tonight,' he said. 'The federal industry minister, Maxime Bernier, is going to be there. I figured since you've been thinking about running, it might help you make up your mind. Not to mention, he's a pretty good-looking guy, and single. Maybe you'll like him.'"*

When I first started working with Kevlar, the contracting procedure for the Quebec City federal building hadn't progressed very far. In fact, the dossier was still only at the request for information stage. Public Works and Government Services Canada had just announced its intention to build a federal office building in Quebec City, providing a number of specifications such as the number of floors and the planned square footage, as well as the maximum perimeter for the building. There were still many steps to be completed before the actual call for tenders would be issued. With the project at this embryonic stage, my assignment was to obtain as much information as possible from the federal government about the project criteria, so that Kevlar would be as well prepared as possible for the subsequent phases.

My agreement with Kevlar wasn't exclusive, however, and during this time I had other clients for whom I was conducting business development, among them a real estate company that specialized in building sports complexes. I also had another group of clients who were interested in prospecting business opportunities in the Middle East, in the United Arab Emirates, among other places. And from time to time I took on work as a real estate agent.

During this period – more precisely, in mid-April 2007 – I happened to run into André Turcot, an old acquaintance I hadn't seen in many years. André, who had once owned a radio station, had long been active on behalf of the Progressive Conservative Party and its successor, the Conservative Party. In fact, the last time I'd spoken to him, the Tories were not in power in Ottawa. We caught up on each other's news; I told him I was working in real estate, and I asked him if he was still active in politics. He said yes, and mentioned that he was now the president of the Conservative riding association for Châteauguay-Saint-Constant, across from Montreal on the south shore of the St. Lawrence River, and that in a few days' time, he would be attending the nomination meeting for the riding's Tory candidate, a man named Pierre-Paul Routhier. He also told me the meeting would be preceded by a cocktail fundraiser, and that I might be interested in attending. "Michael Fortier, the minister of public works, will be there. There'll be all kinds of business people as well. If you want to make some contacts for your real estate business, this would be a great opportunity."

I therefore bought a ticket to the fundraiser, and I gave André a cheque for one thousand dollars. This was the infamous bounced cheque (the only one I've ever written, in my recollection, and it had to be that one!) that got so much play in the media – although few accounts ever mentioned that the bank only tried to cash it a full two months after I'd written it, and that I wrote a new one immediately.

So I went to the fundraiser, which was held in the city of Mercier. There were about fifty people there, including Minister Fortier, who was accompanied by Bernard Côté. I was introduced to the minister, as was everyone else in the room. I also chatted with several business people, representatives from area municipalities, and members of the Conservative Party rank and file. And I met Nelson Bouffard, a Tory organizer for the Montreal region who was also in charge of recruiting candidates for the upcoming election. He asked me whether I might be interested in becoming a Conservative candidate. Running for office was not something I had ever even remotely considered, but I was curious and wanted to find out more, so we agreed to meet again a few days later to discuss the matter further.

As I have mentioned, I had never taken any serious interest in politics, and while I wasn't familiar with all the details of the Conservative Party's philosophy and values, I was quite inclined to support Stephen Harper. I felt that since he had become prime minister the year before, he had been true to his word – which is not something that can be said about all politicians. I also thought that up to then, he had responded quite well to the need for change that had brought him to power in the first place. Although I was nowhere close to making up my mind about running, I wasn't at all averse to committing to his party.

I went to the meeting, which was held in a building on Jarry Street in the city's east end, near the Metropolitan Expressway. I met with three people, Nelson Bouffard and two others whose names I no longer recall, for three separate interviews. The first interview briefly covered my professional background and experience. The second interview was with Nelson, and was mainly about my sense of government solidarity and whether, if elected as a Member of Parliament, I would understand the importance of conforming to party discipline. I was neither surprised nor shocked by any of his questions in that respect. "From time to time, you may not agree with the party line on a specific issue," he said, "but you have to keep looking in the same direction." In principle, I had no issues with that, but I still wanted to find out a bit more about the Tories' main policy orientations before deciding whether to go ahead.

In the final interview, we discussed which ridings might be a good fit for me, and eventually settled on two: one on the island of Laval, where I lived, and the other in Deux-Montagnes, in Montreal's northern ring, where I knew a lot of people. The interviewer also explained in broad terms what was involved in the riding nomination process, electoral campaign financing, the selling of party membership cards, and so on. I was also asked whether raising eighty thousand dollars in funds for my campaign would be a problem for me; I answered that it seemed quite doable. We left it at that, with no firm commitment made by either side; it was agreed that somebody else from the party would follow up with me at an opportune time.

The next day or the day after, I had some business at the Kevlar offices. I took the opportunity to announce to Philippe and René that I was considering getting into politics. "Guess what, guys!" I said. "The Conservative Party asked me whether I was interested in becoming a candidate."

"Why not?" was Philippe's reaction.

I was still taking the whole thing fairly lightly and was a long way from making a decision, but it was pretty exciting for me, of course.

A few weeks later, Philippe called me. "Listen, I've set up a *cinq à sept* and a dinner tonight," he said. "The federal industry minister, Maxime Bernier, is going to be there. I figured since you've been thinking about running, it might help you make up your mind. Not to mention, he's a pretty good-looking guy, and single. Maybe you'll like him."

Before going to the party, I went home, switched on my laptop, and typed Maxime Bernier's name into Google to find out a bit more about him.

34

Meeting Maxime

"It was our first private meeting, the chance for us to get to know each other a little better. We talked in general terms about our respective backgrounds, our careers, the past. I told him that I had been married and divorced, and that one of my boyfriends had been involved with biker gangs, and had been murdered."

The cocktail party was at Suite 701, the bar in the Hôtel Place d'Armes, in Old Montreal. In addition to two or three people I didn't know, and whose names I have now forgotten, Philippe Morin and René Bellerive were there, along with Eric Boyko, who as it turned out was basically the liaison between Maxime Bernier and Kevlar's top management. Boyko had become a multimillionaire before the age of thirty-five thanks to a company called eFundraising.com, which, as its name suggests, specialized in the organization of fundraising campaigns via the Web. He later founded Stingray Digital, a company devoted to digital media. He was good friends with Maxime, who, incidentally, appointed him to the board of directors of the Business Development Bank of Canada in 2007, near the end of his term as industry minister.

I stayed with them for part of the cocktail party and then went on to the Cavalli Restaurant, on Peel Street, where the dinner that Philippe Morin had invited me to was to be held. When I arrived, Maxime was already there, sitting at the bar. I walked up to him and introduced myself: "Good evening, *Monsieur le ministre*. I'm Julie Couillard. We're going to be having dinner together tonight. The others will be here very soon."

"Pleasure to meet you. I'm sorry I couldn't make it for cocktails, I had to finish up some business. I just got here myself," he said.

I have to say he made a pretty good impression on me at that first meeting; he was handsome and self-confident. Quite like-able, but a bit of a poseur. In that respect, I must admit, he fitted in quite well with the decor of the Cavalli. We chatted about this and that for a few minutes while we waited for the other guests. They arrived not long after. We all stayed at the bar a little while longer, and eventually we were shown to our seats.

There were about ten of us around the table. Maxime sat down beside me, with Philippe to his right and Eric Boyko across from him. René Bellerive was there as well. At the last minute the group had been embellished, if I may say, by four young women whom Philippe had brought along. They were very pretty, rather scantily clad, and quite alluring. Philippe had no doubt reckoned that the ratio of men to women would otherwise have been too high.

Early on, as I had planned, I told Maxime that I was think-ing of getting into politics, and I talked to him about it for quite a while. I asked him all sorts of technical and practical ques-tions about choosing a riding, financing, and organization – but nothing too in-depth, of course. He said that if and when I made a firm decision, he could look into which ridings in the Montreal area might offer the best chances for success.

Then, at one point, Philippe left the table momentarily, and Maxime leaned over and asked me, "Who's that guy, by the way?"

"You mean you don't know him? That's Philippe Morin, the real estate broker I'm working for. He's the one who invited me here so that I could meet you and talk to you about politics."

It was at that point that I realized it was actually Eric Boyko who had orchestrated the get-together. That evening, Eric Boyko seemed keen on matching me up with the industry minister. Indeed, he spent quite some time explaining to me how it was difficult for Maxime, as a very visible member of cabinet, to have a meaningful love life in Ottawa, because Maxime thought "people would talk" if he was constantly seen in public with a different woman on his arm all the time. As for Philippe Morin, later that evening, he seemed pleased that Maxime and I were getting along.

In fact, I was quite attracted to Maxime, and Maxime seemed to be quite attracted to me. So much so that at one point – perhaps emboldened by the drinks he'd had, or else titillated by the presence of the young ladies Philippe had invited, who seemed quite accommodating, to say the least – he surreptitiously kissed me on the cheek. I don't mean to appear prudish, but I must say that I found him quite forward, and perfectly unbecoming. After all, that isn't the sort of behaviour one normally adopts with a perfect stranger. I said I was going out for a cigarette, and I asked him to come with me. As soon as we were outside, I got right to the point: "I want you to get something straight. I'm not 'Kevlar's little helper.' It's been great meeting you – you're very nice, and you're a good-looking guy and everything. But I'm not here doing Kevlar's bidding. That's not what's going on here."

"No, no," he said. "Don't take it that way. I wasn't think-ing that at all. Forgive me."

That threw a slight chill over the proceedings, but it quickly dissipated. After dinner, I accompanied Maxime back to his hotel, the W, on Victoria Square. He asked me to have one last drink with him at the bar, and I accepted. We exchanged phone numbers and email addresses, and then I went home. Aside from the little incident mentioned above I couldn't argue the fact that I was strongly attracted to him, and so was he to me. It wasn't love yet but I really hoped to see him again. The very next morning, he emailed me to say how much he'd enjoyed the evening, and to ask if I'd like to have dinner with him the next time he was in Montreal. When that time came, we went to Il Cortile, on Sherbrooke Street West, an upscale Italian restaurant with a courtyard terrace. It was a splendid evening in the month of May, the time of year when it finally starts to feel like summer in Montreal. It was warm, and it was great to be outside.

It was our first private meeting, the chance for us to get to know each other a little better. We talked in general terms about our respective backgrounds, our careers, the past. I told him that I had been married and divorced, and that one of my boyfriends had been involved with biker gangs, and had been murdered. It was very clear in my mind that if Maxime was really interested in me and if we were to have any future as a couple, he would need to know such things. And I certainly preferred that he learn them from me, not second-hand. It was also obvious to me that if ever I became his partner, I would surely be subjected to background checks. No one is going to make me believe that a federal cabinet minister's girlfriend, especially someone he has just met, would be able to attend official functions at 24 Sussex Drive and Rideau Hall, meet other ministers, the prime minister, the Governor General, and so forth, without a thorough investigation into her past having been conducted. If I'm wrong, then Canada's national security is truly in jeopardy. I refuse to believe that the state apparatus would be so incompetent, especially in my case – my name had been in the papers more than once, in stories about the Carcajou sting and Gilles's murder, and I had been mentioned in some magazine interviews that Stéphane Sirois had given.

What's more, that night when I confided those details of my past to Maxime, his reaction – or should I say virtual lack thereof – gave me the distinct impression that he already knew them. There were no "oohs" and "ahhs," not even so much as a raised eyebrow. No questions. He seemed only barely surprised. Say what you will, but not everybody can claim to have had a spouse who was murdered.

That said, we had a very pleasant evening together. After dinner, we went out to a disco, the Funky Town on Peel Street, where we had drinks and danced. Then we retired to his room at the Hôtel Germain, where Maxime usually stayed when he was in Montreal, and what was bound to happen happened.

It is not fair to say, however, that Maxime Bernier and I became a couple after that first night. We began seeing each other more or less regularly, when he came to Montreal on government business. He would call me, usually late at night, and his chauffeur would drop him off at my place in Laval and we would spend the night together. I was okay with this somewhat cumbersome arrangement for a while, but that didn't last. I was starting to get seriously attached to him and I wanted a stable relationship; at my age I had no time to waste on trivial puppy love. I didn't want to get hurt by continuing to have an intimate relationship with him if it was going nowhere. One day, we were talking on the phone and I said, "Listen, Max. The last two times we saw each other, we didn't even have dinner together. If a lover was all I was looking for, I could just find one who lives in the same city as me, who's more available and who doesn't take ten hours to call me back when I leave him a message. I'm just the girl you sleep with when you happen to be in Montreal. It's not enough."

"No, Julie, come on. Please don't take it that way. It's just that I have a lot of work," he said.

"I know lots of people who have a lot of work, people who own who knows how many different companies. They always return my calls on time. So you'd better think about what you really want, Max. The next time you call me, call me because you want to really spend time with me, not just sleep with me, okay? You're going to take me out to dinner, and you're going to treat me right. No more 'wham-bam, thank you ma'am.'"

I hung up, not at all sure whether I'd hear from him again, or how soon.

35

Commitment

*"I said yes, I would go out with him. And when I told him,
he simply said, 'Good. That's a good thing. It'll put a stop
to the rumours.'*

'What rumours?'

*'On the Hill, people have been whispering that I'm gay.
Now they'll see that I have a girlfriend, so they'll stop.'"*

As it turned out, it wasn't long before I did hear from
Maxime again; he called me just days later. He was back
in Montreal on government business. We went out for
dinner, and then spent the night together at the Hôtel Germain.

At this point we had been seeing each other for about a
month. The next morning at breakfast, he asked if I would be his
steady girlfriend. He quickly added that I should take my time to
think about it, because there was a condition. He explained that
given his status as a cabinet minister, if he "changed women as
often as he changed shirts," it would look bad.

"Even if things go sour between us, you would have to officially be my girlfriend for at least a year," he said.

I burst out laughing. I couldn't help it. I'd heard men profess
their love to me more romantically than that, to say the least.

It sounded like a business arrangement more than anything else, and I told him exactly that.

"I know that," he said. "I'm sorry, but what can I say? I'm a public figure. I have to take what comes with the territory."

"So you're saying that even if things don't work out and I can't stand to see your face in the morning, I'm still going to have to pretend to be your partner?"

"You got it. Look, if I start to be seen around town with one woman, I can't be seen a month later with another one, and another one the month after that. Why else do you think I've been single for so long?"

I could see the logic in his reasoning, and I could see why he had no choice but to set that condition. Although the proposal was not what I had hoped for, I really thought we had a very good chance to be happy. So I said, "Okay, but let's say things did get to that point, and I had to keep on being seen by your side in public and 'officially' be your girlfriend. You'd have to do your part to make the whole thing as pleasant as possible. You'd have to keep acting like my boyfriend as well."

"Sure, of course," he said. "No problem."

So I said yes, I would go out with him. And when I told him, he simply said, "Good. That's a good thing. It'll put a stop to the rumours."

"What rumours?"

"On the Hill, people have been whispering that I'm gay. Now they'll see that I have a girlfriend, so they'll stop."

"But why do people think that?" I asked.

"Because I haven't had a girlfriend for two years, and I'm friends with a cabinet minister who's openly gay. So some reporters figure I am, too."

And that was when Maxime and I officially became a couple. He soon introduced me to his two beautiful daughters,

Charlotte and Mégane, who at the time were aged eight and five, respectively. Things didn't go particularly well between them and me, which saddened me very much. It certainly didn't help that, for reasons unknown to me, their mother didn't at all approve of Maxime bringing the girls to my place. She told him they found the trip from their house in Westmount to Laval took a long time – even longer than driving out to the Beauce. (Taking into consideration that it takes forty-five minutes to fly to Quebec City, plus an hour's drive to get to the Beauce, this statement didn't make much sense.) Maxime showed very little backbone with his ex-wife, so his daughters' visits became more and more infrequent, and eventually I never saw them at all.

I remember one of the last times they came over – this was still in the summer of 2007 – Maxime went running in the morning with his eldest. When they came back, he said, "Charlotte asked me if you were used to children. If you'd ever had another boyfriend who had kids. So I told her she should ask you herself."

"Well, of course, I'll talk to her," I replied. "I'll tell her Gilles had a son, Pierre-Paul, that he had shared custody, and that for five years I practically raised him."

"Okay, but you're not going to tell her everything, right?"

"For God's sake, Max, what kind of person do you think I am?" I said.

"Well, what are you going to tell her, then?"

"I don't know. If she asks, I'll say Gilles died in a car accident or something. But I'm certainly not going to tell an eight-year old girl that my boyfriend was shot six times."

I don't understand why Maxime Bernier has repeatedly and publicly said that he was unaware of my past.

It was only after he was sworn in as minister of foreign affairs that Maxime and I started attending official functions together in his electoral riding of Beauce, where he went just about every weekend. But not long after we started going out together, I accompanied him to several private gatherings there. To me, someone who had spent all her life in the city or the suburbs, the Beauce was a completely new world, unlike any I had ever seen. Life there revolved around small, tight-knit communities – nothing like the large urban centres where relative anonymity is the norm.

The Beaucerons I met were, by and large, very down-to-earth, friendly, and kind people. They revered their Member of Parliament, but Maxime was fully conscious of the fact that his father, Gilles – who had represented the riding for years and had even won an election as an independent in 1993 – had paved the way for him. Gilles Bernier, whom I met after Maxime's swearing-in, remained extremely popular in the region. He struck me as a very friendly gentleman, close to the people in his community and very much committed to them. He had a lot of ambition for his son, which was normal. But at the same time, it seemed to me that he was Maxime's severest critic. Specifically, he told him he was neglecting his constituents, saying he didn't spend enough time in the riding, especially after he was named minister of foreign affairs. It seemed very difficult for him to understand that Maxime's duties as the country's top diplomat required him to spend a lot of time abroad, and he obviously couldn't be in three places at once.

It was in Quebec City, on the eve of one of our weekends in the Beauce, that I wore "The Dress" for the first time – the one that became ground zero for the eventual scandal and led more than one journalist to brand me as a "tart." It was a Friday in early August. Maxime had called and asked me to meet him late in the day in Quebec City, where he was due to have dinner with independent MP André Arthur. "Put on something evening-wear-ish," he said. I grabbed a taxi and rushed over to BCBG, a boutique at the corner of Saint-Catherine Street and de la Montagne. I bought that dress as well as a chocolate-brown pashmina shawl to cover my shoulders, and then immediately took the train to Quebec City. I disembarked at the station in Sainte-Foy, and Arthur's chauffeur was waiting to pick me up. He drove me straight to the Michelangelo restaurant, not far away, where we had dinner in a private room.

I had never met André Arthur, although I was aware of his reputation. I knew he was a very controversial radio host in Quebec City, and that he'd won a landslide victory in the federal riding of Portneuf, which was a fairly extraordinary achievement in itself. I also knew that, although he'd been elected as an independent, he was a strong Conservative sympathizer. He was very fond of Maxime in particular, and never missed an opportunity to say nice things about him on his radio show. Obviously, Maxime appreciated him a great deal, because he helped advance Maxime's political career. Arthur was giving him free advertising, and Maxime valued that assistance accordingly. After that night, in fact, Arthur announced on the air that the rumours about Maxime Bernier having a girlfriend were true, that she was a beautiful woman and that he'd been lucky enough to meet her.

The dinner was very pleasant. I found André Arthur to be a kind man, very cultivated, well-spoken, and with a great sense of humour. At the end of the meal, the owner of Michelangelo gave us a tour of the wine cellar, reputed to be one of the finest in Quebec City, and showed us a few rare bottles.

A few days later, Maxime and I flew to Aruba for our first holiday together. It was the first time we had the chance to really get to know each other and get closer. We had an amazing week, full of activities and evenings that always started with a romantic supper. Many times in our relationship, I held on to those wonderful memories to help me excuse certain ways Maxime behaved toward me. And because we had a long-distance relationship and we didn't see each other frequently, every time I would see him it was like our first date all over again. That is how I lasted six months before giving up on love with Max. After that, yes I wanted to keep my word, but I also had to get him out of my system. At the end of the day I am just a girl who met a guy.

36

The Dress

The swearing-in ceremony at Rideau Hall was scheduled for 10 a.m. on Tuesday, August 14. I had never attended that kind of event before, and I had no idea what the dress code was. So that was one of the first things I asked Maxime.

'I've been wondering what I should wear to this thing. What do you think, Max?'

'You remember that dress you wore to the dinner with André Arthur?' he said. 'That was a nice dress.'

'Mm, it was nice. But I'm not sure it would be appropriate . . .'

'Sure it would. Just put a jacket on over it. It'll be perfect.'

When we left for Aruba, in the second week of August, rumours were already swirling on Parliament Hill about a possible cabinet shuffle. Given the choice, Maxime would surely have preferred to keep the Industry portfolio. It was an important department; he handled interesting dossiers and he enjoyed a fair degree of independence in his decision making. We had only been away for a few days, however, when he got a call from the Prime Minister's Office confirming that he would be given a new portfolio.

He immediately grew very nervous. Plenty of pundits were speculating that he would be named minister of defence, and he was less than thrilled at the prospect. In fact, it terrified him. We talked about it at length. Just the thought of a move to Defence upset him a great deal. I remember telling him, at one point, "No, relax, Maxime. I wouldn't worry about it. You have no background in military affairs at all. You know what? I think you're going to be named foreign minister. It would be much more in line with your education and your experience."

He spent the next few days with his fingers crossed. Then, he finally got word that the prime minister had summoned him to 24 Sussex Drive at 2 p.m. on the Sunday prior to the cabinet shuffle announcement. That was the day we were supposed to fly back from Aruba, but the plane would have arrived too late, so Maxime booked a commercial flight on the Saturday so he could be back in Ottawa in time for the meeting. When I flew back on Sunday evening, I turned my cellphone on just before landing at Trudeau Airport; I was too impatient to see what the news was after his meeting with the PM. Maxime had sent me a short text message. Much to his surprise, he had indeed been given the Foreign Affairs job. "*Tu es une visionnaire* (You're a visionary)," he wrote.

The swearing-in ceremony at Rideau Hall was scheduled for 10 a.m. on Tuesday, August 14. I had never attended that kind of event before, and I had no idea what the dress code was. So that was one of the first things I asked Maxime.

"I've been wondering what I should wear to this thing. What do you think, Max?"

"You remember that dress you wore to the dinner with André Arthur?" he said. "That was a nice dress."

"Mm, it was nice. But I'm not sure it would be appropriate . . ."

"Sure it would. Just put a jacket on over it. It'll be perfect," he said.

The day before the swearing-in, I went to meet Maxime in Ottawa, at a restaurant in ByWard Market where he was having drinks with his senior political aides. There were about ten of us in all.

At one point, Deborah Sterling,* a staff member of Maxime's, asked me to step outside with her for a moment.

"So, what do I tell the press?" she asked me.

"What do you mean? About what?"

"Well, we want to know what to say. By tomorrow, the phone's going to be ringing off the hook with people wanting to know who you are."

"Tell them I'm his girlfriend," I said.

"Are you sure?" she asked

"Look, we talked about it, and it's not like I'm going to dump him in the next three months. You and his aides needn't worry," I said with a laugh.

That was the end of that conversation. Earlier, however, as I arrived at the restaurant and Maxime introduced me to everybody, I had sensed that Deborah didn't like me very much.

The next morning, Maxime's chauffeur picked us up at his apartment and drove us to Rideau Hall. My dress had just come back from the cleaners, and the static electricity was making it cling to my body. I remember we even stopped along

* Not her real name.

the way to buy some antistatic spray. Little did I know that was the least of the problems that dress was going to cause me.

I must admit that I have never truly understood the media frenzy that erupted around the dress that I wore the morning of the swearing-in ceremony. I'm quite willing to admit that it perhaps wasn't the most appropriate article of clothing for the occasion. But I clearly recall seeing women at that ceremony wearing outfits with far more plunging necklines than mine, which revealed the curve of their breasts. There were also many younger women whose dresses were literally skin-tight and, under normal circumstances, far more likely to inspire lustful thoughts than what I was wearing. But the press, in its infinite wisdom, decided to focus all its attention on me. Journalists move in mysterious ways, I guess – especially when reputations are at stake.

When we arrived at the ceremony, I was very nervous. It was the first time I had ever been to an event like that, and I really didn't know what to expect. When we stepped out of the limousine, of course, I was completely taken aback by the horde of press people waiting behind the barriers at Rideau Hall, the TV cameras, the barrage of still camera shutters, and the forest of microphones straining to pick up our every word, as dozens of voices rattled off questions all at the same time. They all blended into a dull roar, such that my ears couldn't distinguish any of them.

Once we got inside, though, everything proceeded in a much more calm and straightforward manner. Maxime joined his cabinet colleagues on one side of the room, while a protocol officer came up to me, asked for my name and that of the person I was accompanying, and led me to a seat. The ministers were sworn in, and then it was time for the cocktail reception hosted by the Governor General, Michaëlle Jean. We had the chance to exchange a few words, and I found her very likeable. She came over to Maxime to congratulate him, and we chatted briefly about her forthcoming trip to Australia. Maxime then introduced me to his cabinet colleagues and their spouses, as well as to other people in attendance at the ceremony.

Upon exiting from the Governor General's residence, we had to again negotiate the wall of journalists waiting outside. I remember one of them asking Maxime a ridiculously condescending question, implying that he'd never been anywhere outside the Beauce, and so now that he was foreign minister he'd be able to see the world.

"Yes, you're right. I've been waiting for this moment to be able to travel. I've never been on a plane in my life, you know," Maxime shot back sarcastically.

Then we climbed back into the limousine, a black Toyota hybrid. Within minutes, Maxime's parents, who had been watching the ceremony live on television, called him on his cellphone to congratulate him. His father said we looked like a pair of movie stars. Maxime passed me the phone and I chatted briefly with them; it was the first time I had ever spoken to either his mother or his father. They both said they were looking forward to meeting me. They seemed very friendly and warm.

By the time we left Rideau Hall it was nearly noon, and Maxime said he wanted to go and have a steak. He asked his chauffeur if he knew of a restaurant nearby that served them. The driver said our best bet would be Hy's Steakhouse, a place in downtown Ottawa that was a favourite with the political crowd. But Maxime said, "I'm going to call Deborah and see whether there's anything closer."

He reached her right away and asked her. She suggested we go to an Italian restaurant instead.

"Change of plans," Maxime said to the driver. "We're going for pasta."

I was flabbergasted.

"Maxime," I said, "for the past twenty minutes all you've been saying is how you're dying for a nice, juicy steak, and now, because Deborah tells you to go and have pasta, you change your mind. What's that about?"

In the end, we had steak.

Maxime was thrilled to have been appointed minister of foreign affairs, but his joy quickly turned to disillusionment when the Prime Minister's Office ordered him to dismiss Claudine Bernard,* a woman who occupied a key position in his office at Industry. He was very fond of her and wanted to bring her over to Foreign Affairs, but she was replaced by someone else. This decision caused quite a commotion among Maxime's cabinet staff, starting with Claudine herself, of course, who had no idea why this was being done to her. She had been a skilled and staunch ally of Maxime's, but she also had a reputation as someone who often stood up to the PMO. Maxime himself clearly didn't agree with the move, and it upset him a great deal as well. He admitted to me later that he and Claudine had cried together when they said their goodbyes.

I remember Maxime calling Claudine as soon as he was told of the decision. I also remember briefly telling her on the phone that day that I was sorry I hadn't had the chance to get to know her, and that I wished her good luck. Maxime warned me that his staffers would probably be extremely upset by the firing, and he quite naturally asked me not to express any opinion I

---

* Not her real name.

might have on the matter in front of them, which made sense to me.

Deborah Sterling in particular took the news very badly. She flew into a rage when she heard that Claudine Bernard had been let go. Maxime and I were in his office watching a newscast on TV when she burst in, ranting and raving, tears in her eyes.

"It's not right! They've got no business doing that!" she cried.

After haranguing Maxime for several minutes, she suddenly turned to me and asked, "What about you? What do you think of the fact that the PMO is getting rid of Claudine? Do you think that's acceptable?"

"I don't know, Deborah. I imagine the PMO had its reasons," I replied.

She grew even more furious, spun on her heels, and left the office, slamming the door behind her.

It didn't bode well for the future of our relationship.

37

"A Woman Thing"

"When he called . . . he was incensed. 'Guess what?' he said. 'There's a spouse program after all. There was a dinner tonight at the Sydney Opera House, and all the ministers arrived with their wives. There've been organized activities for spouses all week. You could have come. Deborah lied to me.'"

When Maxime was appointed to Foreign Affairs, among the influential people on his staff was Deborah Sterling, a young woman barely out of university. And Deborah Sterling's youth, no doubt, contributed to her being foolish enough to have to be replaced.

In the days following his appointment, Maxime prepared feverishly for his first trip overseas as Canada's minister of foreign affairs. He was due to attend the 19th Ministerial Meeting of the Asia-Pacific Economic Cooperation (APEC) forum in Sydney on September 5 and 6, 2007. I'd always dreamed of visiting Australia, and hoped I'd be able to accompany Maxime on the trip. But for partners to accompany delegates to this type of event, there has to be a spouse program arranged specially for the occasion. Maxime was told that, unfortunately, no spouse program had been planned for the APEC meeting, and thus I wouldn't be able to go with him. I decided to put a good face on things. I'd have to see the koalas some other time.

Maxime left for Australia. He phoned me every night, happily giving me news about the trip. But one night when he called, after he'd been there a few days already, he was incensed. "Guess what?" he said. "There's a spouse program after all. There was a dinner tonight at the Sydney Opera House, and all the ministers arrived with their wives. There've been organized activities for spouses all week. You could have come. Deborah lied to me."

It didn't stop there. A few days after returning from Australia, Maxime was scheduled to give his first speech in Canada as foreign minister, in Montreal. It was going to be a huge night for him, and he really wanted me to be there. Deborah told him that if I wanted to attend his speech, I was going to have to fork over $125 like any other paying guest. Maxime blew up. He went to see Clifford Dunn,* his chief of staff, and asked him to settle the matter. Clifford called the event organizers, who were well and truly insulted. "Who do you think we are?" they said. "Of course we can afford to pay for the minister's spouse's meal!"

Clifford went back to see Maxime and, referring to Deborah's shenanigans, said, "It must be a woman thing, because I don't understand."

Maxime's speech went over like a lead balloon. A group of people protesting the war in Afghanistan managed to get into the room, and they kept heckling and booing him. In a way, this was a blessing in disguise: Maxime had received the text of his speech at the last minute, and he'd only had time to read it

---

* Not his real name.

through once. So, although he stumbled several times in his delivery, no one really noticed because of the protestors' constant interruptions.

Needless to say, when we got back to his hotel room after the speech, Maxime was pretty wiped out. Even so, he agreed to meet with an old acquaintance – a former university colleague – who was defending some cause or other. He talked to the man for a few minutes, but he didn't feel like seeing anyone else after that. Deborah was also in the room, along with one of his advisers, James Smith.* Deborah went up to Maxime and said, "Listen, there's a reporter I know who wants a word with you, off the record. It'll only take five minutes." Maxime wouldn't hear of it. "No. Forget it," he said. "I can't take any more. We're done for today."

"No, no," she insisted. "It won't take long. It's off the record." Then she turned to me and said: "But we'd like you to leave the room."

"Excuse me?!" I burst out laughing.

"We'd like you to leave," she said again. "Interviews are none of your business."

She may have thought I could be summarily dismissed, but I happened to be the minister's spouse. I was getting awfully close to my boiling point. She was pushing me. And when I'm pushed, it's not long before I push back.

"First of all, Deborah," I told her, a forced smile on my lips, "we're going to get one thing straight. There's only one person in this room who's going to decide if I stay here or not, and that's my boyfriend. If something's likely to come up that's not for me to see or hear, that's his decision. I'm not about to take orders from one of his employees, understand? You know,

---

* Not his real name.

sometimes it's like you don't realize that that's all you are: an employee. You're not the minister, he is."

Maxime stood there, stuck between the proverbial rock and hard place, looking back and forth at Deborah and me. Finally he turned to her and said, "Why are you talking to her like that, Deborah? What's with the attitude?" But she stood up to him, with her usual arrogance, insisting that she was right, and once again decreeing that I should leave the room.

I looked at Maxime. He didn't say a word. By that point I was livid. Either I was going to slap the little bitch, or I was going to leave. I chose option two, but before withdrawing I looked Maxime straight in the eye and told him, quite frankly, "If you think I'm going to stand by while one of your employees insults me and throws me out of the room, well, you picked the wrong girl, Max. Since you obviously can't be a man about this, why don't you just stick with your dear Deborah? I think you make a great team. Goodbye!"

I strode to the hotel-room door, opened it, and walked out. I heard Maxime call after me, "No, Julie! Don't be like that!" He caught up to me beside the elevator and said, "Come back, Julie. The journalist is here; you can stay."

"I don't give a flying shit. Our deal was never that I would let myself be humiliated by a schoolgirl. I refuse to be made into a laughingstock, so get that through your head. If you don't have the balls to stand up and be the boss like you're supposed to, that's your problem, not mine," I said.

"Julie, come back to the room. Please. I'm going to sort this out."

"All right," I said. "But if you want me to go back, I have to talk to her. I'm only going to talk to her once, and she's going to have to understand."

We returned to the room. James Smith was still there. I said to him politely, "James, I'm sorry, but could you please excuse us for a moment? I need to speak to Maxime and Deborah."

He complied, leaving only the three of us in the room. I looked at Deborah and told her, as calmly as possible, "Would you please tell me what your problem is with me? It's just the three of us now. It's time to get it off your chest, all right? Before I met you, Maxime couldn't stop telling me what a great member of his staff you are, but he didn't warn me that you were going to give me such a hard time. It's obvious you have a problem with me. You engineered things so that I wouldn't go to Australia by lying to Maxime. Then, out of pure pettiness, you tried to make me pay for my ticket for tonight. And we all know very well you're trying to keep me from going on the next trip, to New York. Why this obsession?"

I mentioned that I had heard a rumour she was spreading around that I was badgering Maxime to let me go with him to New York, where he was due to attend the opening of the UN General Assembly in a few days. But in fact, it was Maxime who wanted me to accompany him. He'd persuaded me to rearrange my entire schedule – the trip was going to last a week, and I still had to earn a living, minister's spouse or not – and he kept insisting how important it was to him that I be by his side.

Maxime was behind me as I spoke to Deborah. Suddenly, she stared at him and said to me, "Oh, yeah? He asked you to go to New York with him, did he?"

Then I turned around to face Maxime and said, "Did you by any chance tell your staff that I've been begging you to take me with you to New York, when you're actually the one insisting that I go?"

"Of course not. What are you talking about?!" he said.

"Well, if it's not true, then why aren't you saying anything?"

"I don't know why she spread those rumours. I can't answer you. I don't know why she wants to stir up trouble between us."

Well, I knew. It was obvious. As plain as the nose on your face: she had a serious crush on him. I turned to Deborah and said, "There can't be two ways about it: either you're really sick, or you've crossed the line, past the point of no return."

Deborah picked up her things and left. When she was gone, I really let Maxime have it: "I cannot believe your complete lack of balls. What is this circus, exactly?"

The next day, back in Ottawa, he told Deborah straight out that he found her behaviour unacceptable. But he didn't go so far as to fire her. I warned him that I wasn't about to be humiliated at her hands again. I was also thinking of the bigger picture, not just the way she was treating me. "It doesn't make sense for you to keep her around," I said. "What's she going to do to you the next time? If she's got enough nerve to meddle in your private life, make you look like a liar, and manipulate you to serve her personal interests, who's to say she won't end up ruining your career, and you won't see it coming? That girl is bad news, Max. We're talking *Fatal Attraction* here."

Deborah was supposed to make the trip to New York, but instead her assistant, John Miller,* went. That night – this was near the end of the week – Maxime told Deborah that he was going to take the weekend to think about a solution.

The crisis ended up resolving itself, so to speak. On the weekend, Deborah had a serious behavioural problem. Maxime and I were already in New York, and Clifford Dunn went to him and said, "We have a situation." Then he told him what had happened to Deborah.

---

* Not his real name.

In the end, Clifford had to fly back to Ottawa, ask Deborah to surrender her diplomatic passport, and explain to her that she could no longer work in the minister's office.

38

New York, New York

"Our turn came. . . . There was the president of the United States, right in front of us. 'Hey, Maxime! How are you?' he exclaimed. Then he turned and looked at me and, still addressing Maxime, said, 'Well, well, well. Haven't you been keeping good company, now!'"

Maxime flew out of Quebec City early on the morning of Sunday, September 23, bound for New York and the opening of the 62nd United Nations General Assembly. There were actually two legs to the trip, one from September 23 to 28, and the other from October 1 to 2.

The UN trip was to be nothing less than his baptism by fire in the arena of international relations. His agenda was extremely full: he had decided to hold some thirty bilateral meetings with various counterparts during his time in New York, as well as attend the opening session of the General Assembly and take part in various other events.

I took my own flight from Montreal, late on Sunday afternoon, to go and meet Maxime. I was met at La Guardia by Carole Courchesne, the wife of Canada's ambassador, and the deputy permanent representative to the United Nations,

Henri-Paul Normandin. A host of activities had been organized for spouses all week long.

On the Tuesday, the wife of Ambassador John McNee, Canada's permanent representative to the United Nations, Susan, accompanied me to the residence of the UN secretary general, Ban Ki-moon, for tea with his wife, Yoo Soon-Taek, and the other spouses of the ministers attending the General Assembly opening. There were about fifty people there, and as I looked around the room I very quickly realized that people in diplomatic circles don't exactly have it tough. It was wall-to-wall bling, and designer labels abounded: Prada, Chanel, Gucci. I had stepped into another world, with its own codes, vocabulary, and modus operandi. Mrs. McNee, who was of course an habituée of such gatherings, was very kind to me, seeing as how I knew no one in the room and it was the first time I had been in such select international company. She did everything she could to put me at ease.

We had been at the reception for a few minutes when Mrs. McNee turned to strike up a conversation with an acquaintance, and I suddenly found myself looking straight at Laura Bush, who also happened to be alone at the same time. I went over and shook her hand and said, "Madam First Lady, it's an honour to meet you."

Mrs. McNee immediately came over and introduced us, and we got to talking. Mrs. Bush didn't in any way fit the image I had of her. I had imagined her to be fairly reserved, introverted, and aloof. On the contrary, she turned out to be quite friendly and talkative, with a good sense of humour. Among other things, she told me about a documentary she had recently seen about Afghanistan, made by a Canadian filmmaker, and she enthusiastically recommended it to me. Our conversation must have lasted longer than protocol would normally call for, because after ten minutes or so, several of the women present had formed a line and were waiting for the chance to shake the First Lady's hand. But there were also a few who seemed interested in meeting me. Mrs. McNee could barely contain her laughter, and whispered in my ear, "They really think you're well acquainted!"

Just a few hours later, George W. Bush himself hosted a reception for the world leaders and the rest of the diplomatic crème de la crème gathered in Manhattan. It was held at the famous Starlight Roof of the Waldorf-Astoria Hotel. After tea at the secretary general's residence, I went to meet Maxime at the Hotel Élysée, where we were staying, and from there we set out for the Waldorf. Getting there was no mean feat, however. In the United States, of course, security is a very serious matter, especially when it comes to an event bringing together so many heads of state and ministers in one place. Our driver had to park the limousine, adorned with the Canadian flag, two full blocks away from the Waldorf, outside a wide security perimeter that was closed to all motor vehicle traffic. From there, we proceeded on foot to the red-carpeted hotel entrance, stopping not once but twice to run a security gauntlet, where we had to declare our identities, display our UN-issued photo IDs, and walk through metal detectors. Then, as we entered the hotel, there were in the corridors on our way to the roof at least twenty pairs of Marines standing at full attention in their immaculate white uniforms and greeting each passing couple in turn: "Good evening, Sir. Good evening, Ma'am."

When we arrived at the Starlight Roof, I was dazzled by the huge space, which had been splendidly decorated for the occasion. At the back of the room was a huge banquet table brimming with all manner of dishes, while nearby, waiters in livery proffered their wine and champagne suggestions. The room, already packed with invitees, communicated with a small foyer where George W. Bush was receiving his guests. Beside him, an imposing photo studio – tripod, flash umbrellas, and spotlights – had been set up for guests who wanted to have their picture taken with him. And, of course, there was another metal detector. Not only that, but before being allowed to meet the president, all the women had to surrender their handbags to the security detail and then recover them immediately upon exiting the foyer; you don't go near the president with a handbag.

Our turn came. (Luckily Maxime had been told as we came into the room where to position ourselves to enter the foyer before an announcement was made. We were second or third in line.) There was the president of the United States, right in front of us. "Hey, Maxime! How are you?" he exclaimed. Then he turned and looked at me and, still addressing Maxime, said, "Well, well, well. Haven't you been keeping good company, now!" We both shook his hand, exchanged a few words with him, and posed for our photo. Then he said, "See you next time, Max. Take care. Lovely to meet you, Ms. Couillard." It all lasted only a few seconds.

One can say what one wishes about George W. Bush's political leanings. All the same, it is difficult to remain unmoved when you are standing face to face with the most powerful man on the planet. Given the importance of the office he held and despite the brevity of our meeting, I was pleasantly surprised by his friendly, easygoing, almost carefree attitude.

Two days later, I went with Maxime to a dinner reception at the University Club of New York for ministers and ambassadors of the member states of the Francophonie. We were guests of France's Minister of Foreign Affairs, Bernard Kouchner, whom I found charming, funny, and very much a ladies' man – all in all, very French. When we were introduced, he bent and kissed my hand in the purest Gallic tradition, and it went on forever.

What made the deepest impression on me that evening, however, was a conversation that Maxime and I had, before dinner, with an African woman. She was strikingly beautiful, and elegant. With controlled passion, and eloquence, she spoke to us about the difficult situation in her poverty-stricken country, and the potential solutions. For once in these diplomatic settings, I thought, here was a conversation about real things, not vague or disembodied principles. And yet, I also had the distinct feeling that Maxime wanted to be somewhere else. Was he bored? Or was it that he was new to this game, not yet proficient in the issues, and afraid of putting his foot in his mouth? I'm not quite sure. But I know I was somewhat put off by his attitude.

During our stay in New York City, I was not so much impressed by members of the international political elite as by people I met who were involved with various NGOs, or the UN's various humanitarian organizations. At one dinner, I met a woman – unfortunately, I no longer recall her name or that of the organization she worked for – whose job it was to assist in the relocation of child refugees from war-torn regions around the world, including Bosnia, Iraq, and Darfur. I met many people like her, unsung heroes and heroines who will never be awarded medals but who save lives, assuage misery, and really make a difference. It cheered me up, and went some way toward restoring my hope for the future of our world.

I also had some very pleasant meetings with other diplomats' spouses during that long week. For instance, I got on very well with the wife of Srgjan Kerim, president of the 62nd UN General Assembly. Mrs. Kerim is originally from Switzerland, but lived in Canada for many years (in Vancouver, Saskatchewan, Alberta, and Montreal) after first visiting as a student; she even has Canadian citizenship. She is an adorable, beautiful woman, tall and blonde, and very friendly.

Early on the Saturday morning, Maxime and I flew to Montreal together and then returned to New York City late in the day on Monday. The high point of Maxime's diplomatic mission, his address to the UN General Assembly, was to take place the next day, Tuesday, October 2. Naturally, he attached a great deal of importance to the speech, his first before such a prestigious international audience. And he was very nervous.

Among the many ludicrous things that have been written about me over the past few months is the idea that I regularly made changes to the texts of Maxime Bernier's speeches. This is completely untrue, of course. I never would have pretended that I was qualified to intervene in this aspect of his work. What I did do, however, on a few occasions, was help him fine-tune the *way* he delivered his speeches. The most exhausting experience I ever had in this regard was certainly the night of October 1 to 2, 2007.

Maxime was scheduled to give his address to the UN, the bulk of it in English, at ten o'clock the next morning. When he received an "almost final" draft the night before, his watch read 11:30. He was furious with the Foreign Affairs staff, who kept making modifications. Meanwhile, he was busy trying to make his own changes to the copy – specifically, to words that he had a hard time pronouncing in English, a language he doesn't speak very well. In particular, he kept having trouble with the word *world,* slurring the "l" and pronouncing it *word* – rather embarrassing for the country's top diplomat. I tried to calm him down. "Look, Maxime," I said. "You'd better learn the speech as written, otherwise you'll never be ready in time."

"That's it, take their side!" he protested.

"I'm not taking their side. I want you to be able to concentrate on the text, instead of waiting for more changes. At least you'll feel like you're prepared, and you won't be so stressed out."

But he was stressed, and it eventually reached such a pitch that he lost his cool, picked up an iron and threw it across the room. Then he calmed down and apologized, and we sat down to rehearse his speech. More than that, we proceeded with a bona fide phonetics lesson, during which I tried to teach him the correct pronunciation of certain English words. We paid particular attention to placing the stress on the proper syllables, and achieving the right tonalities and inflections. By the time we agreed that his delivery was polished enough, it was five in the morning. I hadn't changed a single word of his speech. But I had spent the night playing diction coach.

Maxime was very well prepared. His speech that morning was one of the finest I have ever heard him give. He had the right bearing, the right emotion, the right intensity. I was very proud of him. Our hard work the night before hadn't been in vain. Afterward, outside the General Assembly Hall, audience members lined up to shake his hand. There were representatives of the Canadian delegation to the United Nations, the Department of Foreign Affairs and International Trade, and the federal cabinet, as well as delegates from other countries. Ambassadors McNee and Normandin had me stand right at the front of the line of people who had come to greet Maxime. He came out, looking proud, standing tall as an oak, and walked straight toward the group, completely ignoring me.

"I'm sure he'll come back over here soon," Ambassador Normandin said, as if apologizing on Maxime's behalf. "He's still a bit nervous, surely."

Maxime was the star that day. He shook everybody's hand, and chatted with everybody: first the ambassadors, then his cabinet staff. Believe it or not, he never came over to see me. Not for a kiss; not to say thank you. I no longer existed in his world. I guess for some people, learning civility is a long process.

39

The Gospel According to Maxime

"Then he started going on about how an independent Quebec was inevitable, and that he was getting ready for it. 'What?' I said. 'Hold on, I'm not sure I heard you right. You, a federal minister?'

'Of course, it doesn't frighten me at all, that's where we're headed. It's obvious. And I have no problem with that. I'm ready. I'm expecting it.'

The people at the next table, who had recognized him and heard every word he'd just said, nearly choked on their soup."

Maxime Bernier saw himself more as a movie star than a politician. His haircut, his skin tone, the neatness of his necktie knot, and the pleats of his trousers – in other words, the image he projected – ranked much higher on his list of priorities than the fate of Darfur or the war in Iraq. He was more vain than ten Hollywood actors put together. Image was an obsession with him. I remember at one point, an Ottawa daily newspaper – or a magazine, I forget which – drew up a list of the best-dressed federal cabinet ministers. Peter MacKay topped the poll. Maxime was deeply upset by this. He went straight to his good friend Eric Boyko for fashion advice, which included wearing a pocket square and similar affectations. Boyko even gave him the address of his tailor.

All in all, Maxime was quite full of himself, and extremely superficial. He didn't seem particularly conscious of his responsibilities, and I never saw him deeply absorbed in his dossiers. He wasn't interested in such things; in fact, I think that apathy in large part explains the gaffes he committed during his time as minister of foreign affairs. He displayed a surprising degree of intellectual laziness for a politician in a position such as his. I have never claimed to be an expert on affairs of state, but it seems fairly obvious to me that to advance a political career, you cannot rely solely on good looks and popularity with your constituents. There are issues to be mastered if you want to be taken seriously – both within your department and in the settings that your duties require you to frequent.

There are people in politics – too few of them, mind you, but they do exist – whose positions are well founded. They ascribe to a vision, to a specific worldview, to clear-cut principles. Maxime Bernier was decidedly not one of them. To him, politics was essentially about charm. Countless times, I heard him say to me, just before an assembly, meeting, or other event, "It's going to be fine, just watch. I'm about to turn on the charm."

That need to charm, at all costs, often led him to not want to disappoint anyone. He would often leave people with the impression that perhaps he agreed with them rather than disagreeing to their face.

Strangely, though, Maxime's need to please often went hand-in-hand with a certain condescending, even contemptuous attitude toward people he spoke to, and even toward his supporters. There is one example that comes to mind that left a deep impression on me; in fact I was downright shocked by it. It happened one weekend at a corn roast in his home riding of Beauce. We were strolling together through the crowd and, in between doling out smiles, he casually leaned down to me and said some disparaging things about his electorate.

Whatever Maxime didn't like about these people, they were still the people who had elected him. It seems to me that, even with me, he should have been more circumspect, and kept his reflections to himself.

Ideologically, Maxime was a conservative, of course. But his beliefs were much more in keeping with those of the former Reform Party than those of the Progressive Conservatives, who had governed under Brian Mulroney. In fact, he was part of what many call the Libertarian wing of the Conservative Party. Libertarianism, which is much more firmly entrenched in the United States than in Canada, advocates the primacy of the individual over the community, reduction of the role of the state to its simplest expression, complete privatization of services (even health and education), and, economically, the preeminence of a free market, unfettered by any regulatory or other constraints. The main proponent of Libertarian ideology in Quebec is André Petit,* who was Maxime Bernier's speechwriter when he was industry minister. Whenever Petit sought to promote a political message, he did so through Maxime Bernier, who placed absolute trust in him and admired him immensely – so much so that when the PMO forced Petit from Maxime's staff after he was appointed minister of foreign affairs,

---

* Not his real name.

Maxime kept him on part-time by transferring his salary to his riding budget.

There was another public figure who was Maxime's role model in terms of political philosophy: Ron Paul, the Republican Congressman from Texas who ran as the Libertarian nominee in the 1988 U.S. presidential election and, most recently, failed in his bid to win the Republican Party nomination for the 2008 election. On two or three occasions, Maxime and I watched Web videos of Paul, who favours, among other things, the abolition of income taxes, the suppression of government subsidies, and the withdrawal of the United States from most international organizations, including the UN, NATO, and the World Trade Organization.

Maxime said things in private that were surprising, coming from the mouth of the minister of foreign affairs of a country so committed, as Canada is, to the fight against the Taliban in Afghanistan. For one thing, he was personally opposed to the posting of Canadian troops in that country. And, in his opinion, the war in Afghanistan had nothing to do with the struggle to replace dictatorship with democracy, nor was it a conflict pitting the values of freedom against those of religious fanaticism; in his mind, it was purely and simply a battle for control of the worldwide heroin trade. Nothing more. He said this to me on numerous occasions.

So it should come as no surprise that he regarded his trip to Afghanistan in the fall of 2007 (when he infamously handed out Jos. Louis cakes to Canadian soldiers) so frivolously. Maxime had told me that a Beauce-born soldier in the Royal 22ᵉ Régiment* had written to his riding office and asked

---

* The Quebec-based infantry regiment, nicknamed the "Van Doos," made up a significant portion of Canadian forces stationed in Afghanistan at that time.

whether some of the cream-filled chocolate cakes, which are made in Sainte-Marie de Beauce, could be sent to his unit. But there is a world of difference between shipping a crate of cakes to the front and handing them out one by one to soldiers, as Maxime did. He later explained to me that it hadn't been his idea; according to him, a young communications consultant from the PMO who had accompanied him to Afghanistan had thought of it, and told him, "You should pass the Jos. Louis round to the soldiers; it'll look good on TV."

Right. You're standing before a group of soldiers who every day run the risk of being caught in a firefight or blowing themselves up on a mine, and all you do to show them compassion and encouragement is hand out a bunch of chocolate cakes. It came off as a tacky backwoods politician move. You'd think he would have seen that one coming.

That wasn't Maxime's only faux pas in Afghanistan. When he publicly called for the governor of Kandahar province to be fired because he was corrupt, he didn't have the slightest inkling that he had put the Afghan government – not to mention the Canadian government – in a very uncomfortable position. Everyone knew that the governor in question (who in fact was eventually removed from power) was corrupt, but if the Afghan government had complied immediately with the request, it would have been an admission that Ottawa was telling Afghan officials what to do.

On environmental issues, Maxime's views didn't differ very much from the majority of people in his party and other members of the Harper government. He saw the whole thing as a huge joke. He claimed that problems like pollution, greenhouse gas emissions, and global warming were non-issues. "Global warming is happening by itself," he told me more than once. "It's not something we can change. It's just fear-mongering on the part of the tree-huggers."

But the one thing that completely flabbergasted me, and that I still can't quite believe, was the day he expressed his opinion on Quebec and the constitution. It was one of the last times we saw each other. We were sitting together one evening at Café Ferreira, in downtown Montreal. The tables there are so close to each other that even the most mildly curious of patrons can easily hear any number of conversations. Maxime had waved to and briefly chatted with a man he knew, who was seated four or five tables away.

Then he started going on about how an independent Quebec was inevitable, and that he was getting ready for it. "What?" I said. "Hold on, I'm not sure I heard you right. You, a federal minister?"

"Of course, it doesn't frighten me at all, that's where we're headed. It's obvious. And I have no problem with that. I'm ready. I'm expecting it."

The people at the next table, who had recognized him and heard every word he'd just said, nearly choked on their soup.

40

Maxime vs. Stephen

"Maxime had no trouble picturing himself as the next Conservative Party leader. At one point, he was even convinced that Stephen Harper would not survive a first term as prime minister, that there would be a leadership convention before the next election call, and that he would win it."

I saw Stephen Harper in person for the first time on September 25, 2007, in New York City, as he spoke to the Council on Foreign Relations in the form of an interview. I sat in the front row, at Maxime Bernier's side. As the prime minister took questions after his interview, I was enormously impressed by his presence, his calm demeanour, and his sense of humour in front of the journalists, some of whom were trying to embarrass him. Every answer he gave was to the point, and his style was relaxed. I was struck by his skilful handling of the situation, and I clearly recall thinking to myself: this man is in his element.

I next saw the prime minister a few weeks later during a private dinner at the residence of the chief government whip, Jay Hill, and his wife, Leah. It was the first time since the

Conservatives' election victory, almost two years earlier, that Mr. Harper had accepted an invitation to dine at the home of one of his MPs. Besides the Hills, the prime minister, and his wife, Laureen, the guests included the minister of human resources and social development, Monte Solberg, and his wife, Deb, along with Maxime and myself.

I was very nervous. It isn't every day you meet the prime minister of Canada, especially in such private circumstances, and I was somewhat overawed. Mr. Harper and his wife arrived last, and for some reason – I imagine it was because I was closest and our hosts were otherwise occupied when the doorbell rang – I was the one who opened the door. I simply said, "Good evening, Mr. Prime Minister. It's a pleasure to meet you." I paid Mrs. Harper the same courtesy, and we all proceeded to the dining room.

Apart from Maxime, the three MPs at the table had all begun their political careers in Western Canada, as members of the Reform Party, during the 1990s. As a result, much of the initial conversation centred on their recollections of election campaigns back then. I was having a hard time keeping track of all the references in the many anecdotes they shared, and I'm sure Maxime was in the same boat. At a certain point, Mr. Harper said, "Okay, I think it's time we changed the subject, otherwise Julie and Maxime are going to feel left out." He was very likeable that night. He didn't speak often, but when he did, it was always apropos. I realized that in private as well as in public, he was extremely calm and composed, and very funny as well.

His wife could be much more loquacious. At one point that evening, she monopolized the entire dinner-table conversation, and no one dared break in; you don't interrupt the prime minister's wife, after all. Mr. Harper, with respect, tact, and discretion

of a kind that I have only rarely seen in the men I have known –
including Maxime Bernier – steered the conversation onto
another topic, giving everyone a chance to participate again.

Throughout the meal – which, incidentally, was very pleasant indeed – Maxime was fairly inconspicuous. He had been far
more talkative before Mr. Harper arrived. After that, he was
very discreet, no doubt because he didn't speak English very
well (at least at the time), and also because he was somewhat
uncomfortable sitting at the same table as the prime minister,
whom he didn't hold in particularly high esteem.

When Maxime was alone with me, he was constantly bad-
mouthing his boss. He criticized Stephen Harper for a number
of things that very often had nothing to do with his abilities as
prime minister: he would say he was fat, had a beer belly, was
out of shape, and drank Pepsi all the time. "You should see it.
Every meeting, he's got these huge bottles of Pepsi. He eats junk
food. He doesn't even take care of himself. He should at least
drink water," he said once.

I remember saying to him, "Is he your wife, or your boss?
What do you care what he eats and drinks, or if he has a beer
belly? What difference does it make to you?" That was the
Maxime I knew: entirely focussed on looks. He thought Mr.
Harper was a poor dresser, had a bad haircut, and projected
an unkempt image. More than once I told him, "Maxime,
you've got to stop saying things like that. This man appointed
you. This man gave you an opportunity you weren't expecting,
to make something of yourself and enhance your resumé. And
all you do is trash him behind his back."

Not only did he make these disparaging remarks about the
prime minister, he also appeared to be openly contemptuous of
Mrs. Harper. At one point there was a function held in Ottawa,
in which the prime minister's wife took part, and to which

Maxime was invited. He showed up late, then ran straight into her. He didn't say "hello" or acknowledge her in the slightest. He turned his head as if nothing had happened, and completely ignored her. If he happened upon a dog, he probably would have acted the same way. I never understood how he could conduct himself so disgracefully – and toward the prime minister's wife, to boot! For a man with as much ambition as Maxime Bernier claimed to have, that was certainly not the right attitude to adopt. There are people in this world, though, who are so full of themselves that they forget what's good for them.

I've often heard it said that it is difficult for politicians to stay grounded and balanced. Maxime was a shining example of this shortcoming. So many people told him he was handsome, kind, intelligent, and all the rest that his head swelled – especially when he was appointed minister of foreign affairs. Maxime had no trouble picturing himself as the next Conservative Party leader. At one point, he was even convinced that Stephen Harper would not survive a first term as prime minister, that there would be a leadership convention before the next election call, and that he would win it. He calmed down a bit after the Harper government enacted the law establishing fixed election dates. But he still thought that would only delay the inevitable: he would one day win the leadership of the Conservative Party of Canada. He pointed to the fact that, traditionally, Canada's two major political parties have always alternated between anglophone and francophone leaders, and he claimed he had started building a power base among party movers and shakers – particularly those who shared his libertarian leanings.

Although he was waging a campaign against Stephen Harper silently, conflict was more open with the Prime Minister's Office. Maxime was on very bad terms with influential people on

Harper's staff, notably Paul Foster* and even more so Mary Gable.† He called them control freaks – which is perhaps not inaccurate – and said they were constantly out to stop him from getting too much media attention. After he was named foreign minister, for example, he was no longer given as much latitude in public as when he had held the Industry portfolio. He was no longer allowed to personalize his speeches. He had to read them as written, and this infuriated him on a regular basis.

In addition, Maxime – like all other ministers in the Harper government, incidentally – was supposed to obtain authorization from Mary Gable before agreeing to any national media interview. Maxime disliked her. On one occasion, he said she had a crush on him and had decided to make his life difficult because he'd never taken her to bed. That was typical Maxime: he thought every woman on the planet wanted to sleep with him. One day – we were no longer a couple by this time, but were still keeping up appearances – he even asked me if I had any objection to his going out for a drink with Ms. Gable to try and patch things up. My sarcastic reply: "No problem! If you think it'll help your career, Max my dear, don't be shy on my account. If you think your stomach can handle it, go for it."

He faced an uphill battle, though. More than once he'd gone ahead and given interviews without the PMO's say-so. Maxime liked journalists a lot. He saw them as a means to advance his career: interviews were like free advertising. If a reporter was critical of him in an article, he'd invite him or her to lunch – usually without the PMO knowing about it – and go into charm mode. Once, in early 2008, we were in Ottawa for an annual awards ceremony called Politics and Pen, the very same event

---

* Not his real name.

† Not her real name.

where Maxime treated the prime minister's wife like she was dirt. Mary Gable had found out that Maxime had been to lunch with Bob Fife, the CTV Ottawa bureau chief, without seeking her authorization, and she had emailed him a reprimand. Maxime decided to have a bit of fun with that. He ran into Fife at Politics and Pen, showed him the message from Mary Gable on his BlackBerry, and offered to forward him a copy. Luckily for Maxime, all this was going on under the watchful eye of another guest at the event, someone who had once been on Prime Minister Brian Mulroney's staff. When he realized that Maxime was about to commit a blunder of monumental proportions, he went over to him and said, "Maxime, you can't do that."

"Sure I can. Don't worry. There's no problem."

"Maxime, I'm telling you, you can't do that."

Then, as Maxime's finger was poised to press the "forward" button on his BlackBerry, the third man laid his hand on Maxime's arm and looked at him, as if to say, "You asshole, don't you realize how much shit you're going to find yourself in if you do that?" Finally, Maxime relented. And the worst thing about that episode was that he was perfectly sober at the time. It wasn't alcohol that had influenced his actions, it was simply lack of judgment.

What Maxime didn't seem to realize was that in his defiance of the PMO, and in keeping up a rivalry with Mr. Harper, he was turning plenty of people against him – and very probably raising the ire of the prime minister himself. Several times, I urged him to find another way, and to try to get into his leader's good graces. "You should quit fighting with the PMO and get some face time with Stephen Harper," I said. "Show him that you're a good servant, and offer him your sincere allegiance. Take what he can give you in terms of experience. Learn your craft. That's how to get ahead in politics." But he was too headstrong. He told me Mr. Harper was impossible to talk to, that he was like some dictator who wanted to control everything.

At any rate, I honestly feel that by that point, after his repeated attacks on the PMO staff, it was too late to try to make amends.

Paris

*"So I headed for the hallway leading to the washroom,
and what should I see but Maxime with his arms around
Suzanne, who was clearly trying to discreetly wrest herself
from his embrace without causing too much of a fuss.
She saw me out of the corner of her eye before Maxime
noticed me, and she managed to break free, at the same
time exclaiming, 'Oh! Julie!'*

*'Excuse me,' I said. 'The last thing I want to do is
intrude. I'm just on my way to the washroom; I'll only be
a minute or two.'"*

To say Maxime Bernier was frivolous in matters of the
heart is the understatement of the century. He was the
most rabid skirt chaser I've ever known. There are
people like that, who have a pathological need to seduce in
order to achieve self-affirmation. Was it vanity? Chronic insecurity? I can't say. But one thing is certain: being with a man
like that was a roller-coaster ride, and didn't exactly do
wonders for my self-esteem. He literally jumped at anything
that moved, with no self-control. I often thought to myself,

This guy's brain is swimming in testosterone. And it wasn't just harmless flirting. He went all the way.

I remember once going to see him at his place in Ottawa. He had returned from a long trip a few days earlier, and we hadn't seen each other for about three weeks. As I walked through the door, I nearly gagged; there was a strong smell of incense cloaking the apartment. "Ah, so you met some girl who likes incense, did you?" I said sarcastically. "'Cause you're not about to make me believe you've taken up meditating after work."

"Come on! I don't know what you're talking about," he said.

"Look, Max. Do you think I'm an idiot? You're a guy. We haven't seen each other for three weeks. You were horny and you couldn't take it anymore."

Finally, he confessed. "Okay, it's true. It was a girl I know. She called me at three in the morning. She'd just come out of a bar and she was drunk . . ."

In other words, the poor man had sacrificed himself to help a soul in distress.

It wasn't the first time he'd cheated on me. (And I have since learned that while he was with me, he was also sleeping with another woman, an Ottawa journalist, on a regular basis.) But this time his infidelity left a more bitter taste in my mouth, because he hadn't even bothered to try and hide the evidence. My misfortunes, however, were just beginning.

In late 2007 – this would have been in November – Maxime had a stopover in Paris on the way to a diplomatic mission in Asia. I flew from Montreal to visit him there. I had always wanted to see Paris, as I've always loved Old Europe, with its cobblestones, fabulous architecture, and lifestyles so different from what we're used to in North America. My flight arrived in the afternoon, and a driver from the Canadian Embassy in

Paris picked me up at the airport and took me to the hotel. A little while later, the wife of Ambassador Marc Lortie stopped by to say hello.

That evening, Maxime and I were invited to dinner at Ambassador Lortie's residence. The other guests were all very *simpatico*, sophisticated folk: a member of Maxime's staff, Clifford Dunn; one of his advisers, James Smith; and a young woman whose name I forget who was also a member of Maxime's staff. There was also a couple, Charles and Suzanne,* who were originally from Quebec and had recently settled in Europe. Charles was a specialist in international business development, and represented a major Canadian law firm. His wife, as it turned out, was someone Maxime had known for some time. In fact, as I would learn later, there was more to it than that – she was an old flame of his. They recognized each other while everyone was having drinks, in the parlour next to the dining room. "Suzanne! Hi! How are you? What are you doing here?" he exclaimed.

"I'm doing great," she said. "My husband was transferred to Paris and we're living here now."

"You're as lovely as ever," he said.

They kissed each other on both cheeks, as is customary between longtime acquaintances. Maxime seemed quite flustered – excited, even. He couldn't stop telling this Suzanne how beautiful she was. He was really overdoing it – so much so that I could plainly see it was making her uncomfortable. Finally, everyone finished their drinks, filed into the next room, and sat down to eat.

Just before dinner was served, Ambassador Lortie stood and

---

* Not their real names.

gave a little speech welcoming the minister of foreign affairs – it was off the cuff, but concise, congenial, to the point, and had just a touch of humour. I could see he was a professional, with a lot of class.

Then Maxime got up to thank him. Some Foreign Affairs staffers had provided him with speaking notes ahead of the dinner, but in the car on the way over to the ambassador's residence, he had emphatically torn them up and muttered, "*Tabarnak!* As if I don't know how to say hello and thank everybody for having invited me. They really take me for a moron!"

Well, that night, Maxime proved them right – in spades. He was pathetic. During his "dissertation," he must have said the word *merci* two dozen times, and he kept repeating the same hackneyed expressions. I have seldom heard someone deploy such a meagre vocabulary. To top it all off, he made a Freudian slip (although, come to think of it, perhaps it wasn't entirely unintentional). Instead of thanking the ambassador on behalf of the government of Canada, he said the government of Quebec. I felt like screaming at him to sit down and shut up.

Maxime and I had worked out a code that we used in such situations. If I put my hand up and touched my right ear, it meant: "Maxime, you're rambling on. Time to wrap it up!" That night – I have no idea whether it was on purpose – he never saw the signal. There was a palpable unease around the table.

In accordance with protocol, Mrs. Lortie was seated to Maxime's right, and I was to the ambassador's right, with Suzanne's husband, Charles, to my right. We chatted at length about his work, which seemed quite similar to mine (but his was at the international level), insofar as his job was to be the go-between for business people who wanted to get certain projects rolling. He spent a lot of time in Africa and Asia, in particular. We got along well, and exchanged business cards.

After the meal, everyone retired to the parlour for coffee and liqueurs. I was chatting with Mrs. Lortie, when I heard my cretin of a boyfriend call me from the other side of the room, "Julie, c'mere!" It was like he was calling his pet dog in an alleyway. I thought I would die of shame. I motioned for him to wait a bit, but he insisted. "C'mere, Julie! I need to talk to you."

Mrs. Lortie jokingly whispered in my ear, "I think somebody's calling you."

I excused myself – as much for having to interrupt our conversation as to apologize for Maxime's discourteousness – and, fuming, strode across the room to where Maxime was talking to Suzanne and Charles. Gesturing to the latter, he said, "Julie, you've got to talk to Charles. He's a consultant and he does pretty much the same kind of work as you, only internationally."

"Uh, Maxime? I've just spent an hour and a half at the dinner table with him. We had a little time to compare notes on our jobs; imagine! I have his business card."

Seeing that I wasn't exactly in the best of moods, Suzanne and Charles retreated to a corner of the room, so they wouldn't have to hear what I had to say to Maxime. "Don't you *ever* call me from across a room like that again, understand?" I hissed. A sheepish face was the only apology forthcoming, and that was the end of that.

Whenever he saw Maxime being rude to me in that way, and he knew that I was angry, Clifford Dunn would do what he could to distract me and take the pressure off. He did the same thing that night in Paris. He came over to me and made small talk, and a bit later Charles joined us. Eventually Clifford said to me, "I'm going outside for a smoke. You coming?"

"Okay. Just give me a couple of minutes. I'm going to use the washroom," I said.

So I headed for the hallway leading to the washroom, and what should I see but Maxime with his arms around Suzanne, who was clearly trying to discreetly wrest herself from his embrace without causing too much of a fuss. She saw me out of the corner of her eye before Maxime noticed me, and she managed to break free, at the same time exclaiming, "Oh! Julie!"

"Excuse me," I said. "The last thing I want to do is intrude. I'm just on my way to the washroom. I'll only be a minute or two."

I didn't make a scene. I certainly wasn't about to humiliate myself by making a spectacle in front of everybody – and in the home of a Canadian ambassador, at that. At any rate, it was becoming quite clear that if Maxime wasn't even bothering to conduct his little affairs in secret any longer, it was because he had stopped caring about me. I soon got that message.

I realized that, basically, what I had thought was a need to charm others – fairly common in a certain type of man but usually harmless – was in fact a sort of uncontrollable illness with Maxime. And now I saw how, even in the course of his official ministerial functions, in a Canadian diplomat's residence, he wasn't able to restrain himself.

Maxime boarded a plane the next day, in the late afternoon, bound for Laos. As for me, I stayed in Paris for a few days before leaving for Dubai and Abu Dhabi, on private business.

Suzanne seemed genuinely ill at ease about what had happened and, since my boyfriend's libidinous ways had now become fully obvious to me, I was sure that when she had found herself in Maxime's arms, it was against her will. When we said our goodbyes that night, she invited me to have dinner with her and Charles, knowing that I would be spending a few more days in Paris, alone. I was delighted to see the two of them again. They have an adorable little girl, and seemed to me to be a stable, happy couple. The same could hardly be said of my relationship with Maxime.

After the Paris episode, I decided I had given enough. Maxime had simply gone too far. A few weeks later, around December 15, with the holidays fast approaching, I put an end to our liaison. "It's over," I told Maxime. "I won't be coming to your place. I won't be visiting your family. I'll keep my promise, and play the game in public for a few more months, but I won't keep up this charade in front of your parents, your daughters, and your family over Christmas. I'm not interested."

From that moment on, I would be nothing more than Maxime Bernier's "official" girlfriend – his arm candy to keep the rumour mongers at bay.

42

Call for Tenders

"I never asked Maxime for help with regard to Kevlar's plans for the Quebec City federal building tender. I didn't expect anything from him. In fact, I hoped he wouldn't get involved – that he wouldn't try to throw a wrench into the works."

When I met Maxime Bernier in May 2007, I had a job, as well as several clients for whom I was engaged in business development, and I was still working as a real estate agent. I wasn't about to suddenly quit earning a living just because I was going out with a cabinet minister. At any rate, he didn't have the means to support me, and even if he had, I wouldn't have been interested. I have never depended on anyone but myself for support, and I would never have it any other way. In other words, in between the assorted tasks and frequent travel – to Ottawa and elsewhere – that my role as a minister's partner required, I kept on working to earn my keep, just like anybody else.

After the short visit to Paris that I described in the previous chapter, I flew to Dubai and Abu Dhabi in the United Arab Emirates. I was headed there on a one-week trade mission that

I had organized, with support from Export Development Canada, on behalf of clients working in the fields of commercial and industrial construction. More precisely, my clients were two companies that had formed a consortium with a view to exploring the development potential for sports complexes in the Emirates.

The trip was quite challenging. We took part in something like thirty-five separate meetings with promoters, investors, and executives of companies both private and public. Our trade mission coincided with the week-long Big 5 Show, the biggest construction trade show in the entire Persian Gulf region. We toured several work sites and looked into all kinds of projects in various phases of completion. My clients and I discovered an area of the world experiencing amazing economic growth – a staggeringly rich region enjoying a construction boom like nothing I had ever seen elsewhere, on a scale that was difficult to fathom on our shores. We saw building sites employing a thousand workers in the middle of the desert. In short, it was an exhausting but very instructive trip.

It concluded on a sour note, however: the morning I was due to fly back to Montreal, I woke up with a fever of 103°F. I'd caught some kind of bug, and was in a considerably weakened state. I'd never felt so rotten in my entire life. I felt like I was dying. Worse, I had an eighteen-hour flight to look forward to. I took a lot of ribbing from my travelling companions, who said I'd know what a "real man's flu" felt like. But they'd contracted the same virus, and two days later, after they'd returned to Montreal, they were just as sick as I was. I was laid up for a good week, and I even had to decline an invite from Laureen Harper to visit 24 Sussex Drive with other cabinet ministers' partners. A few days later, though, on December 10, I was well enough to resume my hostess role, as Maxime, in his capacity as foreign minister, welcomed the entire Canadian diplomatic corps for a Christmas reception at the Museum of Civilization just outside Ottawa.

The litany of absurdities that has been written about me since May 2008 includes the accusation that I was guilty of influence peddling – specifically, that I used my connection with Maxime Bernier to help my client, Kevlar, in the matter of the land contract for a federal office building in Quebec City. The truth is an entirely different story, and it is high time I revealed it.

I never asked Maxime for help with regard to Kevlar's plans for the Quebec City federal building tender. I didn't expect anything from him. In fact, I hoped he wouldn't get involved – that he wouldn't try to throw a wrench into the works. As I have said, on the evening of our first meeting in Montreal in May 2007, Maxime was aware that Kevlar was one of my principal clients. After that, it wasn't long before he also knew that I was representing Kevlar in the matter of that major call for tenders in Quebec City; what's more, he was made aware of the details of the project, as well as the clauses of the contract binding me to Kevlar in that project.

It was in Montreal in the summer of 2007, at the end of an evening during which a fair amount of alcohol had been consumed, when he asked me straight out, "So what's this deal you're working on with Kevlar that's related to the government?" I explained the complex project to him in detail, including its objectives, how far along it was, and my role in it as Kevlar's representative. He also asked me about the nature of the contract I'd signed with Kevlar, and specifically about the amount of the commission to which I was entitled if Kevlar's land was selected.

"Your job pays pretty good money," he concluded, somewhat surprised.

"Maybe," I said, "but it's nowhere near a done deal. We're not the only ones bidding, you know. Everybody's after that contract."

Confiding in Maxime like that may have been a serious mistake on my part, because from that moment on, it would seem that he did everything in his power to keep Kevlar out of the call for tenders process that was then underway. Maxime sat on the Treasury Board, and in that capacity, he had a say in the government's decision as to whether to approve the budget already earmarked for the project and to agree to the RFP process, per the parameters established by Public Works and Government Services Canada, or to modify those parameters and start the tendering process over from scratch. The government chose the latter option. The criteria for the call for tenders were redrawn, forcing all the companies in the running – not just Kevlar – to go back to the drawing board, and in the process waste precious time and lose all the money they had already invested in their bids. In fact, the criteria became so convoluted, and the required bid amounts so high, that even companies on the firmest of financial footings pulled out of the competition.

I quickly learned, from a reliable source, that Maxime Bernier may have played a crucial role in that government decision, the practical outcome of which was to considerably lower Kevlar's chances of being awarded the tender, and in turn wipe out any chance I had of earning a generous commission.

In spite of this, I tried to protect Maxime vis-à-vis the people at Kevlar: I neglected to tell them the role he may have played in that decision. But I was furious with him because everything led me to believe that he would knowingly do me harm, and would even use my private admissions to him to force my clients out of a competition they had an excellent chance of winning – not because of political pressure but solely on the merits of their proposal. When he is lying, Maxime tends to clear his throat and enunciate more clearly. That's what he did when I confronted him about this. "Ahem! Ahem! Ahem! Come on. I don't know what you're talking about," he pleaded.

"Don't play games with me, Maxime," I said. "You know very well what I'm talking about. I know what you said in that meeting, word for word."

He soon spilled the beans: "Look, it's because if ever word got out that you have a client who's bidding on a federal government contract, it could be bad for my career."

"I was working on this deal before I met you," I said. "It has nothing to do with you! I'm a realtor. I'm in the business – it's my job. It's perfectly normal for me to be involved in real estate projects."

"Yeah, but you know how journalists are . . ."

"Well, in that case, it was up to you to tell me in the first place. You knew what I did for a living. Why didn't you tell me that going out with you would disqualify me from representing clients on government projects? What was stopping you from telling me that?" That was the first but not the last time that he hurt my career to protect his own.

That is the real story behind the allegations of influence peddling levelled against me without a shred of evidence to back them up. The truth is that Maxime Bernier not only didn't lift a finger to help me, he actually may have put his fist on the table to hinder me. Worst of all, the last time I ever went out with him in public, at a thousand-dollar-a-person cocktail fundraiser in Montreal attended by Kevlar's top executives, he had the nerve to ask Philippe Morin, "So, Philippe, how's that Quebec City deal going?"

"Ah! It's going round in circles," Morin said. "They're making me spend all kinds of money and it's not going anywhere. I've never seen a government deal that was so complicated."

"It's dragging on, huh? Tell you what, I'm going to check into that for you. I'm going to see if there's anything I can do about it."

As I explained above, it had already been quite some time since Maxime may have done something about it.

43

The "Forgotten" Documents

"Just before leaving – he often did this – Maxime opened his attaché case and pulled out a bunch of documents and other papers. I was sitting in the living room, not really paying attention to what he was doing. He dumped the stack of papers on the kitchen counter and asked, 'Could you put all this in the garbage for me?'

'Okay,' I said.

Then he took two steps toward me and added, 'But you know, I'd rather you waited until garbage day to do it. After all, they are confidential documents . . . '"

From mid-December 2007 onward, though I was no longer his girlfriend, I continued playing my official role as Maxime Bernier's partner. I had made that commitment at the start of our relationship, and I intended to keep my word. From that point on, I no longer accompanied him on any foreign trips, but I did attend a number of official functions in Canada, occasionally in his home riding but mostly in Ottawa.

I recall that we took a few commercial flights together, and every time, I simply could not believe how strict airport security measures were for Canadian government ministers, even worse than for ordinary citizens, because we weren't just searched sometimes but rather every time. Maxime even complained about it happening when we weren't travelling together. I still can't get over it. I have travelled a lot, in Canada as well as abroad, and I have never been subjected to such thorough searches as when I flew in Maxime Bernier's company. He had to go along with this ridiculous circus every time, and submit to a full search. After all, if one believes that ministers of the Crown and people travelling with them are potential terrorists and constitute a threat to air safety, who in this country can one trust? The security officers would make me take off my coat and jacket; they would go through my handbag and wallet; we had to empty our pockets, of course; and I had to take off my boots in winter, or my shoes, so they could pass the metal detector under my feet. The same went for Maxime, who had to remove his shoes and even his belt. The guards seemed to get quite a kick out of wielding a little power over a cabinet minister. Maxime told me that he had raised the issue one day at a cabinet meeting, and the feeling was that citizens would be extremely insulted if they were to learn that any exceptions were granted to their duly elected representatives. What a country . . .

About a month before our last meeting, Maxime and I were in bed – for, although we had broken up, we still occasionally slept together – and he asked me, "How would you feel about working as an Immigration and Refugee Board commissioner?"

Puzzled, I didn't say anything.

"At least you'd be able to count on a stable salary for a few years."

Maxime knew that, possibly thanks to his kind work, there was no longer much chance of me ever seeing a commission from Kevlar, and I suppose he felt a bit guilty about that. So he was offering me an IRB position, which is generally accompanied by a three-year contract and is always awarded to friends of the party in power, or through them.

"Okay, and what exactly does an Immigration and Refugee Board commissioner do?" I asked.

"Well, it's kind of like a judge. You listen to immigrants and refugees who want to enter the country and you decide whether they have what it takes. I think you'd be good at it."

I was tempted. The position would involve long hours, but the pay would be good, and I thought the experience would be interesting. He told me to fill out an application form and recommended that I purchase a copy of the annotated version of the *Immigration and Refugee Protection Act* so that I could read up on how the whole process worked – which I did. Then he entrusted the file to his colleague Diane Finlay, the minister of citizenship and immigration. I considered the possibility very seriously, and I was even fairly enthusiastic about it.

A few weeks later – the last time we saw each other, in fact – Maxime said to me, "*Ah! toi, là, ma grande krisse . . .*"*

That was the "affectionate" nickname he sometimes called me by.

"What?" I replied. "What's wrong?"

"Well, I've been meaning to tell you that I think it would be best if we no longer saw each other in public."

"How come?"

---

* An approximate rendering in English might be "Aw, you, my big tall babe," but it is virtually impossible to convey the flavour of the Québécois expression.

"Well, you know, you're applying for a government position. If we're seen together, people will talk. We'd be better off not seeing each other. But looking at you now, you're so damn gorgeous, it's making things pretty difficult!" he said.

I told him that as far as I was concerned, our agreement had pretty much run its course anyway.

The last time I was seen in a more-or-less public setting with Maxime Bernier was April 18, 2008. It was at the cocktail fundraiser to which I referred in the previous chapter, held in the offices of the company Pomerleau in Old Montreal. Besides Maxime and me, there were ten people there, and each had paid one thousand dollars for the privilege of meeting the minister. They included Philippe Morin and René Bellerive of Kevlar, along with Eric Boyko.

After the cocktail party, Maxime and I went to have dinner at Ferreira Café – where he spoke about Quebec independence – and then we went back to my place to spend the night.

The next morning was a Friday, and the House was not sitting. Maxime had slept in a bit, and he was getting ready to go to Westmount to pick up his daughters and take them, if I recall correctly, to a birthday party at his brother's place on the South Shore. By the time he was ready to leave, it must have been about ten o'clock.

Just before leaving – he often did this – Maxime opened his attaché case and pulled out a bunch of documents and other papers. I was sitting in the living room, not really paying attention to what he was doing. He dumped the stack of papers on the kitchen counter and asked, "Could you put all this in the garbage for me?"

"Okay," I said.

Then he took two steps toward me and added, "But you know, I'd rather you waited until garbage day to do it. After all, they *are* confidential documents . . ."

That blend of vanity and flippancy was just like the Maxime I knew. It was as if he had said to me, "Look at me, I'm a minister of the Crown. I'm somebody incredibly important walking around with ultra-confidential documents in his brief-case, but I'm above all that. You see what I'm doing with them?" It wasn't the first time he'd left documents at my house like that, for me to dispose of them. It had happened maybe two or three times before.

I must explain that Maxime Bernier was not exactly a whiz when it came to information technology. He had his BlackBerry, of course, which he could use to make phone calls and to send and receive email. But he didn't own a laptop, which meant he carried a lot of printed documents around in his attaché case, which inevitably would wind up being too full. My house had become a second office for him. When he was at my place, he would ask me to do his secretarial work from my computer. People in his office, the Department of Foreign Affairs, regularly communicated with him using my personal email address. Countless documents he carried around in his attaché case had been printed out on my own printer, forty and fifty pages at a time. He had briefings, analyses, and speeches sent directly to my computer, which was no more secure than that of any ordinary citizen. He received them all as if they were grocery lists. Looking back on it now, I can't help but smile when I think that, in the eyes of some observers, I supposedly constituted a threat to national security and state secrets! I could have wallpapered my house in confidential documents. Mind you, it would have lacked a certain aesthetic appeal . . .

Consequently, on April 19, 2008, when Maxime Bernier left those documents in my house and asked me to throw them in the garbage, I didn't pay any more attention to his request than usual. When someone tells you, "Put this in the garbage," the message is fairly clear: it can't be all that important.

As almost anyone who lives alone can attest, a kitchen counter is often a makeshift filing station, where all kinds of papers pile up: newspapers, bills, flyers, and who knows what. For two weeks following that morning, I never gave another thought to those documents sitting on my counter. When Maxime left them there, it was a Friday morning, and the next garbage pickup wasn't until the following Friday. In the meantime, other papers piled up on top of them, and I forgot all about them. But I was soon to be reminded of their existence in quite brutal fashion.

44

Panic

"I was immediately gripped by panic. I'm no expert in international affairs. I didn't know what was in those documents and I didn't want to know. But to my mind, they were red-hot. I was sure they contained explosive information about countries that take their security very seriously indeed. I thought of the CIA. *I thought of the Mossad. And at that moment, I started fearing for my life."*

Ten days or so after he'd left the documents in my home, Maxime called me. "Julie," he said, "I just got a call from Paul Foster. He says a reporter from the *Globe and Mail* called him, alleging that you have past ties to people in organized crime."

"So what did you tell him?" I asked.

"Well, I denied it. I said I knew nothing about it."

Then, after a moment's silence, Maxime added, "I have a pretty good idea where that came from."

"Me too," I said. "But I'd still like to hear it from you."

"I'd say it came from Caroline," he said.

Caroline was Maxime's ex-wife. Among other things, Caroline felt that I wasn't worthy of being a minister's partner. Maxime was convinced that she was the one who had started the ball rolling by leaking information about my past to reporters.

In fact, rumours had been going around Parliament Hill for a few weeks already. This was confirmed to me by Claude Poirier, whom I called immediately after I got off the phone with Maxime.

"I'm glad you called," he said right away. "I haven't said anything to you because I didn't want to upset you, but I've had three calls from *Globe and Mail* reporters about this. I haven't told them anything, but I know for a fact they've been on this story for two months now. They've even got two reporters working on it. Listen, everybody on the Hill's talking about it."

The story was the talk of the town, and the man at its centre was the only person not in the loop? I found that highly unlikely.

About ten days before the story that was eventually dubbed the "Bernier-Couillard Affair" broke, I made it clear to Maxime not only that I was putting an end to my "assignment" as his official girlfriend, but also that I no longer wished to be intimate with him. We could remain friends, but I wasn't interested in seeing him in that way anymore. I spent the weekend in Quebec City, where I attended the annual convention of the Union des municipalités du Québec. Maxime was in the Beauce, and called me to say he wanted to come and see me, but I refused. He didn't take it well. That was the last time we spoke to each other before the media firestorm erupted.

It happened late in the evening of Wednesday, May 7, 2008. The news that the partner of Minister of Foreign Affairs

Maxime Bernier had past links to criminal bikers was trumpeted on radio and TV newscasts and on the websites of every major media outlet in the country. According to the reports – I wasn't identified by name, but that would come soon enough – I had been romantically involved with two criminal biker gang members, and married to one of them. They even implied that I had been nothing less than "planted" at the core of the Canadian government apparatus by elements of organized crime. My world had just been turned upside down.

At five in the morning on May 8, I sent a text message to Maxime: "Call me. Urgent." But he never called. Later that morning, my best friend, Nathalie,* came over to my house to keep me company in these difficult circumstances. Early in the afternoon, we sat down in front of the TV to watch the CPAC network's coverage of question period in the House of Commons. We heard opposition MPs – namely Denis Coderre, the Liberal national defence critic, and Gilles Duceppe, leader of the Bloc Québécois – assert that I was a potential national security threat, and that I might even have had access to, or be in possession of, confidential government documents.

Suddenly, a light went on in my head and I remembered the documents that Maxime had left at my place a few weeks earlier, for me to throw in the garbage. I ran to the kitchen counter where I had forgotten them, and found them under a pile of newspapers. There were three of them: one pocket sized document that said the word *Secret* on the cover; a larger one that also said *Secret* on it, both addressed to The Honourable Maxime Bernier, Minister of Foreign Affairs; and a third that was also pocket-sized but didn't have any *Secret* indication on

---

* Not her real name.

it and was addressed to Mr. Harper. All three concerned the
NATO Assembly in Bucharest, Romania, at the beginning of
April 2008. The first thing that came into my mind was: the
happy-go-lucky fool; why did he leave this stuff in my house?

But then I was immediately gripped by panic. I'm no expert
in international affairs. I didn't know what was in those documents and I didn't want to know. But to my mind, they were
red-hot. I was sure they contained explosive information about
countries that take their security very seriously indeed. I
thought of the CIA. I thought of the Mossad. And at that
moment, I started fearing for my life.

I didn't know which way to turn. What should I do with
the documents? Throw them out? Burn them? Hang on to
them? In doubt, I decided to keep them and wait to see what
happened next.

For three whole days, I stayed hunkered down in my
house, with the door locked and the shades drawn. I didn't
have any choice: the house was literally besieged by a horde
of journalists. Their cars and trucks were parked outside. TV
cameras were trained on the house continuously, ready to
record the slightest sign of life. It was sheer hell. The doorbell
rang constantly; the phone rang every thirty seconds. I was
starting to go insane. I will never forget those three days,
during which my house was photographed and recorded on
video from every possible angle, and my address was broadcast to the whole world. My privacy and my intimacy were
violated in a way I never would have believed possible.

Around nine-thirty in the evening on Friday, May 9, I
received a text message from Maxime: "If you want to talk
to me, you can call me." I was infuriated; I had been trying to
reach him for nearly two days without success, and rather than
call me, he had sent me a text message asking me to call. I

immediately texted him back to tell him that I couldn't believe he had taken so long to answer. But he didn't call me back.

Maxime gave another sign of life late in the afternoon the next day, again via text message. It said that Rona Ambrose, the minister of intergovernmental affairs, had contacted him to say that what was happening was terrible, and that she felt for me. She had also asked him if she could call me. I immediately replied that, yes, Rona could call me if she wanted to. Maxime texted me again, asking me what number she could use to reach me. I immediately became suspicious, because he knew my phone numbers. It was as if he was trying to find out whether I was at home. I answered that she could call me at my cellular number. Then he forwarded me the message Rona had sent him, as if he needed to prove to me that she had really been in touch with him. He was behaving very strangely, I thought.

Rona Ambrose never called me. But Maxime finally did, at around six in the evening. Needless to say, I really let him have it: "What is all this shit? You really have no balls at all! I've spent the past three days in misery, I've been trying to call you and you won't even call back. This entire mess is your fault."

"Listen, Julie . . . I didn't know how to react. With everything you've been through in your life already, you're a lot stronger than me," he said.

"You didn't know how to react?! Come on! It was me calling. It's not like you were mulling over some official response to I don't know who. You could've at least sent me some sign – 'Hang in there,' or whatever – so that I'd know I wasn't alone in all this. That you, at least, hadn't abandoned me."

Maxime reacted the way he always did when he felt he'd been caught out: he offered profuse apologies. They didn't strike me as particularly sincere. Then he started telling me how horrible and ridiculous all the allegations about me were. But he wasn't speaking normally; the longer the conversation went on, the more I got the impression that he wasn't alone, and that someone was listening in. At one point, he asked me whether I was at home. No, I was with friends, I answered. Why did he want to know that? A bit later he said – and I could sense he had an embarrassed smile on his face when he said this – "When I think there are people claiming you've seen documents . . . you never had any documents in your possession, right?" I was somewhat surprised that he would lie like that, and then, after a brief silence, I said, "Of course not, Maxime. Anyway, we were seeing each other so seldom that we had other things to do when we did get together." I felt a sense of relief on the other end of the line.

Then I asked him what we could do to put a stop to this whole circus, and he said I should sue all kinds of people, starting with the Montreal daily *La Presse* and the Bloc Québécois. "That bastard Duceppe," he said. "He gets his hair cut in the same salon as me and he's been blabbing to everybody for months about how he's going to crush Maxime Bernier because his girlfriend is a mafia moll. He's to blame." I couldn't help replying, "For someone who said he didn't know how to react, it seems to me you're on top of a lot of things."

At that point the line went dead. He called me back about three-quarters of an hour later saying the battery in his BlackBerry had run down and he'd had to go to his office to charge it. We continued our conversation where we'd left off. "We're going to sue them all," Maxime told me. "What they said in the papers . . . they have no right to do that. We're going to take the Bloc Québécois to court, and we'll fix it so the trial date falls during the election campaign and Duceppe'll lose his job. They're going down."

"Oh, sure, Max. 'We'll sue them all.' You do know it takes money to do that, don't you? I'm going to sue *La Presse*? Do you have any idea what Power Corporation's profit was last year? Do you know how much a lawyer costs?" I said.

Then Maxime told me, "Don't tell anyone, but I'm going to talk to the party president. Every year there's a huge budget set aside for attack ads against the other parties. A lawsuit against the Bloc would make for a pretty effective attack ad. I'll ask the party to pay for your lawyer under the table."

"The party would pay my legal fees? Go ahead, Maxime. All I want is for this whole business to stop."

Then I asked him why the government had reacted the way it had, asserting that the whole affair was a private matter and denying all knowledge of my past. "I was investigated by the police a long time ago," I said. "They've known for years that I had nothing to do with that business. It happened a decade ago. That's an eternity. And even when I was close to people who were close to the underworld, I was never involved in their business. The police know that. Why didn't the government say so?"

"They can't do that, Julie. It's unconstitutional. If they want to investigate you, you have to sign a document authorizing them to do so."

"What are you talking about? The police can investigate whomever they like – you know that."

"Look, Julie. The government had no choice but to respond the way it did."

The conversation ended with Maxime promising to call me back two days later, after he'd spoken to the Conservative Party president.

45

Alarmed

"I told them what had happened with my alarm system the night I'd left the house. They both laughed, and one of them said, 'Ma'am, some "cleaners" have obviously paid you a visit. You've been under surveillance. Someone waited till you left the house to come and recover microphones that had been planted here. They've removed the evidence.'"

On the third day of the siege, Saturday, May 10, my friend Nathalie invited me to have supper at her place. The journalists' surveillance had eased off a bit, so I took a chance on leaving the house. I had decided that the documents Maxime had left in my house would never leave my possession as long as I hadn't disposed of them in some way. That evening, I slipped them into a recyclable grocery bag, put them in my car, and drove to Nathalie's. It was there that I had my long telephone conversation with Maxime.

When I got back home, around eleven-thirty that night, I noticed that my alarm system was no longer armed, though I was positive that I'd activated it before leaving the house a few hours earlier. There was no sign of forced entry, though. I immediately called Nathalie and, while she stayed on the line, checked every room in the house. Nothing. "So what are you going to do now?" Nathalie asked.

"Well, there's nobody here. If anybody *was* here, they've left. They must not have found anything."

I said goodbye and, before going upstairs to take off my makeup and get ready for bed, set the alarm system to "Night" mode, as I always do. But I had a nagging doubt. To make sure everything was working properly, I opened the front door. No alarm sounded. The system wasn't working. I started to panic. My heart racing, I called the alarm company.

The man at the call centre said that on his end, everything appeared fine. "But my door's wide open and there's no alarm sounding," I said. He ran a few more checks, and told me everything was still displaying normal. Then he said he was going to test the communications link between the centre and my house. Just then, the phone went completely dead: no dial tone, nothing. I learned later that this was normal, but at the time I was terrified.

I grabbed my cellphone and called my brother to tell him what was going on. "Don't take any chances," he said. "Get out of there and call the cops." I grabbed my running shoes and jumped in the car, remembering to pick up the bag with Maxime's documents in it, and drove to a Couche-Tard corner store near my house. On the way, I called 9-1-1 and asked the police to come and meet me. A squad car arrived within five minutes. "Look," I told them, "there's something strange going on with my alarm system. I have to go back home to pick up some stuff, but I don't want to go alone." They didn't seem to understand exactly, but they said they'd come with me. "There are a lot of strange things going on in my life," I added, "and what's happening to my alarm system can't be a coincidence."

Then I showed them some newspapers from the past few days, and they realized who I was. They checked the entire house and realized that although the LED indicator on the alarm panel said "Fully Armed," the motion sensor wasn't working. In the meantime, the alarm company called back and asked me to help them do some more tests, but all we could establish was that the system still wasn't back up. The alarm-company employee kept repeating that everything appeared to be fine, and he didn't seem to believe me. At that point, one of the two police officers, a bit annoyed, came close to the phone and, speaking loudly enough for the employee to hear, said, "Listen, there's definitely a problem here. It says the system is armed, but the door's wide open and I've been walking back and forth in front of the motion sensor and the alarm isn't being tripped." Later, one of the police officers went outside, walked around the entire house, and came back. "There are exposed wires outside. They've been freshly cut," he told me.

By now, it was three in the morning. Before they left, the police officers advised me to go and stay somewhere else for the night. They waited while I collected a few things, and left the house at the same time as I did. I went back to Nathalie's to spend the night there. Needless to say, I didn't get much sleep. At five o'clock, I sent Maxime a text message asking him to call me. He did so around six-thirty, and I told him what had happened. "It's got to be people from your past, bikers, who did this," he said.

"That doesn't make any sense, Maxime. I've lived at the same address for ten years and my name's listed on 4-1-1. If those people had anything against me, they would have done something a long time ago."

"Well, who else would it be, then?" he said.

"You tell me. It's all too professional," I answered.

An hour later, I got a call from an employee at the alarm company, who told me my alarm system was defective and all the batteries would have to be changed. I asked him to send a technician the same day; he answered that, it being Sunday, there was nobody working in my sector – and that even if there were, it would cost me more than three hundred dollars. "I don't care what it costs," I said. "I want to be safe tonight."

A technician came to my house in the afternoon. He put in a new control panel and restarted the system. And, to my surprise, it didn't cost a penny. The company was never able to provide me with a satisfactory explanation for my malfunctioning alarm system. The technician who repaired it simply said, "Oh, you know, these systems, they can stop working overnight without us ever figuring out why." Bravo for the thorough investigation! A few days later, the company sent me a hopelessly vague report, riddled with factual errors, which shed no more light on what might have happened.

In the end, it was a pair of security experts from the Garda company – which is one of the biggest, if not *the* biggest, private security contractor for the government, so they cannot all of a sudden be incompetent because they are conducting an analysis of *my* house, even though the media tried to discredit me when I told my story in my interview – who solved the mystery, a few weeks later, and told me exactly what had gone on in my house that evening. The two were seasoned professionals, both former police officers. Armed with state-of-the-art electronic equipment, they swept the entire house and searched everywhere they thought they might uncover an anomaly. Eventually one of them called to me from the bedroom and asked me to come and see what he'd just found under the bed. "See right here?" he said, pointing to a tiny cut that had been made in the fabric covering the box spring, next to the wood frame. "There was probably a microphone attached to the frame of the box spring. They cut into the fabric and then folded it over again so nobody would suspect anything. There's nothing there now, but based on my experience, I'd say there was at some point."

I told them what had happened with my alarm system the night I'd left the house. They both laughed, and one of them said, "Ma'am, some 'cleaners' have obviously paid you a visit. You've been under surveillance. Someone waited till you left the house to come and recover microphones that had been planted here. They've removed the evidence."

Obviously, I never found out who might have done it, and I probably never will. But one thing was clear: I hadn't been imagining things. It's possible someone wanted to scare me, but I have no idea who or why. It's also quite possible that the target of the surveillance operation was Maxime Bernier. Indeed, when the specialists from Garda told me of their conclusions, I remembered something Maxime had once said to me. When he was appointed minister of foreign affairs, Stockwell Day – who was a good friend of his – had warned him about just such an eventuality. "You have to realize from now on that when you're in a hotel room in a foreign country, you'll be under audio surveillance, and probably video as well," he said.

"You've got to be kidding! You mean when I rent a movie, everyone will know what movie I'm watching and what I'm doing?" Maxime asked.

"Yeah, of course. It's not exactly fodder for a scandal!"

46

The "Biker's Chick"

"I could live with them writing about my past. Yes, I had gone out with Gilles Giguère, who'd been murdered. Yes, I had been married to Stéphane Sirois, a one-time full-patch member of the Rockers. I had come to terms with that period in my life. But I would not accept these dogged efforts by people close to the government – obviously unnamed sources providing quotes to journalists – to brand me as some sort of tawdry slut. The press was no longer printing truths about the past; these were untruths about the present."

As agreed, Maxime called me back on Monday, May 12. It was late in the afternoon. He said he hadn't been able to reach the Party president; apparently he was in Toronto until the following Wednesday. He played that stalling game with me all week until, on the Friday, I told him, "Look, Maxime. I'm sorry, but this whole thing is starting to stink. You're messing with me. Never mind, I'll manage by myself."

Meantime, the pressure was mounting ever higher. Not a day went by without its share of new "revelations" flooding the newspapers: I had shown up in Maxime's office wearing leather chaps; I chewed bubble gum at official functions; I demanded changes to Maxime's speeches; I insisted on being present at private meetings; I'd smoked in an ambassador's limousine; and who knows what else. By that time I knew that it was government sources who were bringing this fresh grist to the journalists' mills.

I could live with them writing about my past. Yes, I had gone out with Gilles Giguère, who'd been murdered. Yes, I had been married to Stéphane Sirois, a one-time full-patch member of the Rockers. I had come to terms with that period in my life. But I would not accept these dogged efforts by people close to the government – obviously unnamed sources providing quotes to journalists – to brand me as some sort of tawdry slut. The press was no longer printing truths about the past; these were untruths about the present.

And yet these were people who knew me very well. They had considered me worthy of accompanying the Canadian minister of foreign affairs to official functions, and of hosting or attending all manner of receptions during which I had occasion to converse with ambassadors, ministers, and even the First Lady of the United States. Then, overnight, I was suddenly pond scum. A nobody. A former "biker's chick."

There were essentially two people doing damage control at that time: John Miller and Mary Gable, a government official who worked in the Prime Minister's Office, whom I have already mentioned. Obviously, Maxime's former employee, Deborah Sterling – to whom I have devoted an entire chapter and who was very close to Mary Gable – was never far away either. This was all confirmed to Maxime sometime in May by Zarkis Vedan,* who was part of the prime minister's cabinet. At the same time, Zarkis said that Paul Foster and Mary Gable

---

* Not his real name.

were about to be fired from the PMO – and a week later, that's exactly what happened.

But none of that solved any of my problems. More and more lies were being printed about me, adding to my reputation as a "biker's chick." Eventually, I realized that people were willing to believe anything about me. Sooner or later, my credibility would be so completely eroded that I would not only be easy prey for anyone wishing to attack me, but I would also end up bearing all the blame for the whole business. I had to do something to reestablish my credibility, and my dignity.

On Monday, May 12, I got a call from Claude Poirier, who told me that some people from TVA wanted to talk to me. He asked me whether he was allowed to give them my telephone number. I told him he could. Then, someone offered me the chance to be interviewed by TVA. Later, Éditions de l'Homme approached me about writing a book.

These proposals made a lot of sense to me; at least this way I would have my say. More and more people had this image of me as some kind of lowlife tart with no morals. Here I had a chance to show the world the real me – not perfect, necessarily, but certainly not the vulgar and debauched woman some were making me out to be. Of course, the idea of publishing my auto-biography before I had even reached the age of forty bothered me to some extent. I was well aware that it could be thought of as pretentious. But I wanted to set the record straight, and I was being given the opportunity. *Verba volant, scripta manent*: "Spoken words fly away, the written word endures." I don't mean newspaper articles, which everyone eventually forgets about, but a real book, written by me, that would stand the test of time and in which I would tell my story. The true story.

Clearly, Maxime had started to worry in the days since I had told him that I was going to straighten out my problems myself, and would no longer count on him to help me out of my bind. Smelling a rat, he began calling me regularly to find out what my plans were. When I told him I had met with a crisis management expert and I was going to let him handle things, he bombarded me with questions. Who was it? Who did he work for? What had he advised me to do? I told him that I preferred to remain discreet about the matter. Every time he called, he would also ask me where I was, but I never told him.

The truth is that I was now virtually convinced that Maxime Bernier was ready to do anything to save himself – including, if need be, remorselessly sacrificing me on the altar of his ambition. And indeed, he was to prove this later by claiming that he couldn't recall having forgotten any documents in my home, thereby insinuating that I must have stolen them. It soon became quite clear to me that placing any trust in him would set me on the road to ruin.

On May 20, Maxime telephoned me in the early evening to say he'd been invited to a University of Ottawa alumni gathering and that it would be nice if I could go with him and spend the weekend in Ottawa. I was dumbfounded. I couldn't believe what I was hearing. "Maxime, are you crazy?" I said. "The last thing I need in my life right now is to be seen in public with you. Have you completely lost your mind?"

The last time I heard Maxime Bernier's voice was on the morning of Saturday, May 24. The day before, I had signed the contract with my book publisher. I had embarked down a path from which I had no intention of straying. He called me, and I opened my cell but didn't say a word. For a reason that I still can't fathom, all I heard was his panicked voice saying, "You didn't give me the right number. It's not answering." As if he didn't know my number?

And then the line went dead.

47

Quandary

"I met with Mr. Hébert [my lawyer] that day. . . . He said, 'I would be very surprised if the fact of having had these documents in your possession caused you many problems. Especially if you surrender them at this time. For Mr. Bernier, however, it's a different story.'

'What would be the consequences for him, then? Worst-case scenario.'

'In theory, he could go to prison.'

'What? You're joking,' I said.

'As I said: in theory. I don't think that will happen. But the fact remains that these documents were his responsibility, and he has sworn a solemn oath to protect the information in his possession. He had no business leaving them at your home. He's committed a serious error, and he'll certainly be forced to resign as minister.'"

From May 8, when I remembered they were on my kitchen counter, until May 25, 2008, when I entrusted them to my lawyer, Jean-Claude Hébert, so that he could return them to the government, the documents that Maxime Bernier had left in my house never left my sight. I did everything in my power to safeguard them and, in so doing, ensure that no one would become apprised of their contents. Today, I can attest to the fact that during this time, neither I nor anyone else read them.

Nevertheless, I felt a gnawing fear about what those documents really contained – and what harm might possibly come to me as a result of my possessing them – coupled with a growing anxiety about what I should do with them. As the days passed, it seemed increasingly obvious to me that it would be dangerous to put them in the garbage or the recycling bin. If I chose that option, I had no way of knowing in whose hands they might end up. There were no guarantees at all. And if those hands happened to be the wrong hands, and the documents contained extremely sensitive information about foreign countries – as I initially believed they might – I would run the risk of causing my own country great harm.

Eventually, something else became quite clear to me as well: if I held on to the documents, I could, in a way, protect myself. In the House of Commons, the opposition parties were having a field day with their assertions that I was a potential threat to national security. Of course, that was part of their respective game plans, but the problem was that more and more people were tending to believe the claims. And articles had started to appear that mentioned my work in the security business, whether with DRP or my own firm. That only served to lend credence to the accusations and theories (which were, of course, patently absurd).

I had seen my share of government documents during the months that I was going out with Maxime Bernier, but none were stamped "Secret" – not until he decided to leave one at my house. Setting aside the fact that we now know its contents were (thank goodness) inconsequential in terms of national security, I naturally thought: you don't stamp a document "Secret" unless it's important. So my eventual reasoning was as follows: What if the document were to disappear? People could easily blame it on me and fabricate all manner of outlandish stories about what I might have done with it. They'd say I'd sold it to the Israelis, or the Russians, or the Hells Angels. Or who knows what. And then what would happen?

You can insist all you like that we live in a free society, and not under some junta, but I must say that during those few days, the thought crossed my mind that it might be very easy for certain people to do away with me and blame it on the Hells Angels. Therefore, I felt that as long as the document was intact and in my possession, it was my protection. Charity begins at home . . .

If, when this whole affair first erupted, Maxime Bernier had bothered to come and see me – if only to lend me some shred of comfort while my life was falling apart – I would have covered for him. I would gladly have given him back his damn documents. If he had done something other than wait until three days after I had left him an urgent message, until there were who knows how many other people listening in on our conversation . . . If he had not simply denied, in the first place, that I had ever had government documents in my possession . . . If he had come to me and offered to sit down and discuss the situation frankly, so that we might find the best way out of the crisis (both for him and for me) . . . But he did none of those things, as everyone knows. He stalled, he dangled false promises in front of me, and he tried to save his own ass while I kept sinking deeper into trouble.

He could have issued a public statement to the effect that he condemned the hounding that I was being subjected to in the media. He could have come out and said that I wasn't at all like the woman being described in the newspapers. He could have shown himself to be as honourable as would befit the title conferred upon him as a federal cabinet minister. Instead, he behaved like a soulless, petty politician. Had there not been documents and photographs to prove the contrary, I think he might even have gone so far as to say he had never met me.

After conducting some research, I got in touch with Jean-Claude Hébert, a well-known Montreal lawyer whose abilities and integrity were universally acknowledged. I explained the situation I was in, and he agreed to represent me; among other things, he would return the documents I had in my possession to the federal government. I gave them to him on May 25, the same day that I was interviewed for the TVA network by journalist Paul Larocque.

When I met with Mr. Hébert that day, I asked him to explain what the consequences would be for me, in the worst-case scenario, if I were to surrender the secret documents to him. He said, "I would be very surprised if the fact of having had these documents in your possession caused you many problems. Especially if you surrender them at this time. For Mr. Bernier, however, it's a different story."

"What would be the consequences for him, then? Worst-case scenario."

"In theory, he could go to prison."

"What? You're joking," I said.

"As I said: in theory. I don't think that will happen. But the fact remains that these documents were his responsibility, and he has sworn a solemn oath to protect the information in his possession. He had no business leaving them at your home. He's committed a serious error, and he'll certainly be forced to resign as minister," Mr. Hébert said.

I started to panic. "Listen," I said, "I don't want to tell any lies. But I don't want Maxime to go to prison because of me, either. Yes, he's lying to me. He's manipulating me. He's standing by and doing nothing while I'm drowning. But I want him to be able to emerge from this with some dignity."

"Your wisest course of action," my lawyer replied, "is to simply say that he came to your home, and when he left, the documents remained behind. You don't provide details, or circumstances. That way, you aren't lying, and you give Mr. Bernier the opportunity to provide his own explanation, and possibly salvage whatever career he has left."

That was the line of conduct I followed a few hours later, during my interview with TVA. In doing so, I was telling the truth. Yes, the documents had been in my possession, but I had done my duty as a citizen: I had ensured they would be returned to their rightful owner, knowing full well that no one had so much as seen them, let alone read their contents – and as a result, Canada's national security had never been compromised, not even for a second.

In light of what has transpired in the ensuing months, I have come to the conclusion that I let Maxime Bernier off far too easily. For his part, he never ceased in his underhanded attempts to damage my credibility and make me bear the blame for his incompetence – to the point where he has now cast doubt on my integrity and spread utterly ridiculous rumours to the effect that I stole the documents in question. The Department of Foreign Affairs and International Trade report on its internal review of the matter, made public on August 1, clearly implies this.

That report states that Maxime Bernier resigned from his position acknowledging that he had forgotten a classified document; it was only later that he said he did not recall having forgotten it, and insinuated that he had been the victim of theft.

How many people resign from their position because they have been the victim of a criminal act? And now, in a recent Radio-Canada interview on the program *La fosse aux lionnes*, he has gone back to the claim that *he* forgot the documents at my house, probably after hearing the comments that my lawyer made to the press refuting the allegation that I had stolen them and saying that he had proof.

As far as I am concerned, my version of the facts, unlike Maxime Bernier's, has never changed. The reason is simple: I have told the truth about this affair all along.

Epilogue

I had no choice but to write this book. Last spring, I was cat-apulted into the media spotlight overnight, without asking for it, nor ever imagining that such a thing could happen to me. Without displaying the slightest decorum, these people set about rummaging through every corner of my life and my past. They harassed my family. They videotaped my house. They published my home address, the locations of the places where I've worked, most of my social insurance number, my credit history. And they publicly scrutinized my personal rela-tionships, going back to when I was twenty.

We live in an age when people are quick to invoke privacy rights in expressing reservations about making public the names, addresses, and likenesses of convicted pedophiles. And yet no one has expressed shock or dismay at the widespread publication of a vast array of private information – not to mention all manner of falsehoods – about an ordinary citizen who has never been charged with any sort of crime.

And it didn't stop there. For weeks, journalists felt obliged to devote pages upon pages to anyone who had anything to say about me. Whether the statements they reported were true or false was the least of their worries; nor did they care a whit about the motivations of their "anonymous sources." It was alleged that I had showed up in government offices wearing leather chaps; demanded changes to the texts of Maxime

Bernier's speeches; chewed gum at public events; and smoked a cigarette while riding in the Canadian ambassador's car in Paris. Worse, it was claimed that I was at the centre of an influence peddling scandal, that I had met with a close associate of Maurice "Mom" Boucher as late as 2007, that I had once been a nude dancer, and that I had run a prostitution ring. I was branded a schemer, a gold digger, a con artist – even a thief.

When I read and listened to these inanities, it was as if these people were talking about someone else. But no, that was really me in those stories. Countless people believed the lies, and I have had to live with the consequences of all that media mythmaking.

It would seem that I have been naive in my belief that no one has the right to spread lies about other people, be it verbally or in print. I was under the impression that there was a word for such behaviour: *defamation*. I know better now; the newspapers can say and write whatever they want about anyone, with complete impunity. But there is an even more absurd aspect: even though my private life has been shamelessly splashed across the front pages of the newspapers, here I have had to refrain from using the real names of the majority of the people I describe, for fear of lawsuits.

This entire affair has also made clear to me that, even in our day and age, there is still a bright future ahead for misogyny and sexism. If the roles had been reversed – if this story had been about a man in a relationship with a female cabinet minister – no one would ever have said the things that were said about me. That stubborn determination to make me out to be some sort of vulgar courtesan, a woman of easy virtue and loose morals, is perfectly in keeping with the prejudiced notions that so many people continue to entertain about "feminine nature" – in particular, the idea that it is only by scheming and seducing that a woman can get ahead. Most appallingly, even a commentator who considers herself a feminist felt obliged – in an article that she clearly cobbled together based solely on the malicious gossip that had been written about me – to describe me as suffering from "escort syndrome," when I have never relied on anyone but myself to earn my living.

This same type of sexist, backward mentality prevailed on June 10, 2008, at a meeting of the Standing Committee on Public Safety and National Security in Ottawa, when one Michel Juneau-Katsuya – whom I would describe as a photo-op-seeker masquerading as a security and intelligence expert – said the following about me:

> At her own initiative, she told the media that she had selected an event attended by Mr. Bernier, that she managed to be at his table that evening, that she had dined with him and that she had been nice to him all evening. She even revealed that that evening she wore the same dress that she had on at Mr. Bernier's swearing in because it showed off all her assets.

Nothing in Mr. Juneau-Katsuya's perfidious, condescending statement is true – except, of course, for the fact that I had dinner with a group of people that included Maxime Bernier. The rest was sheer fabrication. And to think people were surprised by my refusal to answer questions at that same meeting! No one would ever have said the same things about a man. Most shocking to me in that regard is that these words were spoken before a committee of the Canadian Parliament, and that none of the MPs present seemed offended by this blatant sexism. Indeed, some of them were even amused by it. But once again, these statements lent credence to the image of me as an unscrupulous Mata Hari weaving her web, the better to ensnare her prey. Where does this idea come from, that as soon as a man is introduced to a beautiful woman, he automatically becomes a victim, even if up to that point he was presumed to be intelligent enough to be a cabinet minister?

Had I been given any choice in the matter, I would much rather have preserved, until my dying day, the anonymity I enjoyed before May 7, 2008. But in the face of the lies and delusions perpetrated about me, I had no option but to speak out – to set the record straight and attempt to recover the dignity that had been taken from me.

My work is done now. I have told the truth. Those who choose to believe me may do so; I cannot do any more. I can only try to pick up the pieces of my life and bring some semblance of meaning back to that life – both personal and professional – after having survived these hellish few months. I know that it will take time. As a result of the media firestorm touched off this past spring, I no longer have a job – and I can't really blame anyone who might normally be prepared to offer me one for steering clear of me, for fear of seeing whole swaths of their own lives subjected to public scrutiny as well. And as for the likelihood of my enjoying, any time in the next few months, a romantic relationship worthy of the name, I dare not even think about it. What man in his right mind would dream of going out with the Julie Couillard that journalists have taken such pleasure in portraying these past few months?

Today, what I long for most of all, with every fibre of my being, is to find peace of mind, to get to the point where I can look to the future confidently and with serenity. I dream of truly enjoying life again, of being able to walk down the street without feeling watched and judged, without hearing the laughs and whispers behind my back: "Hey, did you see? It's that Couillard girl."

I only want to get back to being Julie. Is that too much to ask?

Julie Couillard
Laval, September 2008

Acknowledgments

I would like to thank Serge Rivest, for his tremendous job of listening, summarizing, and writing, which has helped me to recount my story in the most faithful manner possible.

I also extend my thanks and appreciation to the many people who have expressed their sympathy and encouragement throughout this ordeal.